"Former FBI agent Mike Campi's exceptional integrity, insight, and irrepressible sense of humor shine in this groundbreaking book. An historic undercover investigation was born when Campi joined forces with the charismatic rising Mafia star Michael 'Cookie' D'Urso, who was hellbent on avenging a family murder and an attempt on his own life. Together they upended the singularly powerful and secretive Genovese crime family. Campi is a most trustworthy guide into the mob underworld, laying bare the treachery and hypocrisy of 'the life' so unlike Hollywood depictions. At the same time, Campi bravely focuses scrutiny on the FBI and a long-hidden scandal that threatened his greatest professional achievements."

—Kati Cornell, former federal court reporter for the *New York Post* and public information director for New York City's Office of the Special Narcotics Prosecutor

"Fuhgetaboutit! This book has it all. The history of the Italian Mafia and America's Cosa Nostra. The five families. The unmasking and takedown of Vincent 'the Chin' Gigante, a.k.a. 'the Oddfather,' boss of the powerful Genovese crime family. Follow the investigation of mobsters by one of the FBI's most respected and legendary organized crime agents. You won't be able to put this book down as it is packed with never revealed info on these mobsters, their informants, and what led to their capture. Hollywood will definitely be knocking on Campi's doors."

—Joaquin "Jack" Garcia, retired FBI agent and author of *Making Jack Falcone*

"Campi's strategic tenacity as a mafia-busting FBI agent comes through page after page as he reveals the gruesome, twisted reality of the American mafia—where there is no honor among thieves, only treachery. *Mafia Takedown* is a captivating insider's account of the gangsters that have infiltrated and controlled many aspects of American life for over a century. I couldn't put it down."

—Katya Jestin, former AUSA and deputy chief, Organized Crime Section, Eastern District of New York

MAFIA
TAKEDOWN

MAFIA
TAKEDOWN

THE INCREDIBLE TRUE STORY OF THE FBI AGENT
WHO DEVASTATED THE NEW YORK MOB

MIKE CAMPI

FOREWORD BY TOM ROBBINS

Skyhorse Publishing

Skyhorse Publishing books may be purchased in bulk at special discounts for sales promotion, corporate gifts, fund-raising, or educational purposes. Special editions can also be created to specifications. For details, contact the Special Sales Department, Skyhorse Publishing, 307 West 36th Street, 11th Floor, New York, NY 10018 or info@skyhorsepublishing.com.

Skyhorse® and Skyhorse Publishing® are registered trademarks of Skyhorse Publishing, Inc.®, a Delaware corporation.

Visit our website at www.skyhorsepublishing.com.

Please follow our publisher Tony Lyons on Instagram @tonylyonsisuncertain.

10 9 8 7 6 5 4 3 2

Library of Congress Cataloging-in-Publication Data is available on file.

Hardcover ISBN: 978-1-5107-8316-4
eBook ISBN: 978-1-5107-8317-1

Cover design by Brian Peterson

Printed in the United States of America

I can do all things through Christ that strengthens me.
If God be for me, who can be against me?
—Anthony Campi
(often quoting Philippians 4:13 and Romans 8:31)

If you're afraid to fail, you'll never succeed.
—Dan Gable

CONTENTS

Disclaimer

In accordance with my obligations as a former FBI employee pursuant to my FBI employment agreement, this book has undergone a prepublication review for the purpose of identifying prohibited disclosures but has not been reviewed for editorial content or accuracy. The FBI does not endorse or validate any information that I have described in this book. The opinions expressed in this book are mine and not those of the FBI or any other government agency.

—Mike Campi

A Note on Redactions

Several passages in this book are blacked out, or "redacted." This was done by the FBI's Prepublication Review Office. They argue that these passages are not releasable to the public. Although we disagree, we elected to keep the redactions in the text and blacked out for the purpose of continuity.

A Note on Names

Some names have been changed to protect the identities of certain individuals.

FOREWORD

BY TOM ROBBINS

Outside a Brooklyn courtroom a few years ago, I remember encountering a veteran federal agent who was waiting to take the stand in a mob trial. It wasn't Mike Campi, the author of this compelling tale, but it was a senior colleague, a decorated lawman in charge of a squad investigating one of New York's five Mafia families. I was struck by how the agent was dressed: He was decked out in the height of mob fashion—a dark double-breasted suit, a red pocket hankie, gleaming cufflinks, and a large expensive-looking ring. As we spoke, his speech was peppered with the lingo of the street-wise hoodlums he was paid to pursue. I remember thinking how odd it was that someone tasked with bringing down mobsters should choose to emulate their style and look.

That the customs of the American Mafia can rub off even on those charged with bringing wiseguys to justice is a reminder that the mob still casts a strong spell, aided by a continuing stream of movies and books. Even as the power of the Mafia has receded, the image persists of the so-called secret society, composed of men of honor heeding their own creed, modern-day pirates loyal to their brotherhood, making their own rules.

What's confounding is that this romantic portrait has endured despite the steady parade of turncoats who have emerged from the mob's ranks in recent years, bringing with them grisly tales of the deceit, cruelty, and duplicity they experienced in "The Life" as the Mafia's soldiers like to call it.

Despite what Hollywood would have us think, those are the true attributes of this society that is not-so-secret anymore, thanks to the scores of informants who deserted their would-be families in the Mafia. That twisted brotherhood is the relentless focus of this powerful book by Campi, a former FBI agent who spent more than twenty years investigating the underworld without ever feeling the call to dress or talk like the men he chased.

That may have been because, as Campi writes here, the conclusion of his many investigations, in addition to the dozens of indictments and convictions he helped win, was that "life in the mob is all about treachery, fear, greed, and hypocrisy."

Campi's lessons about that life came courtesy of diligent study of how mobsters operated, where they went, and who they met. In order to discreetly tail gangsters, he obtained a hack license to drive a yellow taxi. To locate the gambling operation of an elusive crime family figure, Campi pulled up his parking tickets. He listened to every tip, no matter how unlikely the source, sitting patiently with a junkie locked up in Rikers who, it emerged, knew someone who knew someone significant in the Mafia. Asked by fellow investigators why he was never found in the FBI squad room, he said, "I follow wiseguys. I haven't seen one come through the squad."

Along the way, Campi met a gangster who had learned in bitter personal experience just how deceitful the mob was. Michael D'Urso had been playing cards, surrounded by friends from the powerful Genovese crime family when one of them shot him in the head. D'Urso survived, but his cousin, seated across from him, was shot dead. The killers had a simple goal in trying to rub out two of their friends: money. They wanted to avoid paying tens of thousands in debts they owed them. So much for the honored society.

D'Urso kept his outrage to himself but quietly went looking for a way to wreak revenge, and when he met Mike Campi, he found it. For almost three and a half years, D'Urso wore a secret wire for the FBI, recording thousands of conversations with his Mafia associates. He was "our own

Trojan horse," Campi writes of his infiltration into the mob. It was also a perilous high-wire act in which the agent and his undercover juggled constant threats of exposure. Yet D'Urso was so convincing in his role that top mob figures took him into their confidence, detailing their criminal schemes, and confessing their own jealousies and feuds. "You're cut out for it," an admiring mobster told him. "You've got the brains and the balls." He was assured that he was going to become a made member of the mob any day now.

Before that could happen, Campi pulled in his net. Falling into it were many of the top figures and dozens of soldiers and associates of News York's crime families. Faced with D'Urso's devastating recordings, almost of all of those charged pleaded guilty. The result of the operation, said the United States attorney whose office prosecuted the cases, was "breathtaking."

In his quest to defeat the mob, Mike Campi became a close student of the history of organized crime in this country, much of which is related as his dramatic story unspools. But don't look for any tales of swaggering hoodlums, of men forced by poverty into lives of crime, or for that matter of leaders who inspired their troops. The morals of those at the top of the mob's pyramid, Campi learned as his undercover mission dug ever deeper into the Mafia's upper echelon, were if anything far more corrupt than those of the ambitious young men they recruited with false promises of wealth, power, and prestige. At the end of the day, Campi warns, there is "no loyalty, no brotherhood, no honor" to be found inside the mob. Just ask Michael D'Urso.

HOW AND WHY THIS BOOK
CAME TO BE

This is the story of my career participating in some of the most relentless and successful attacks on organized crime in America—including putting a conclusive end to the biggest mafia con of all time.[1] It is also a story that lays bare the hypocrisy and cruelty of life within the American mob—routinely glamorized in film and other media—but where in fact there is very little honor, loyalty, or sense of family. It is only an engine intent on destroying the American way of life for selfish gain. *Mafia Takedown* will prove this point—providing you with facts and statements, often from *the gangsters' own mouths*, that betray the fiction and reveal the truth—life in the mob is all about treachery, fear, greed, betrayal, and hypocrisy.

This is the real mob, not the one you have seen portrayed in Hollywood. I pull back the curtain, take you deep inside their real worlds, and explain how I put them away.

Why have I chosen to step forward and write this book now, more than fifteen years after I moved on from my days in federal law enforcement? Although many have recommended that I write about my experiences, I didn't really plan to do so. Why now? The answer to this question is a

---

1 It goes without saying that countless other members of law enforcement likewise have struck the mob deeply. This is the story of my contribution.

bit winding, but it also helps show what makes this story so unique and interesting.

After the mafia battles, you'll read about here, long after I left my work in law enforcement, I periodically kept in touch with an ex-gangster named Michael "Cookie" D'Urso. D'Urso had been a rising mafia power whose ascent was temporarily interrupted when he was shot in the head and left for dead in 1994, his assassinated cousin's prone body lying beside him. In stark illustration of the mafia's hypocrisy and always-present treachery, their murders were planned and executed by mobsters they considered trustworthy friends.

After recovering, D'Urso sought vengeance—despite explicit orders to the contrary from the country's most powerful mafia family—which further risked his life and hindered his progress up the ranks. A couple of years after that, he threatened to rip out and eat the heart of a complete stranger, who unbeknownst to him, turned out to be the acting boss of his own crime family, the Genovese. D'Urso was almost killed for this as well. By this point, in 1998, he'd had enough. He'd played by what were supposed to be the rules, and yet his life always seemed to be hanging by a thread. D'Urso had his attorney surreptitiously approach law enforcement, asking to arrange a meeting with me. D'Urso pled guilty to murder and secretly began working with me, wearing a wire and recording the crimes of his fellow gangsters on a scale never seen before or since. He did so for three years—risking his life on a daily basis and showing spectacular courage. Our work succeeded to such a degree that even while working for the FBI, D'Urso rose so far up the criminal ranks that his superiors openly compared him to John Gotti and discussed him becoming the future Genovese boss. This all culminated in 2001 in one of the largest and most decimating mob takedowns ever.

FBI bigwigs described this as perhaps "the *most significant and successful undercover operation* in law enforcement history." It resulted in the arrests of dozens upon dozens of high-level mobsters, including the *entire* ruling Genovese administration—the leaders of the most powerful criminal gang in America.

The end result was historic. The government's sentencing letter for Cookie D'Urso reflected this, describing the resulting prosecutions as *"among the most successful and far ranging in the history of the prosecution of*

American organized crime. By any measure . . . Michael D'Urso's cooperation is virtually unprecedented." The public knows very little about this, but by the end of this book, you'll know it all.

After our work together concluded in the early 2000s, D'Urso and I periodically stayed in touch. Years after D'Urso was sentenced, he also revealed to me absolutely stunning and horrible details (discussed in the main body of this book), of what had taken place behind the scenes—stuff that even I knew nothing about—and which had all along threatened to derail the entire operation from its very outset.

Fast-forward to the end of 2019. D'Urso reached out for my assistance with something unrelated, which I agreed to provide. That led to us spending time together in person, culminating in a holiday meal where we reminisced about the case and its historic impact. As the public knew virtually none of it, D'Urso suggested he write a book after his son asked him one day if he was a gangster. The next day we met with a book publisher who offered a contract on the spot, requesting that we write it together instead, to contribute our various perspectives: a gangster, and his handling FBI agent. I was unsure if I wanted to tell my story because I'd had so many issues with inexperienced and incompetent FBI management. At the same time, my family and friends had been encouraging me to do a book for years. D'Urso stated he wanted his children to learn about his shadowed past, and as I understood, to discourage them from following in his footsteps—and to see how much he had accomplished as a cooperating witness. Ultimately, we agreed to move forward.

Unbeknownst to us, at about this same time mobsters *still* had their eyes on D'Urso and were talking about him—even though *twenty years had passed* since he'd wrecked them. They held one such meeting at an Upper East Side Manhattan restaurant. D'Urso found out about this and responded by writing to the mafia at large, which the *New York Post* published in a two-page spread on January 10, 2020, under the headline "Former Mob Rat Michael "Cookie" D'Urso Writes Open Letter to Mafia." His letter featured messages such as: "a bat and a knife won't help you . . . you'll have to use a gun." Needless to say, this type of open communication to the American mafia was unprecedented, unique in gangster history.[2]

Film and television figures, along with Hollywood agents, took notice. They became intrigued and expressed interest in a potential movie and/or television show depicting D'Urso's story, our lives, and how we had retained a relationship over the decades. In fits and starts, these discussions continued for two years. We met with the head of a movie studio, and major Hollywood players confirmed their potential interest. My interest in large part was because I wanted a chance to set the record straight about the real mob. This would hopefully assist with opening the eyes of young men who believe this is a life of honor.

Then everything changed. At the last moment, D'Urso wanted me to include one thing in the book that was blatantly false. From the very first day of our very first meeting, I always cautioned D'Urso to tell the truth. That rule was set in stone—D'Urso in fact often repeated these words as the best and most priceless advice I had ever given him. Yet the intended falsehood betrayed that foundation. I also felt it was a betrayal of our relationship and I was disappointed that he wanted me to coauthor a book where my name would stand behind something untrue. He was clearly trying to manipulate me based on his inaccurate belief that I was interested in a movie or multiyear TV series. I also felt it would send the wrong message to his kids. I immediately severed my relationship with D'Urso.

The movie people were contacted and informed we were stepping away from the project. We also advised the book publisher to let them know that my relationship with D'Urso had ended, and the project was now unfortunately over. The movie people responded that all projects have ebbs and flows and suggested that I would work out our differences. But I said no—that a line had been crossed and it was over.

The publisher of *this* book in your hands, responded that it was extremely unfortunate, as I still had an important story to tell. I ultimately decided that I would move forward without D'Urso's participation.

---

2   Jerry Capeci, "Former mob rat Michael 'Cookie' D'Urso writes open letter to the Mafia," *New York Post*, January 9, 2020, https://nypost.com/2020/01/09/former-mob-rat-michael-cookie-durso-writes-open-letter-to-the-mafia/.

D'Urso's cooperation was epic and unprecedented. It facilitated others to also cooperate.

So this is the untold story of my work fighting the mafia, culminating in me and my team developing the remarkable and unparalleled Cookie D'Urso case.

Hard work and passion, combined with a firm knowledge that I was addressing the crimes of a sophisticated criminal organization, aided by a bit of luck, facilitated a devastating blow to organized crime. I take you behind the scenes and hope you enjoy this insider's account of battling the mob, with all of its ugly bumps and bruises. The cases I built succeeded against what at times seemed overwhelming odds (imposed as you'll learn by both external *and* internal forces). I take you deep inside all of it, where you'll figuratively stand alongside my investigative challenges and choices. Along the way you will learn about the real American mafia.

As I alluded to above, toward the end of the book you will also learn about some truly explosive related events, heretofore never told.

CAST OF CHARACTERS

This book contains a fairly comprehensive review of multiple gangsters and cases concerning all five crime families. The below list, unless otherwise indicated, is of positions held during the time period covered in this book. Please consult it freely to help you follow the action.

Elio "Chinatown" Albanese—Genovese associate and later a soldier
Vinny Aloi—Colombo acting boss
Vic Amuso—Lucchese boss
Sammy "Meatballs" Aparo—Genovese acting capo and D'Urso mentor
Vinny Aparo—Genovese soldier
Ralph Balsamo—Genovese soldier
George Barone—cooperating witness and ex-Genovese soldier
Tommy Barrett—Genovese associate
Dino Basciano—cooperating witness and ex-Lucchese associate
"Vinny Gorgeous" Basciano—Bonanno acting boss
Barney Bellomo—Genovese acting boss and later official boss
John Borelli—murdered gangster
Dominic "Fat Dom" Borghese—cooperating witness and ex-Gambino soldier
Nelson Boxer—SDNY AUSA
Ben Brafman—criminal defense lawyer
Adolfo Bruno—murdered New England boss

Anthony Bruno—cooperating witness who ran into a burning building and saved children after serving his sentence

Jim Bucknam—SDNY AUSA

James Caan—actor, close friend of Colombo acting boss Andrew Russo

Vincent "Fish" Cafaro—Genovese soldier and incomplete cooperating witness

Tommy Cafaro—Genovese associate, son of "Fish" Cafaro, and close to acting boss Barney Bellomo

Frank Campanella—Colombo associate

Patricia Cappozzalo—surviving victim of attempted hit and sister of cooperating witness and ex-Lucchese capo "Fat Pete" Chiodo

The Honorable Zachary Carter—U.S. attorney EDNY

Anthony "Gaspipe" Casso—Lucchese underboss and failed cooperating witness

Paul Castellano—murdered Gambino boss

John "Boobie" Cerasani—Bonanno soldier

Anthony Cerasulo, a.k.a "Rookie"—cooperating witness and ex-wannabe

Tommy "Gigali" Cestaro—Genovese soldier

"Fat Pete" Chiodo—cooperating witness and ex-Lucchese capo

"Quiet Dom" Cirillo—Genovese administration member and former acting boss

Ralph Coppola—murdered Genovese capo

Frank Costello—survivor of hit attempt and ex-Genovese acting boss

"Wild Bill" Cutolo—murdered Colombo underboss

Harold Daggett—ILA president

"Little Al" D'Arco—cooperating witness and ex-Lucchese acting boss

The Honorable Raymond Dearie—EDNY federal judge

Bobby DeBello—Genovese soldier

Joe Defede—Lucchese acting boss

Tommy Defiore—Bonanno capo

Pasquale "Scop" Deluca—Genovese administration

Frank DeMeo—Genovese soldier

Robert De Niro—actor

Joe Dente—Genovese soldier

"Little Larry" Dentico—Genovese acting underboss

Jackie DeRoss—Colombo acting boss

"Petey Red" DiChiara—Genovese capo and later acting boss

Anthony "Hickey" Dilorenzo—murdered Genovese soldier

Bob Doherty—FBI agent

Craig Donlan—FBI agent

Michael "Cookie" D'Urso—cooperating witness and ex-Genovese associate who historically brought down dozens of powerful gangsters from all five New York crime families

Louis Eppolito—ex-NYPD murderer for Luccheses

Olympia Esposito—Vincent "Chin" Gigante paramour

Vincent Esposito—convicted felon son of Vincent "Chin" Gigante

Albert "Chinkie" Facciano—Genovese capo

Patty Falcetti—Genovese capo

"Johnny Green" Faraci—Bonanno capo

Mark Feldman—EDNY chief of Organized Crime unit

Mario Fortunato—Genovese associate

Michael Franzese—former Colombo capo and son of Colombo capo Sonny Franzese

Nicky "the Blond" Frustaci—Genovese soldier

Ross Gangi—Genovese capo

Jack Garcia—FBI agent

Mickey "Dimino" Generoso—Genovese acting underboss

Vito Genovese—Genovese boss

Enrico "Red Hot" Gentile—Genovese soldier

Paul Geraci—Genovese soldier

Andrew Gigante—convicted felon son of Vincent "Chin" Gigangte

Father Louis Gigante—priest brother of Vincent "Chin" Gigante

Rita Gigante—daughter of Vincent "Chin" Gigante

Vincent "the Chin" Gigante—Genovese boss

The Honorable Leo Glasser—EDNY federal judge

Jack Gordon—Genovese associate

John Gotti—Gambino boss

Peter Gotti—Gambino acting boss

Sammy "the Bull" Gravano—terminated cooperating witness and former Gambino underboss

David Grossman—cooperating witness and former Genovese associate, attorney, and New York State Trooper

"Fat Gerry" Guadagno—Gambino associate

Vito Guzzo—Colombo associate and later a soldier

Lenny Hatton—FBI agent

Kathryn Hudak—EDNY paralegal specialist

James "Little Jimmy" Ida—Genovese consigliere

Joey Ida—Genovese capo

John "Gingale" Imbrieco—wannabe

The Honorable Sterling Johnson—EDNY federal judge

Tommy Krall—FBI agent

Danny Leo—Genovese administration and future acting boss

Phil Leonetti—cooperating witness and former Philadelphia underboss

Martin Light—cooperating witness and former criminal defense lawyer

Sally "Dogs" Lombardi—Genovese capo

Tino Lombardi—murdered Genovese associate, Michael D'Urso's cousin

Alan Longo—Genovese capo and used as messenger within Genovese and between other families

Danny Longo—Genovese associate

Pat Maggiore—NYPD Detective

Allie "Shades" Malangone—Genovese capo

Sal Mangiavelano—cooperating witness and former Gambino associate

Joe Massino—cooperating witness and former Bonanno boss

Roslyn Mauskopf—EDNY U.S. attorney

Glenn McCarthy—Genovese associate

John McEnroe—tennis great

Brian McLaughlin—New York City assemblyman and criminal defendant

Butch Montevecci—Genovese soldier

Glen Muenzer—FBI agent

Ernie "the Bear" Muscarella—Genovese capo, later acting boss and current underboss

The Honorable Eugene Nickerson—EDNY federal judge

Artie Nigro—Genovese acting boss convicted of Adolfo Bruno murder

Mike Norrito—Genovese associate and ex-NYPD

Vic Orena—Colombo acting boss

Danny Pagano—Genovese capo

Pasquale "Patsy" Parello—Genovese capo

Pete Peluso—cooperating witness and former criminal defense lawyer

Alphonse Persico—Colombo acting boss

Carmine Persico—Colombo boss

Randy Pizzolo—Bonanno associate

Carmine "Pizza" Polito—Genovese associate and later acting capo

Gary Pontecorvo—FBI agent

Angelo Prisco—Genovese capo

Jack Quinn—Genovese associate

Dominic Rabuffo—Genovese associate

Edward Reich—court referee, lawyer, former president of the Brooklyn Bar Association, and criminal defendant

Louie Restivo—Bonanno capo

Alex Rudaj—Albanian gangster

"Baby Carmine" Russo—Genovese associate and later a soldier

"Fat Tony" Salerno—Genovese street boss

Bobby Santoro—Genovese associate

Peter Savino—cooperating witness and former Genovese associate

Irwin Schiff—Genovese associate

Frank "the German" Schwamborn—Genovese associate

Frank "Farby" Serpico—Genovese acting boss

Carmine Sessa—cooperating witness and former Colombo consigliere

Gerry Shargel—criminal defense lawyer

Joe Simone—NYPD Detective

Frank Sinatra—singing great

Anthony Soldano—wannabe

James Soldano—wannabe and Sammy Aparo godson

Dave Stone—FBI agent

Anthony Tabbita—cooperating witness and ex-Lucchese associate

Peter "the Tax Doctor" Tarangelo—cooperating witness and former Genovese associate

Joseph Toddaro—Buffalo boss

Gary Uher—FBI agent

"Tony Green" Urso—Bonanno underboss and later boss

Joseph Valachi—cooperating witness and former Genovese soldier

Dr. Wilfred Van Gorp—neuropsychologist

Salvatore "Good Looking Sal" Vitale—Bonanno underboss

Bob Vosler—NYPD detective

Bernard Wechsler—doctor to Genovese figures

Abe Weider—convicted felon

The Honorable Jack Weinstein—EDNY federal judge

Johnny Zero—Genovese associate

Joe Zito—Genovese soldier

CHAPTER ONE

THE REAL AMERICAN MAFIA

"I wish I could tell them what it really *is."*
"They're suckers—we just use them."

Let's begin with a primer on the real mob. Much of what you think you know about the mafia comes from Hollywood and television, such as through *The Godfather* and *The Sopranos*—and it is wrong. Some may be loosely based on facts; however, the glorification of mobsters as loyal to their "brothers" and living by a valuable "code of honor" is simply not accurate. I'll try here and throughout this book to set the record straight and to give you a fair and complete account of the truth.

Because of the glorified depictions, you may picture suave and debonair dons and bosses. You imagine them as ruthless, but also perhaps as men of honor, a world of brothers who live and die by a code and would not betray one another. A world in which seniority and the wisdom of years are honored by the rising generation. And criminals, yes, but they generally only prey on one another.

There's a reason for these unreal, generous, and falsified portrayals. The mafia has historically infiltrated and wielded great influence and control over how they are depicted in film and elsewhere. Their infiltration of Hollywood dates as far back as a century. Gangster Willie Bioff, who was close to infamous Chicago mobster Al Capone's ally Frank "the Enforcer" Nitti, was a key player. Through him and others, the mafia gained control over the International Alliance of Theatrical Stage Employees, whose members were critical to the film industry's ability to operate. The mob planned to go even further and gain control over every union involved with the film industry. At one point, Bioff threatened a nationwide theater strike to achieve their aims, enabling the mafia to extort millions of dollars from the major movie studios that were desperate for labor peace. The studios could not risk the threatened worker problems that would shut down their film productions. The gangsters also exerted occasional control over movie content. For instance, Capone was concerned about his fictional portrayal in the original 1932 *Scarface* movie, so he sent gangsters whose threats assured his satisfaction with the film.

Bioff and his confederates were eventually arrested, and Bioff chose to become a witness rather than rot in prison. However, his ego apparently did not permit him to fade away quietly and avoid the spotlight. Because of this, the mafia eventually was able to identify him under his new name and identity. They murdered him by blowing him up in his truck.

A critical example of mafia influence over Hollywood depictions involves the legendary film *The Godfather*. Mob boss Joe Colombo used his control over the Italian American Civil Rights League to apply pressure on Paramount against the proposed movie. He also made clear that he would exploit the mafia's control of unions and other leverage to interfere with its making. In addition, the mob threatened the film's producer and other executives and stole expensive movie equipment. After following this up with bomb threats, Paramount folded to their demands. A silent deal was made, and the movie's story was adjusted to the mob's satisfaction. Not only did they manipulate the story, but they embedded their own members within the film. For instance, Lenny Montana, who was affiliated with the Colombo crime family, played Luca Brasi in the film. Likewise, James Caan was extremely close with then-Colombo capo[3] Andrew Russo. Caan's character was said to have been based on Russo.

---

3   A term I will explain later.

The end result was a film that gangsters everywhere fell in love with since it falsely portrayed them as glamorous men of honor and loyalty. Once the movie came out, mobsters walked with more pride, chests thrust out. Knowing no better, the public ate it up as well.

Other examples include a Robert De Niro movie, *Analyze This*. Rumors have long circulated about De Niro's relationships with powerful gangsters.[4] De Niro reportedly consulted with Gambino capo "Fat Andy" Ruggiano for his role. Michael "Big Mike" Squicciarini, affiliated with the New Jersey–based DeCavalcante crime family, appeared in both *Analyze This* and *The Sopranos*. Likewise, Tony Sirico, "Paulie Walnuts" on *The Sopranos*, was with the Colombos. Sirico also appeared in *Goodfellas*, as did Louie Eppolito, the disgraced ex-NYPD mass murderer for the Lucchese family.

One of the most famous alleged mob-affiliated celebrities was Frank Sinatra. Rumors long circulated that he was close to gangsters and that they boosted his career from the outset. There is abundant evidence to support this claim. Among other things, Sinatra's name and home address was once found by Italian authorities in Charles "Lucky" Luciano's possession, and Sinatra was alleged to have once delivered a suitcase stuffed with cash to Luciano in Cuba. Sinatra was also good friends with Louie "Dome" Pacello, a longtime Genovese soldier[5] who operated out of an office above Veniero's Bakery in New York City. Pacello once refused to answer under oath whether he even *knew* Sinatra, citing his Fifth Amendment privilege against self-incrimination. After being immunized and legally compelled to respond, Pacello still refused to answer—voluntarily choosing to be incarcerated rather than respond to this simple question.

When the film *From Here to Eternity* was made, Columbia Studios was reputedly closely aligned with the mob. Sinatra requested a role from Columbia's head, Harry Cohn, who turned him down. Sinatra then apparently approached an intermediary to Genovese power, Frank Costello, who handpicked Chicago mobster Johnny Roselli to deliver a message.

---

4 You will read in chapter 5 how, knowing this, I attended an opening for another of De Niro's movies. As expected, mobsters were invited and present at the opening.
5 Another term I will soon explain.

Along with Bioff and others, Roselli had been previously convicted for his role in the mafia's massive movie studio extortion described earlier.

Roselli ensured that Cohn cast Sinatra. Although Cohn reputedly warned Roselli that he was connected to other powerful mobsters, Roselli had better connections and was said to have replied that Cohn was a "fucking dead man" if he didn't do as he was told. Sinatra ended up winning an Academy Award for his role. In apparent partial appreciation, he years later sponsored Roselli for membership in the Los Angeles Friars Club.

Genovese soldier George Barone (discussed at length in chapter 11), provided me personally with further details of Sinatra's affiliation with the Genovese family. According to Barone, at one point Sinatra was becoming too friendly with other crime families (Sinatra was famously photographed with multiple Gambino members). Genovese street boss "Fat Tony" Salerno summoned Sinatra to a meeting in Harlem. Barone was instructed to be there before Sinatra's arrival. Salerno instructed Barone to kill Sinatra depending on the meeting's outcome. Sinatra begged for his life, was reprimanded, and committed not to violate his relationship with the Genovese. His life was spared.

The mob's infiltration of Hollywood was even discussed during my investigation with D'Urso. D'Urso was closely aligned with Genovese capo Sammy "Meatballs" Aparo. Aparo's son Vinny is a Genovese soldier. Vinny's son Michael, in turn, is an actor who among other things, appeared in the movie *The Harvard Man*. In one conversation secretly recorded during the investigation, Sammy recounted how James Caan was with a Colombo family crew. Sammy stated that Bonanno family capo Johnny Green Faraci's son Vinny, a Bonanno soldier, aided Michael in obtaining his role in the film by introducing him to Caan. Faraci also related how he had the contract to supply the limousine service for the film.

The list of the mafia's affiliations with the industry and with celebrities goes on and on. The result is a multitude of portrayals that overwhelmingly emphasize the fictional positive and glamorous side that mobsters themselves loved.

This myth of men of honor still persists.

There have been rare exceptions. *Angels With Dirty Faces,* made in 1938, showed America that mobsters tend to die horrible deaths and deeply regret their involvement in "the life." Few other mob movies made since have dared to reveal this reality, although *Donnie Brasco* did a good job.

Law enforcement has no equivalent mechanism or public forum to combat the public relations machinery of movies/film/TV. Instead, we quietly catch and imprison these men for the destruction they bring upon the law-abiding public.

I participated in this process for many years and witnessed mob members behaving dishonorably toward each other at virtually every turn. I have experienced the hypocrisy of this treacherous life, which is often unknown to aspiring gangsters and to legitimate society. Details of secretly recorded mafia conversations that you will read about also demonstrate evil, callousness, baseness, and disorganized cruelty. I heard a capo describe his own son not in a loving, sane, normal manner, but as "some sperm" injected into a woman. Too many of these men are not only vicious criminals; they are not normal men with normal values.

Amoral mobsters without honor are not the exception—they are the rule. Each generation of young men who seek to join in hopes of achieving honor and status—and finding a new "family" to join—are instead likely victims of the ongoing con. Despite what they may have heard, they are joining a glorified gang where there is virtually no honor and very little loyalty. Mob members will and have killed their best friends and family members without hesitation whenever it was in their interest to do so. They freely con and plot against one another, and they additionally spend their time conning, threatening, and hurting others—their victims—who are not a part of "the life." The single most disingenuous expression spoken by them is "I love you." Never believe this statement if you hear it. One of the driving forces for telling my story is to make this all clear.

Young men joining a crime family are lucky if they can cultivate three or four truly trustworthy friends. That small group has to fend for itself in an ecosystem of a few hundred other often hostile and scheming members, alongside tens of thousands of associates. And even this small band of men may turn on one another. The men involved are thieves and liars, many of them violent, willing to do anything to boost their personal status in the chain of command, and it may well come at your expense. These men would violate omertà (their code of honor and silence). They would kill you without a second thought if they were ordered to—as has happened countless times. Moreover, these men bring sadness, death, financial stress, and family stress upon virtually everybody in their orbit. Most of them don't realize the inherent hypocrisy until years after joining. Then they observe over time the stream of lies to each other. It is by then too late and/or risky to leave, unless you cooperate with law enforcement.

There are gangsters who love and value their children. However, this life can cause extraordinary untold trauma even for their own family members. Genovese Boss Vincent "Chin" Gigante's daughter recently revealed witnessing her father brutalize another man and step on his face while she hid in terror and watched blood trickle down under the family's dining room table at just five years old. She became petrified of her own father and for years suffered from debilitating anxiety along with other disorders that plagued her. Her mother paid a terrible price as well from a deep lifelong depression. One has to wonder whether mobsters ever pause to consider the unspeakable damage they inadvertently inflict on those they love most. As former Colombo capo Michael Franzese has explained: "Any lifestyle that does that to families has to be evil and that is the bottom line."

And while some mobsters generate significant money, and their children live well from the father's criminal conduct, the lifestyle is achieved only by victimizing others; neighbors gossip and cause stress to young children. Normal friendships are limited for the children, as Gigante's daughter tellingly described, other children "were not allowed to hang out with me," and "rumors [followed] in school, everybody talking about you." Sons are more likely to follow in their father's criminal ways, placing their own lives in jeopardy. Law enforcement surveillance also can draw unwanted attention to them in the neighborhood.

Michael and John Franzese can speak to the destructive impact of the mob as the sons of a powerful member of the Colombo family. Michael was able to eventually extricate himself from the mob's gravitational tug and has publicly declared, *"I don't know one family that's part of that [mob] life that hasn't been totally devastated."* John was desperate to leave, too, and eventually helped gather evidence to send his own father away.

On top of it all, the one guy you consider your closest and most trusted friend may be reporting your activities to the FBI, or may even be recording you for them. No matter how it may seem from afar, living among that level of ongoing stress is simply not worth it. Many mobsters go to bed with concealed weapons in their homes in the constant awareness that their end might come at any time, and they may be summoned to meetings from which they know they may never return.

The relationship involving Frank Campanella, a.k.a. Frank Campy and D'Urso was a lengthy one originating with a dispute involving competitive business. Frank Campy, Colombo associate, was very close with Billy Cutolo, acting underboss. Jackie DeRoss, was representing Campy and Cutolo in meetings with Sammy Aparo. One day, Cutolo disappeared. It was immediately obvious that he was killed. Campy cited in a recorded conversation with D'Urso how everybody loved him, but one guy didn't like him. This referred to Carmine Persico. Cutolo's murder related to Carmine Persico's dislike of Cutolo—that related to a previous Colombo war. Vic Orena was placed as the acting boss subsequent to Persico's conviction in the Commission case. Orena, in this capacity as acting boss, believed this should transition to official boss since Persico received a one-hundred-year jail sentence. A hostile division led to another internal war. Billy Cutolo sided with Orena. Orena was subsequently arrested and was sentenced to life in prison for murder during the war.

Persico wanted his son, Little Allie Boy Persico, to become the next official boss of the Colombo family after he passed away. He made his son the acting boss. Since Cutolo sided with Orena in the war, I imagine Carmine Persico maintained a grudge and hatred of Cutolo. However, after the war was settled, Persico agreed to Cutolo being placed as acting underboss of the family. This may have appeared as a fair settlement for the war. However, it may have also provided Cutolo with comfort as though matters were settled. The reality, Persico feared Cutolo could become boss, preventing his son from running the family. Persico also held a grudge and Cutolo was killed. Jackie DeRoss and Little Allie Boy Persico were convicted and sentenced to life in prison for this murder. A little more hypocrisy, as I understand, DeRoss had Cutolo as his best man for his wedding. Durso's recordings about Cutolo's murder with Aparo, Campy, and others provided a foundation for the murder convictions.

The horrors of such a lifestyle were summarized by a gangster recorded in one of my investigations describing the sudden disappearance of someone close to him. "I was told he ain't around, that that's it. What am I going to do? *That's it, that's the life. One day you're here, the next day you're gone.*" Moreover, you have to bury any anger or sadness because otherwise they might murder you too. "If a friend of yours ain't around and they turn around and say 'how do you feel he ain't here?' your answer has to be 'he ain't here, he ain't here. We going to eat now.'" The gangster further related, "It's over, it's over. It's just like I lost my best friend, which I did, you know. You know what? *Everybody loved him. But one guy didn't like him.*"

Young men who consider joining a crime family need to be made aware of all of this, before it's too late. They should ask themselves, is it really worth it? They should know that they are not signing up to work with the best and the brightest, and they are certainly not signing up to work with men of honor. Rather, they will cause misery and suffering for others, in exchange for which they can hope to profit and hope to dodge the above-described land mines. They will also learn to dehumanize their fellow human beings in order to prey upon them without hesitation, and so become dehumanized themselves.

One mobster who rose to the highest ranks of organized crime once summarized the situation in open court: "I hate everything about the life I led, and I hope that it ends soon because it keeps destroying families and kids who are infatuated with it and can't wait to be 'goodfellas.' *I wish I could tell them what it really is.*"

Supported by those that spread their supposed mystique, the mob projects an outward appearance of order and strength. However, as you'll learn in this book, behind closed doors lies a very different reality. Beside the ever-present internal strife and backstabbing, law enforcement crackdowns hit the families hard, crippling them deeply, sometimes for generations. Prosecuting the top of the family hierarchy has proven extremely effective. Capable mobsters are replaced by less competent and inexperienced underlings which in turn weakens the gang's structure and effectiveness.

Heat from law enforcement, both real and perceived, also creates great paranoia and fear, alongside the knowledge that fellow gang members may be quietly turning over evidence and/or recording their conversations for the FBI. Sometimes the paranoia spirals out of control, as mob leaders mistakenly order the murder of others who they wrongly believe to be cooperating, or simply use this as an excuse to justify murdering a rival or somebody that they dislike. This in turn increases the collective paranoia and ironically creates additional mobsters-turned-witnesses or informants. After a takedown, the mob members who do remain are often too paranoid to be fully effective in their crimes. When informers and cooperators decimate a crime family, that family is less able to know who to trust, making it much more challenging for them to conduct their business.

There is also the ludicrous myth that mobsters only harm other mobsters, and therefore, don't really impact regular citizens. That is pure nonsense. Government, business and commerce, even philanthropy can all become stifled and corrupted—have their very lifeblood sucked out—if organized crime is allowed to thrive.

In sharing my story, I will display—often citing the mobsters' own words—just how powerful and useful government decapitation of a crime family can be and why it is so very important for law enforcement never to relent, and to keep turning up the heat.

My career intersected with the so-called Five Families that are synonymous with organized crime in America. Since 1931, in various forms, these five New York City–based "families" have been responsible for some of the most damaging crimes in our country. They consist of what are now known as the Genovese, the Gambino, the Bonanno, the Colombo, and the Lucchese. Although each refer to themselves as a "family," they share absolutely nothing in common with real families—except for those in which murder, theft, violence, blind greed, treachery, hypocrisy, and backstabbing are the norm. I will at times in this book refer to them as "families" because it is the common parlance, but please keep in mind that they represent the polar opposite.

Here is a basic primer of what they are and how they are structured: The Genovese, historically the most secretive, successful, powerful, and deceptive, are regarded as the "Rolls-Royce" of the group, while the Gambino are the next most powerful. Each family shares a core group structure consisting of "members," who sit atop the hierarchy, but who also make the whole organization vulnerable to their personal foibles, failings, and indiscretions. The Genovese often take additional steps to attempt to insulate its boss such as by using an acting boss, street boss, or straw boss. Sometimes they do not even share this information with their own members. As you will learn vividly in this book, that has advantages but has also led to utter disaster for them. The Genovese also use messengers to communicate with other families and internally, so that their most powerful members rarely occupy the same room.

In terms of hierarchy and structure, here are the basics:

At the bottom rung, with the most people by far and in the aggregate numbering in the many thousands, are what are known as associates. Associates can be of any ethnic background, Italian or otherwise. An associate is not a "member" of a crime family, but they work to help enrich both themselves and a crime family. Some associates find it useful to be in a reciprocal relationship for the advantages this brings, such as lack of competition, because competitors will be threatened or hurt until they go away. Others consciously hope to one day become a made member. Others have no desire to have any relationship with the mob, but in the course of doing business or doing a favor for someone, before they know it, that relationship is imposed upon them. It then almost inevitably becomes too late for them to extricate themselves, and they become resigned to a partnership they never sought, and which will likely bring them only misery. Some businessmen get compromised this way. They allow the made member to treat them favorably. But once he grants you a favor, you're his. You belong to him. It's now too late to get out. Many young men want to be in an organized crime family. However, one needs to understand this decision rests with the gangsters. Gangsters often lead others to believe they have a future, just to profit from and use these "wannabe" guys.

Acting Colombo boss Jackie DeRoss once concisely summarized the relationship in a statement secretly recorded in the D'Urso investigation. DeRoss said that associates may *believe* they are in "the life" but in reality, they "*are suckers—we just use them.*" So, if you're reading this book and are considering that way of life, just know he's describing *you*.

Many associates' lives are at constant risk, whether or not they know it. Most can be killed by mafia members without the member necessarily needing to obtain any permission from their crime boss to do so. A host of reasons have led to such murders. Some have been killed because they are viewed as "weak links" who might cooperate with law enforcement, even though at times there is no objective basis to think that this will take place. Interestingly, sometimes associates are killed after being proposed to be "made."[6] This is because a crime family may learn or suspect that the associate previously cooperated with law enforcement or committed some similar transgression. The murder of Ralph DeSimone, a Genovese associate proposed for induction, is a textbook example, occurring after the Genovese learned that DeSimone once provided assistance to law enforcement. One of my investigations led to the conviction of Genovese consigliere Jimmy Ida for this murder. And sometimes associates are murdered simply because another mobster is settling an old score or looking to gain some kind of advantage. Since associates are low men on the totem pole, they often have no protection against such a plot. One such murder played a major role in the D'Urso case, as I will discuss thoroughly in this book.

Another violation that has led to associates' deaths involves sex with a made guy's girlfriend or wife. Associates have also been killed for pushing back against the relationship they've been thrust into, voluntarily or not, with the mob. Many have lost their lives when they realize the extent of the money the gangster is taking, and they resist in some form. Even adopting a tough-guy attitude can be viewed as arrogance that could lead to a death sentence due to a perceived lack of respect.

Above an associate is a member, also known as a soldier, made man, wiseguy, goodfella, button man, and friend of ours. Each crime family, depending on its size, can have anywhere from around a hundred soldiers, up to several hundred. These numbers are fixed and not permitted to change although, being criminals, they cheat on this rule as I will show you. Soldiers must be males of Italian descent on the father's side. Because

---

6 Defined on the next page.

this requirement excludes many otherwise valuable associates, there have been some notable instances of powerful and successful associates who were treated as though they were made men, and in rare cases even commanded the respect accorded to the most highly placed gangsters.

Soldiers typically control associates, who are said to be "with" them, and control their activities. Soldiers have the protection of the entire crime family to which they belong. For this reason, they generate a lot of fear and deference on the street. Unlike an associate, a soldier cannot be killed without permission from the boss of the family.

When an associate becomes a soldier, a secretive initiation ritual takes place, and he is inducted as a "made" member. Though there are some variations, the induction ceremony generally involves calling the initiate into a room filled with senior members of the family. There, the initiate is asked if they know why they are there. The proper response is "No" because this is a secret ceremony, and they are not supposed to know. They are asked if they wish to join the crime group, to which they must pledge their absolute loyalty. In many ceremonies, a gun and knife are present, and the initiate is told that he will live and die by these weapons and, if ordered, must kill for the family or himself be killed. The initiate is instructed that he must place the interests of the mafia family above his own blood family. Mob business takes priority over every other priority, including the initiate's wedding, the birth of his child, even the hospitalization or imminent death of a spouse: if his wife is dying in the hospital and he is called, he must leave her and go where he is told. Then the initiate's finger is pricked, and a few drops of his blood are placed on a saint's prayer card, or a napkin. He then holds the card while it is lit on fire and burned in his hand. He is told that if he ever betrays the secrets or any of the rules of the family, he will be killed and burn in hell like the saint burning in his hand. Among other things, he is instructed that there is a code of omertà, meaning "silence."

That being said, there has apparently been some slippage in the formality of this ceremony. I had D'Urso record a Genovese soldier's critique his own induction ceremony: *The induction ceremonies depicted in the movies are done better than the real inductions.*

The initiate must deny the existence of the mafia and *never* reveal any of its secrets. Betrayal of this omertà vow is supposed to meet with death.

Despite this, and as alluded to immediately above, I will present you with mafia members describing the induction ceremony—in their own words.

You will learn of so many routine violations of the mob's rules as to question the very notion of true omertà.

The next rung up the ladder, above the soldier, is the capo, also known as captain, caporegime, or skipper. A capo is generally placed in charge of a "crew" of soldiers (and the associates under each of them), usually between a small handful up to around twenty, and the occasional powerful associate who may not answer to a soldier. Soldiers underneath a capo must put "on record" with the capo all criminal conduct they and their associates are participating in, and with whom. They receive the capo's protection and his support in the event of a dispute. Capos can also serve as a "bank" for their crew. For example, a capo may lend money to a soldier for loan-sharking at an interest rate of 1 to 2 "points" per week. Points are the same as "percentage," so 2 "points" per week means 2 percent of the loan per week must be paid—a rate of over 100 percent per year—not including repayment of principal which must be repaid separately. The soldier (or an associate) will then charge whatever they can get above that rate from the borrower, so the ultimate borrower is paying far in excess of 100 percent per year interest. Particularly because such extortionate rates are exceedingly and obviously hard to repay, violence and the threat of violence attends this arrangement and ensures repayment. Those who borrow often are driven to desperate street-level crime such as car thefts, robbery, drug dealing, etc., in an effort to pay off their loans. An associate may work in the financial sector and assist with stock fraud to help the gangster. This is part and parcel of the criminal ecosystem of new crimes created by organized crime, which damages society's collective daily safety and standard of living.

Capos are usually in charge of large criminal projects, and in most crime families they report directly to the boss, underboss, or consigliere who together constitute each crime family's ruling "administration."

Soldiers typically kick up a portion of the money they make to their capos, and the capos share some of that with the boss and the administration. Hiding money and criminal activity is punishable by death.

The consigliere is usually appointed by the boss and serves as his advisor. He also addresses disputes involving other crime families, along with internal disputes within their own family. Above the consigliere is the underboss, who is like the vice president. He will usually become boss or acting boss if something happens to the boss, such as incarceration or assassination.

At the very top, then, is the boss, who is the unquestioned head and decision-maker.

Decades ago, Lucky Luciano attempted to prevent the constant murders, infighting, and wars plaguing these criminals (discussed more in chapter 2). This included creating a ruling body, known as the commission. The commission imposed order, resolved disputes, identified controlled territories, and oversaw and governed organized crime operations on a national scale. It originally consisted of the five bosses from New York City in addition to the Chicago and Buffalo bosses. Murder of a boss without the commission's consent was punishable by death. The commission was decimated by significant prosecutions over the years. As a result, the five families function in a more disjointed fashion, compared to the previous historic commission composed of their bosses. They do still coordinate resolutions of disputes and violations of omertà. However, they clearly lack the trust due to the historic cooperators from former high-ranking members.

The goal of this entire criminal structure, of course, is making money through crime. All the rest of us in their worldview are "suckers," ripe for the potential picking. The mafia makes money through a variety of rackets—some of which change with the times, and some of which are evergreen. In addition to loan-sharking, they run sports gambling (legalization of this industry increasingly eats into their profits), extort "protection money" from business owners large and small, commit fraud, deal in counterfeit and stolen goods, and they perpetrate financial crimes of all types. They infiltrate legitimate businesses until they come to control them, often to the terror of the original owners. This has famously been seen in extremely lucrative examples of controlling multiple labor unions and businesses that depend on their labor such as construction companies, the carting industry, and the garment industry. Every dollar they take is an inflationary extra dollar, a tax that regular law-abiding citizens must pay. Every terrible worker they send to mess up the work of those that don't "play ball" with them is a potential building that collapses, or at the very least, a more expensive project whose cost will once again be passed on to the law-abiding public. And if a mob-controlled carting company can get away with it, they'll not hesitate to dump toxic waste that may poison a community or its water supply. Although it is officially forbidden within their rules due to lengthy prison sentences and the subsequent possibility of cooperating with the law, many mafia crews quietly traffic in drugs, unable to resist the temptation of easy profits.

But there are lots of other ways they make money. There are bank robberies, control of the seaports, home invasions, control of significant centers of commerce such as JFK Airport, the Fulton Fish Market and Hunts Point Market, running nightclubs, participating in stock fraud, controlling strip clubs, controlling street festivals, making pornography, and more. The list goes on and on. It would take an entirely separate book to explain how these crimes impact the rest of us, but as one small illustration, through their control of JFK Airport, the mafia has historically been able to steal an enormous amount of money and goods. For instance, if they steal millions of dollars of computers in transit, then the seller has to raise its prices to make up for that loss, or pay increased insurance premiums. And guess what, those costs are passed on to the rest of us, who pay ever so slightly more for the next computer we buy. If you dislike inflation and taxes, an inflationary tax to the rest of us is embedded in virtually every mafia scheme. Their control of the construction industry in New York was known as the "mob tax" added to every significant construction project. Not only do their crimes come at a significant financial cost to the rest of us, but many also have real victims, real people who suffer, such as honest businesspeople who don't want to "play ball" with mobsters and who are then threatened, hurt, killed, or economically damaged.

As alluded to above, controlling unions generates huge money for the mafia. When law enforcement arrests a gangster affiliated with a corrupt union under their control, the mob does not simply walk away from this union. Similar to the NFL, when a player gets injured and is removed from the game, the team does not stop playing or play with a man down. They replace this player with another player who may not be as good, and then they continue with the game. Their schemes allow favored contractors to win jobs, either against contractors who are not connected, or against contractors who are affiliated, but who do not generate the same amount of money for the mob. They may also use contractors to facilitate bid rigging schemes with an increased cost passed on to the average citizen. To enforce this approach, unions controlled by the mob cause problems with contractors by strikes, destruction of property, union noncompliance with audits, etc. Controlling unions also gives the mobs access to their funds, such as pension funds and health and welfare funds, which can be skimmed, and mob-connected companies are inserted to handle these funds for extortionate fees. I participated in the investigation that involved Genovese capo James Messera, who used millions of dollars belonging to the Mason Tenders District Councils Union Pension Funds to purchase properties based on fraudulent real estate appraisals. One of those transactions was for the sale of Messera's mother's property in Miami, Florida. Honest union members obviously suffer because their hard-earned pension funds are used to benefit gangsters who swindle their money.

To put more meat on the bones, here are just some of the unions historically linked to the mob.

The International Longshoremen's Association (ILA): Around fifteen separate Locals have historically been controlled by the Genovese and/or Gambinos. These unions have huge memberships, with some placed there by the mob, and they kick back a portion of salary in exchange. Shipping containers' contents disappear, and shipping companies learn that they must abide by rules set down by the mob for their profit. At least two Associations have also been under mob control. The Associations relate to companies that do business at the seaports. Over decades, investigations have made numerous recordings that detail the corruption.

Construction unions: About eighty separate union locals, district councils and associations are affiliated with four of the New York mob families in addition to the New Jersey–based Decalvacantes. These locals include carpenters, laborers, mason tenders, bricklayers, operating engineers, electricians, plumbers, truckers, concrete, painters, and drywall tapers.

The Teamsters Union Warehouse Division: There are more than twenty separate locals and a couple of associations affiliated with all of the New York mob families.

In addition to the above, there are unions for the hotel workers, restaurants, waste haulers/sanitation, Jacob Javits Center, and others who present opportunities to generate money and jobs for the mob at public expense.[7]

The mob uses violence and the threat of violence to enforce each of their rackets. Few are willing to defy them, as they will threaten, hurt, or kill those who get in their way. One infamous example was the murder of two honest carters, Robert Kubecka and Donald Barstow, many years ago.

Their reach used to expand across the entire United States, with crime families established virtually everywhere. But law enforcement launched successful attacks across much of the country, and in many places the mob has either been eliminated altogether or is now an empty shell of what it used to be.

Yet even outside of New York, the mob still exists in some cancerous form or another in places like Philadelphia, New Jersey, Chicago, Arkansas, Florida, Texas, California, Colorado, New Haven, Providence, Boston, Buffalo, and New Orleans. Mob members also don't hesitate to travel to other locations, and even to other countries, when there is an opportunity to steal.

---

7   Law enforcement should make greater use of forfeiture to seize assets, reduce criminal profits, and to pay the expense of investigations. Assets subject to seizure include corrupt union members' retirement funds, corrupt contractors' equipment, trucks, buildings, homes, and corporate assets.

CHAPTER TWO

THE MAFIA'S ORIGINS AND HISTORY: HYPOCRISY, TREACHERY, AND DECEIT

The mob likes to present itself as filled with men of honor, loyalty, and principles. The reality is that its foundation—its very origin—was built instead upon a slippery base of hypocrisy, betrayal, and deceit. Let me take you on a little history lesson, bringing you back to the true beginning of the New York mob and its "five families." The treachery I will outline will make your head spin, and it describes the underlying reality. One of the original bosses was Joe Masseria. Lucky Luciano, Vito Genovese, Frank Costello, Meyer Lansky, and others who reported to him, killed Masseria off. That is some treachery for you. They coordinated this with Masseria's enemy in the bloody and vicious Castellammarese War, Salvatore Maranzano. The agreement was that Luciano would take control of Masseria's operations.

Months after Masseria's murder, however, Maranzano made plans to murder Luciano and Genovese because he became envious of Luciano's popularity among the ranks. More treachery. Maranzano's coconspirators in the murder plot, however, backstabbed him and shared the details with Luciano and Genovese. They murdered Maranzano in 1931, and this led to the creation of the five original "families":

Luciano family: Boss—Charles "Lucky" Luciano (this later became the Genovese family)

Mangano family: Boss—Vincent Mangano (this later became the Gambino family)

Gagliardi family: Boss—Tommy Gagliardi (this later became the Lucchese family)

Profaci family: Boss—Joe Profaci (this later became the Colombo family)

Bonanno family: Boss—Joseph Bonanno (still known by that name although it briefly changed to the Massino family)

Luciano worked to develop an overarching structure to prevent the constant cycle of murder, betrayal, infighting, and wars. This included creating a ruling commission, consisting of the five New York bosses, the boss of Chicago, and the boss of Buffalo. Buffalo was later replaced by Philadelphia due to Buffalo's violation of the commission's first self-preserving rule—no murdering a boss without the commission's consent. Additional rules were made to coordinate criminal activities, resolve disputes, and approve future members through joint background screening (sharing the candidates' names on lists provided to each family, for their input). If details emerged from this process that posed a red flag, such as the candidate was a suspected informant or had assisted or worked in law enforcement, the candidate should be killed.

Although by its definition, membership was limited to Italian male "brothers," Luciano likely had a closer, more trusting relationship with Jewish gangsters Meyer Lansky, Bugsy Siegel, and Louis "Lepke" Buchalter than with some of his Italian so-called "brothers in the life," like Joe Bonanno. Luciano was eventually arrested in 1936 on charges of running a large-scale prostitution ring. Rarely ever mentioned is that New York Assistant District Attorney Eunice Carter was instrumental in the case against Luciano. She was the first African American female to ever work as a prosecutor in New York. In coordination with others, she designed a discreet strategy to raid a couple of hundred brothels, and she obtained the trust of many prostitutes who testified as witnesses.

After Luciano's arrest, Dutch Shultz attended a meeting with Luciano, Meyer Lansky, and other powerful New York figures. Schultz wanted to kill New York District Attorney Thomas Dewey for overseeing the investigation. Luciano and others responded this would be counterproductive because law enforcement would become much more aggressive in response. Schultz wanted to follow through on his plan anyway and discussed this with Mangano family underboss Albert Anastasia. More treachery because unfortunately for Schultz, Anastasia was also close with Luciano, and Schultz was murdered.

Luciano was convicted in 1936 and sentenced to a term of thirty to fifty years. His underboss, Vito Genovese, became the acting boss. Vito temporarily abdicated the throne, however, in 1937 when he fled to Italy to avoid a murder charge, and Frank Costello was promoted to acting boss (or "street boss") to run things while Vito was unavailable.

According to cooperating witness and former Lucchese acting boss Al D'Arco, mob members are prohibited from ever assisting law enforcement in any capacity. The U.S. Navy is a government agency with law enforcement capabilities. Sharing information with the Navy posed risks to organized crime, allowing Navy intelligence the ability to share details learned about this secret, criminal organization. However, during World War II the Navy, in coordination with New York State authorities, requested Luciano, Lansky, and others' assistance through their relationship with the ILA and the Seafood Workers Unions. Obtaining the ILA's assistance would ensure timely delivery of crucial military supplies. Mangano and his underboss Anastasia controlled the Brooklyn waterfront while Luciano and his underboss Genovese controlled the Manhattan and New Jersey waterfront. Joe "Socks" Lanza, a member of Luciano's crime family, headed up Local 359 of the Seafood Workers Union. Union members could assist with early notification of possible German submarine threats. The men on ships coming to port would also be the eyes on the sea, in addition to the U.S. Coast Guard.

Genovese had fled to Italy and aligned himself with Benito Mussolini's administration. But he was also willing to double-deal Mussolini and assist with Navy Intelligence for the invasion of Italy. He became an interpreter with the U.S. Army and in this way also aided Luciano. The purpose of the double-dealing was to try to ensure that they win either way.

Apparently, the reward for these efforts was an early release from prison for Luciano, and his deportation to Italy. As for Genovese, he was arrested by the military after they learned of his murder arrest warrant in the states. Murder charges against him were dropped in 1946, however, because prosecution witnesses appeared to have been killed.

When Vito returned to the states, his acting boss, Costello, was loath to give up his title and the power that attended it (because Luciano had been deported, he could not participate in daily operations). They grew to hate and distrust one another, as they each laid claim to the throne. As you'll see, backstabbing, treachery, and machinations of betrayal operated at their peak.

Costello was close with Anastasia, who was also bumping heads with his own boss, Mangano. Mangano envied both Anastasia's close rapport with Costello, Luciano, and Tommy Lucchese, and also resented Anastasia making decisions without consulting Mangano or his brother, consigliere Phil Mangano.

As usual, the "brotherhood" resolved their differences with brutality. In April 1951, Vincent Mangano disappeared while his brother Phil was found shot dead in Brooklyn. These murders were not sanctioned by the commission. Underboss Anastasia was elevated to boss, with the commission's approval. Many gangsters nonetheless believed that Anastasia orchestrated the murders without the commission's authorization to become the new boss—a clear violation of the rules.

Anastasia was also infamous for the probable murder of a key witness in a case charging Anastasia with murder. Abe Reles, a hit man who turned government witness, was being protected at a Coney Island hotel by six police officers before he was to testify at Anastasia's trial. Reles plummeted out of the hotel window to his death, supposedly opting to kill himself. This was prior to the establishment of the federal Witness Security Program.

In any event, perhaps impressed by Anastasia's forceful seizure of power, Costello plotted with Anastasia to murder Genovese so that Costello could take his place. Much of this information was personally corroborated to me by soldier George Barone (see chapter 11), a longtime member of the Genovese family who had been in Vito Genovese's crew at that time. They also met with Luciano consigliere Michael Miranda because they must have viewed him as a strong potential ally. They shared their plan to kill Vito, and asked Miranda for his support. Miranda left them with the impression that he would consider it but instead went directly to Genovese and others. More head-spinning layers of betrayal. Miranda identified Colombo member Sonny Franzese as having observed this meeting, which Franzese corroborated. As a result, the commission sanctioned the murders of Costello and Anastasia.

Vito Genovese assigned the assassination to Vincent "Chin" Gigante, a soldier close to him. Gigante shot Costello in 1957 as he returned from a night out on the town. The grazing shot did not kill Costello. Afterward, mafia members who authorized the sanctioned hit discreetly met with the shaken, still-living Costello. In an effort to save his own life, he confirmed his and Anastasia's plan to kill Genovese. He also confirmed that he would do his best to prevent Chin's conviction for trying to murder him, as he wanted to preserve his own life. Costello was permitted to live based on his cooperation with the mafia and was placed in an inactive status.

Costello most likely deceived Anastasia into believing that his shooting was not related in any way to Genovese discovering their joint plot to kill him. Because he was unaware that his life was at risk, a few months later Anastasia was easily killed while sitting in a barber's chair at the Park Sheraton hotel.

The above details all vividly illustrate nearly mind-boggling levels of backstabbing and treachery, and the complete absence of any remnant of "honor," "loyalty," or "family." In fact, just the complete opposite.

More treachery took place a few years later, in 1961, when Profaci member Joe Gallo decided to take over his own crime family. He kidnapped underboss Joe Magliocco, the boss's brother Frank Profaci, and two other high-ranking Profacis. Gallo had allegedly been one of the shooters in Anastasia's homicide, and I imagine his ego and arrogance may have emboldened him to conduct these kidnappings. After several weeks of negotiation, he released the hostages. During this same time, Gallo was convicted of an unrelated extortion, and he served a prison sentence until 1971. He was killed after his release while dining at Umberto's Clam House in Little Italy, on April 7, 1972.

Joe Colombo became boss of the renamed Colombo family. Profaci had died from cancer in 1962, and Magliocco was broken (a term used to describe how a gangster is prohibited from participating in the gang's affairs) by the commission after admitting his role in a plot to kill other bosses. Colombo was himself shot in 1971. This was because he organized and participated in a demonstration by the so-called Italian American Civil Rights League in Columbus Circle. The commission did not appreciate the attention Colombo brought to the mob with these demonstrations. The shooting left him paralyzed and bedridden until his death. The Colombos have had numerous internal wars involving mass killings since then.

The Bonannos were also involved in high-level treachery, deceit, and betrayal. In the early 1960s, Joe Bonanno planned to assassinate some of the other commission bosses. The intended victims were to include Carlo Gambino and Tommy Lucchese. Bonanno sought the aid of others in this plot, including Profaci boss Joe Magliocco, who replaced Profaci after his death, and then-high-ranking Profaci member Joe Colombo. However, just like Genovese consigliere Michael Miranda went to the commission with the plot to kill Genovese, Joe Colombo also decided to go to the commission rather than participate. When confronted, Magliocco confirmed Colombo's information, and Magliocco was permitted to live but made inactive as a mobster. This in turn led to another internal war, this time among the Bonannos, in the 1960s. As part of a negotiated truce, Joe Bonanno and his son Bill, the former Bonanno consigliere, were broken and relocated to Arizona.

In another instance of hypocrisy, Bonanno then wrote a slanted auto-biography revealing many supposed secrets—clearly a violation of omertà, the mob's code of silence never to disclose details of this criminal organization. He also appeared on an episode of *60 Minutes* to discuss the book. Two Luchese family members, capo Sal Avellino and boss Tony Ducks Corallo, were secretly recorded discussing Bonanno's violation of omertà.

Mob treachery has not been limited to New York. The Philadelphia family was known as the Bruno family after its boss, Angelo Bruno. He was historically aligned with the Gambinos. Anthony Caponigro was Bruno's consigliere. He had a gambling operation in which he became involved in a dispute with a powerful Genovese member Funzi Tieri. Their dispute escalated to the commission, which sided with Caponigro over Tieri. Tieri may have held a grudge over this.

Years later, in 1980, Caponigro reached out to Tieri, by then the Genovese acting boss, to coordinate what he thought would be the commission's consent to murder Bruno. Caponigro believed Tieri gave him (Caponigro) the impression the commission authorized the plot, and Bruno was killed. Genovese consigliere Bobby Manna, then traveled to Philadelphia and declared that Bruno's murder was not sanctioned and that the commission was conducting an investigation. They summoned Caponigro to New York, and he told how Tieri represented that the commission authorized Bruno's murder. Tieri, however, maintained that he never confirmed authorization but instead had told Caponigro that he would share Caponigro's request for authorization. Caponigro was killed in a brutal manner.

Phil Testa became Philadelphia boss after Bruno's murder, but Testa too was killed shortly afterward. Nicky Scarfo then assumed the boss title. He installed his nephew Phil Leonetti as underboss. Scarfo also had Phil Testa's son Salvatore killed because Nicky was jealous of him. Scarfo had Salvatore's best friend carry out the murder. Think about that for a moment. Killing your best friend. As I've said often, there is no brotherhood, loyalty, or honor. Only treachery and betrayal.

For further insight into how poisonous "the life" can be, Leonetti later described his uncle Nicky as pure evil. Scarfo's own son Mark did not want to be involved in organized crime. Instead of supporting his son's decision, or just staying out of the way, Leonetti described how Scarfo regularly insulted Mark in front of others. As a result, Mark committed suicide by hanging himself. A graphic demonstration of the damage that can be caused by valuing the mob family over your biological family.

After eventually leaving the life and becoming a cooperating witness, Leonetti often described how great his new life was, no longer being in the mob, and that it was the best thing for his son to live a normal life.

So there you have it. This is the wreckage of a foundation upon which the mob was built.

With this background, here are some thoughts. Historically, I have had empathy, not sympathy, for old-time gangsters, members, and close associates. Many were involved in this criminal life based on their family's immigrant status, as they or their parents came from Italy. As immigrants they were often mistreated by the police, and for many there was no trust in law enforcement. For more recent mobsters, completely unrealistic fantasy depictions like *The Godfather* serve as a powerful recruiting tool. Gangsters also typically grow up in an environment where they observe how mobsters are treated in the neighborhood. The fine clothing, attractive ladies on their arms, expensive watches, coiffed hair, fancy cars, jewelry, etc. can be powerful draws to poor kids. Neighborhood kids also may have gangster relatives who appeared larger than life.

Joining such a group initially appears to be such a huge honor and achievement. However, reality quickly intrudes and is the exact opposite of what they think. Mob life hypocrisy is typically not realized until it is too late. As former Colombo capo Michael Franzese described, "One of the horrors in that life, you make a mistake, your best friend walks you into a room [and] you don't walk out again. Unfortunately, I've witnessed that."

That relative who appears to be so powerful may not share the details of abuse and deceptions that he experienced or witnessed in this alleged "brotherhood," or the fact that, like many in the mob, he has to sleep with a gun under his pillow every night in an effort to defend himself against some anticipated or unanticipated attack. The "wannabe" may also not realize that when a neighborhood gangster no longer appears in the neighborhood this may be because he was murdered or has quietly gone away to serve a significant prison sentence. In turn, the investigation that led to this result most likely originated from one of his "brothers," who served as an informant or witness.

Moreover, young, naive initiates quickly learn that the mob family comes first, even before their blood family. Depending on the "family," there are a hundred to hundreds of made members, along with thousands of criminal associates. They are instructed to trust and value their criminal "brother" in the mob over their blood family member. Think about that for a few seconds. You're joining a criminal organization and—upon penalty of death—you are told to trust hundreds of deceitful and often murderous criminals over your closest friends and family. Think about how upside down that is. As Kevin McCallister stated in *Home Alone,* "I don't think so."

Some gangsters nevertheless place their blood family before their mob "family." Ironically, although every made Genovese member (like all mob members) is told when initiated that they must value the Genovese over their own wives or children, the boss, Vincent "Chin" Gigante, didn't apply these rules to himself. And nobody was going to call him on this hypocrisy. His blood family and a small group of his friends came first. Chin did not induct his sons, knowing it might draw law enforcement scrutiny and significant prison time. Famously, at a meeting with John Gotti, when Gotti proudly informed Chin that he had inducted his own son, Chin replied, "I'm sorry to hear that." Although Chin did not make his family members, he did provide them with mobster benefits— lucrative employment at the seaport he controlled through the ILA. They could earn a half million dollars a year without ever leaving their home. Some were paid as shop stewards who supposedly worked twenty-seven hours a day, seven days a week. They were related to, or close to, Chin, and were therefore respected and feared. Nevertheless, I wonder if Gigante ever regretted his crazy act and the inconvenience it caused in his family life. I imagine they may have had some laughs over the years, but was it worth it?

Young men fascinated by "the life" like to view themselves as tough, but this is another misunderstanding. In my experience the most treacherous gangsters can be short in stature, and they don't resolve differences through a fistfight. They'll shoot you if they like you, and you'll never see it coming. They will torture you first if they hate you. And often, the one you think likes you actually hates you, as D'Urso and Lombardi discovered too late.

And then there are all of the informants and cooperating witnesses. Many of them, or a very close friend of theirs, have been screwed, deceived, and/or abused in some capacity and decided to cooperate with law enforcement. During my career, I have made numerous recordings and reviewed source communications that capture the seething hate and contempt for supposed "brothers." In the corporate world there is similar envy and jealousy, but it doesn't end with murder or prison.

My hope in writing this book—by being completely honest about mob life—is to convince young men never to join in the first place. There is no glory in that life. There may be a temporary financial gain, but it comes at enormous cost, and once you are in the life there is no backing out. They will kill you rather than let you leave because of the risk that you'll give away their secrets. It is a world of vipers who prey not only on the public, but on each other. It is a world of men who will both literally and figuratively backstab one another whenever they think it's in their best interest. It is a con that convinces aspiring young men that they have found a place of honor and family, and then uses them—grinds them up and spits out whatever is left of them.

CHAPTER THREE

THE ODDFATHER

"Can you argue with the king? When you're the queen?"

While I made my way into young adulthood, a figure whom I've referenced above came from a very different world. He secretively stood at the very top of the crime family to which I would devote much of my professional career. Vincent "Chin" Gigante was on the rise.

He was much older than me, born in New York in 1928, the son of working-class Italian immigrants. When Vincent was a boy, his mother often called him "Vincenzo"—the Italian version of his first name. This was sometimes shortened to "Chen-zo" and when the other kids on the playground heard this, they apparently simply started calling him "Chin."

Chin went to grade school in the West Village and started high school in Chelsea but dropped out. He was a doughy, meaty kid who was good at sports. Chin boxed and thought he might make a career of it for a while. Tommy "Ryan" Eboli, a future acting boss and another older member of Vito Genovese's crew, was a professional boxer who may have influenced Chin as an aspiring gangster. When he was just nineteen years old, Chin left boxing behind with a 21–4 professional record. Some believe his nickname "Chin" arose from his boxing career, because he had a good chin. Though he was a very capable boxer, he had other, less legitimate and much more violent ideas about a career path.

While growing up, local mobsters who lived in his neighborhood took note. They took a special interest in him as he engaged in petty theft. He also may have thrown a fight or two to generate income in gambling bets for his mentors. Chief among these men was Vito Genovese, arguably the most powerful man in the mafia at the time. Vito was head of the Genovese and when Frank Costello challenged Vito's leadership, Vito assigned Costello's assassination to Chin.

Here are some details of what took place: On May 2, 1957, Costello returned to his apartment building on Manhattan's Upper West Side after dinner out on the town. Interestingly, this building was directly across the street from where John Lennon would be killed many years later. Chin was lurking nearby and followed Costello into the building's lobby. According to some of the witnesses, Chin announced, "Hey Frank. This one's for you," as he opened fire.

Decades later, Chin became the most powerful, canny, sophisticated, and feared of all mafia bosses.[8] But back then, an inexperienced Chin had not yet honed these skills and appeared to have done everything possible wrong. The scene is almost reminiscent of the Keystone Cops.

He fired at Costello only once, and may have believed he'd scored a perfect headshot. However, his bullet only grazed Costello along the side of the head. Chin also did not conceal his face from other people in the building's lobby, including the doorman, who got a good view. As a boxer, Chin knew all about cutting weight or bulking up as the situation called for. He apparently had decided that his "disguise" for the hit would be to simply become as overweight as possible, and then go on a weight-cutting regimen directly afterward until he resumed his normal size and looked like a different person.

---

8   Gigante's decision to pursue life as a mafioso contains a powerful and horrible irony. His daughter recently revealed that Gigante's grandfather killed himself. He had apparently witnessed a crime by the mafia in Italy, and they threatened him and his family so that he would be quiet. He was a pharmacist, and he chose to poison himself with strychnine due to their threats. So when Gigante himself chose to become a mafioso, for his own mother "it was like the nightmare all over again for her."

After Gigante fled the scene in a black Cadillac—believing he had killed his target—Costello got up and simply took a cab to the hospital. What was worse, witnesses had the license plate of the getaway car, and the police quickly learned that Chin had purchased the vehicle just two weeks before the attempted murder.

Chin moved to an undisclosed location where he began his crash diet. However, word quickly spread that law enforcement knew exactly who they were looking for. The diet plan was probably a complete waste of time. Years later, Chin came up with another outlandish plan to avoid prosecution for his crimes, one literally much more crazy than eating his way to a criminal defense—but this new plan ironically would succeed and buy him freedom for decades.

Months after shooting Costello, a much thinner Chin Gigante turned himself in to the police. The ensuing trial was an embarrassment, as the witnesses laid out how truly inept he had been. Things were looking bad until Costello testified. The existence of organized crime was not well known at the time. The prosecutor—who apparently did not know how the mafia worked and had assumed Costello would promptly finger Chin—was confounded and furious. Costello firmly maintained that he didn't know who'd shot him. Moreover, he knew of no reason why Gigante should want to shoot him. Of course, by testifying in this manner Costello kept his word—which helped save his life—to the commission that he would not help in Chin's prosecution. Gigante's life was also spared. Oftentimes, mobsters who bumble a murder assignment are themselves killed, but as his daughter Rita has explained, Chin was not killed because "Vito loved him."

When Costello finally stepped down from the stand and passed Gigante on his way out of the courtroom, several trial observers heard Chin remark, "Thanks a lot, Frank."

Costello's performance apparently sufficed to create reasonable doubt in the minds of the jury, although it is not known whether mobsters bribed or threatened any of them. After a short deliberation, they returned a verdict of not guilty. Despite perpetrating one of the most bumbled hits in history, Chin Gigante was a free man. Few could have predicted at the time that such a prominent stumbling start would culminate in the rise to power of one of the most deadly, powerful, and utterly strange men ever to rule the criminal world.

For his part, although Costello quietly retreated into the background, he remained available to assist the Genovese when called upon. According to Genovese soldier George Barone and others, Costello made overtures to President Kennedy to convince his brother, Attorney General Robert Kennedy, to refrain from pursuing organized crime. JFK is said to have responded, "I can't control my brother. Nobody can control him. He would indict our mother, Rose."

* * *

After his acquittal, Chin went back to work for Vito Genovese. But this did not last long because just forty-one days later, they were both arrested as part of a larger takedown of Genovese's criminal operations, including running heroin. Chin was called to testify in Vito's trial, but he took the Fifth Amendment on every question and refused to testify. Vito was eventually sentenced to fifteen years and died in prison. Gigante was likewise convicted of his involvement in peddling narcotics, serving just five years of a short seven-year sentence, which was much lighter than he was expected to receive. Looking for a reason to account for the judge's puzzling mercy, trial observers pointed to the large number of letters, many from Chin's friends and neighbors in Greenwich Village, attesting to Chin's upstanding character. After his release, Chin rejoined the Genovese crew and was promoted to capo. He held court inside a club he christened The Triangle Civic Improvement Association. It was located across the street from an apartment owned by his mother. From this outpost on Sullivan Street, Chin ascended the ladder that ultimately resulted in his becoming boss by 1981. During this time, he also participated in several unusual activities. Though most mobsters have girlfriends or mistresses on the side, Chin harbored an entire secret other family—replete with separate family homes, one in a townhouse in New York and one in a house in New Jersey—with two wives and children that, at least initially, had no clue of each other's existence.

By far the most eccentric facet of Chin's rise—and eventual domi-
nance of the mafia—arose from what on its surface appears like sheer
idiocy. Gigante created the ludicrous impression that he suffered from a
complete and debilitating mental illness. This was an effort to create an
insurance policy against future prosecutions. Unparalleled in the annals
of crime and just plain silly on its face, his decades-long stunt defied
common sense yet actually succeeded for almost the entire time that he
maintained the act.

He started in about 1966 by periodically checking himself into mental
hospitals and psychiatric treatment centers. Chin began to create the utter
illusion that this was real. At intake sessions, he complained of symptoms
that most would associate with paranoia, schizophrenia, and disassocia-
tion. But he made it all up on the fly based on films he had seen, books he
had read, and also by "mimicking the cartoons" he saw on television, as
explained by his daughter Rita. He simply sought to create a long record
of fraudulent treatment and care. Rita further elaborated that if a doctor
gave him a pill, Gigante would "show them he swallowed it. They would
leave. He'd spit it out in a tissue, give it to my mother and say, 'take it
home and flush it.'"

This crazy act could not have worked without the active assistance of
psychiatrists and other mental health professionals. Some were complicit
and understood that the man before them had no legitimate mental illness.
Some were gullible and did not have the ability to distinguish between an
act and a sincere mental illness. Combined, they insisted vigorously that
Chin was indeed insane. Over the course of decades, Gigante collected a
fat stack of medical files, with a substantial number of medical professionals uniformly swearing that the dangerous mobster suffered terribly from
debilitating mental illness.

Consistent with the act, when Chin appeared in public, he began walking the streets of Little Italy and conducting mob business in a bathrobe.
He had several among which he alternated, including one that was pink.
Chin knew full well that he and his crew were under observation by the
FBI and other law enforcement. Because of this, he and his colleagues also
were exceedingly careful to avoid having their voices recorded. He made it
clear that mentioning his name aloud could result in the speaker's death,

so his crew and others almost always invoked their boss by silently touching their own chin.

Because mobsters are wary about discussing their crimes inside of a building where a listening device could be installed, they often have such discussions outside, in what they term "walk/talks." However, outside, they are subject to being photographed or filmed. Gigante conducted his business outdoors in the bathrobe, sometimes putting on a showy physical performance as though he were both severely mentally and physically impaired. The resulting FBI photos from the era are sometimes surreal. Gigante is often surrounded by mafia members right out of central casting, while he appears to have been deposited from another movie entirely, leaning on their arms for support, looking disheveled and dribbling from the mouth. There are also surveillance photos of him appearing normal as he walks and talks with members of his crew in his neighborhood. When he conducted his business occasionally inside the apartment, he took every available precaution. Gigante's daughter recently brought us inside Chin's methods: the shades were always pulled down over the barred windows, he never spoke on the telephone, he always left the phone off the hook, he only talked in whispers, he kept cartoons blaring on the television, he left the radio on as well, and he had everyone tear up every piece of paper they reviewed, followed by either burning them or flushing them down the toilet.

Chin did all of this to prepare his defense for the next time he found himself in handcuffs. His lawyers would point to years of reports from psychiatrists unequivocally opining that Chin was a mental vegetable, could not possibly understand any charges against him, and that the trauma of a trial would likely kill him. "This man is not a criminal mastermind," his lawyers and physicians would say. "He's a victim himself . . . of profound mental illness. You don't need to punish him with a long sentence—or even with any sentence at all—because God's already done that. Have pity on this poor, unwell man."

That was the card that Chin strengthened in his back pocket at all times. It was a wild plan, seemingly out of a silly comic book plot, but somehow it worked. Whatever his criminal colleagues thought of it privately, only in rare and hushed private conversations would they question his choice to appear crazy. None were brazen enough to question him aloud except for a few who were captured on FBI bugs.

As he walked the streets of Greenwich Village issuing instructions to a massive and sprawling criminal organization while appearing a madman, Gigante ordered murders and designed and approved of criminal plots for others to carry out. He inherited and enhanced a criminal network that ran across the city. In addition to evergreen rackets like gambling and loan-sharking, Chin inveigled the Genovese into positions to collect profits from major New York institutions like the Javits Center and the Fulton Fish Market, along with much of the waterfront. These institutions had been historically controlled by the mob, but Chin managed them skillfully to ensure the Genovese saw maximum benefit.

He also inserted the Genovese (alongside other mafia families) into labor unions and the construction industry; developers in the city knew that they needed to quietly insert money into a project's budget for payoffs to the mob. These costs would ultimately be passed onto their law-abiding tenants and others. Teamsters, laborers, cement and concrete workers, bricklayers, carpenters, operating engineers, roofers, drywall tapers, plumbers, electricians, painters, building services workers, hotel employees and restaurant workers, bakery and newspaper unions—just to name a few—all saw themselves infiltrated by the Genovese and other mafia families. To this day, there are over one hundred locals controlled by and or affiliated with a La Cosa Nostra (LCN) family in the New York metro area. Chin's son-in-law, Joseph Colonna, was being paid hundreds of thousands of dollars as a union shop steward while never actually having to leave his residence to do any work. There are approximately a dozen other members of Chin's personal family who benefited from mob-arranged positions—with high salaries and little work—along the New Jersey waterfront.

The New York Waterfront Commission Hearing Report for 2012 cites the ongoing organized crime influence and control generating money for them. I partially quote from this hearing below:

> Shop stewards are conferred a large amount of responsibility, yet the
> hearings uncovered what appears to be widespread ignorance, neglect,
> undemocratic practices, and organized crime connections . . .

Mr. Gigante's limited knowledge about the Collective Bargaining Agreement (CBA), which he is charged with safeguarding, is also concerning. When asked whether he was familiar with the CBAs, Mr. Gigante simply replied, "I have no idea what you're talking about." He actually required clarification that "CBA" stood for "collective bargaining agreement," a troubling admission for an individual whose responsibility it is to enforce the rights of employees under the agreement. He also indicated that he had "not really" read the pertinent CBA . . .

Salaries ranged from $60,000 a year to over $400,000, the latter earned by Ralph Gigante, nephew of former Genovese crime boss Vincent "Chin" Gigante, of ILA Local 1804 1. Mr. Gigante apparently also has, to a certain degree, unlimited paid vacation. . .

But the most troubling shop steward connections belong to the family and relatives of Vincent "Chin" Gigante. First, there is Ralph Gigante, who succeeded his cousin Andrew Gigante, Vincent Gigante's son, as shop steward in 1995. Ralph Gigante ran unopposed for shop steward, was elected by "affirmation," and testified that he is shop steward "for life" or until he retires. There is also Robert Fyfe, Jr., who was Vincent Gigante's son-in-law. He, like Ralph Gigante, is an ILA Local 1804–1 shop steward. Joseph Colonna, another son-in law to Vincent Gigante, is also a shop steward at ILA Local 1804–1. He succeeded Vincent Gigante's brother-in-law, John Bullaro, and was among the highest-paid shop stewards, earning about $400,000 in 2009.[9]

All of the above is corroborating evidence of the recorded conversations made by D'Urso and Barone's testimony.

Gigante had other innovations up his sleeve. In a kind of belt-and-suspenders approach to trying to insulate himself from the law, he inserted Anthony "Fat Tony" Salerno as the "front boss." This meant that while

9   "Special Report of the Waterfront Commission of New York Harbor to the Governors and Legislatures of the States of New York and New Jersey," WCNYH, March 2012, www.wcnyh.gov/news/Waterfront%20Commission%20of%20New %20York%20Harbor%20Special%20Report.pdf.

Gigante issued the orders and held all of the true power—in his bathrobe, between mental health appointments—Fat Tony was officially known as the Genovese head. Everyone referred to Salerno as the Genovese boss. Only a select circle at the top knew the truth. As confirmed by Gigante's daughter Rita, Gigante "always had someone in front of him saying that they're really the head."

Salerno himself clarified this relationship in a covert FBI recording in which Salerno discussed the arrangement with fellow Genovese gangster Giuseppe Sabato.

Salerno: He stays there like a dictator. He dictates.
Sabato: Tony, can you argue with the king? When you're the queen? The queen? You can't argue with them.

Employing a front boss (sometimes called a "straw boss or street boss") kept law enforcement off-balance. This plan worked as well, because when the famous commission case from the mid-1980s was brought, targeting the bosses of each of the crime families, the government asserted Salerno—not Gigante—was the Genovese boss.

And so, during a period when mob influence in New York City was near its highest point, one of the strangest mafia dons of all time, Vincent Gigante, managed a vicious and terrible criminal empire. His actions caused misery and ruin. He carved out incredible riches for himself and his blood family, yet was well-liked by the other Genovese because he did not demand particularly heavy payments from those beneath him in the power structure. As described by his own daughter, "It was never about the money for him. It was always about the power."[10]

---

10 Legendary Colombo capo Sonny Franzese likewise told his son, "Just remember who the real power in New York is. And that's Chin."

CHAPTER FOUR

BEGINNING THE FBI CAREER

As Chin Gigante was making his final moves to solidify his position at the top of the Genovese power structure, I was starting my career with the FBI. I joined the agency in 1978, and for several years essentially worked as a kind of low-level office clerk, handling administrative tasks while learning the culture. I was not yet an FBI agent.

Though my position might have been lowly, the effects of joining the FBI were felt in my family immediately.

My uncle Johnny worked in the carnival business, traveling around the country organizing shows and county fairs and so forth. He was also something of a character, and as I understand, had once been a champion Golden Gloves boxer.

Only a year after I joined the FBI, I ran into Johnny at a funeral. "Now you stay on that side of the fence, and I'll be on my side of the fence," Johnny joked. Years later, my father and grandmother filled in some blanks in the family history for me. Johnny, they explained, was good friends with Angelo Dundee, the prominent boxing trainer and corner-man for Muhammad Ali. Dundee's brother Chris was a boxing promoter who was connected at various times to mobsters like Frankie Carbo of the Luccheses and Frank "Blinky" Palermo, who was regularly charged with fixing fights.

My work status changed in 1983. I had been married for less than a year, and one night took my wife, Nancy, out for Chinese food. The fortune cookie told me that I was in for a career change, and we both agreed it was a good omen because I had by then been seeking employment outside the FBI. Nancy always had some reservations about how my becoming an FBI agent would impact the family, and after we wed, her brother offered me a corporate job at Chase Bank, which I turned down at the time. That same night as the fortune cookie, however, as we got home our phone was ringing. It was the call I had spent years waiting for. They invited me for new agent training at Quantico.

During the first part of Quantico training, I was away from home for a solid month. The FBI conducted a thorough background check on all prospective agents. This included interviewing my neighbors, who were a young couple with young daughters. FBI agents made an unannounced visit and asked questions about me without explaining the purpose. We had only lived next door to them for a few months at that point. Since the neighbors had not seen me for about a month (I was at Quantico), and the FBI was asking about me, they concluded I must be a fugitive or criminal of some kind.

When I finally returned home, the neighbor rushed her children inside the house when I tried to speak with them. I told Nancy about this odd behavior. Later that week as she came home from work, the same neighbor asked her where I had been. Nancy responded, "at the FBI academy training to be a new FBI agent." The neighbor burst out laughing. "I thought he was an FBI fugitive. I was on the verge of calling the FBI . . . to help get him arrested."

* * *

My first assignment was in Cincinnati, and those nearly two years were important and formative, in addition to sometimes being very strange. Back in the 1980s, for a guy from the East Coast, Cincinnati was a bit different than Northern New Jersey.

For example, I went to meet my first federal prosecutor, known as an Assistant United States Attorney (AUSA) regarding a new investigation.

As I crossed the street a police officer sprinted down the sidewalk looking as though he had just witnessed a major crime. I looked around to see if there was a purse snatching or assault of some sort. Then I noticed that the officer was slowing down and coming to a stop on the curb right where I was about to step on. He looked at me and said, "Do you know what you just did?

"I crossed the street," was my answer.

"You jaywalked," he stated.

I had not heard this expression since I was a child. I had heard of it, of course, but had never seen it enforced. Seeing a cop trying to enforce jaywalking was like glimpsing a rare animal that was supposed to be extinct. However, the officer's tone was like he had witnessed a rape or a serious assault. He then asked if I was on the job, an expression used to identify if I was law enforcement, as though this would excuse my serious offense. I explained who I was and that I was on my way to meet an AUSA in the federal courthouse. The officer did not seek to charge me.

When I shared the story with my new FBI colleagues, they had a good laugh. I would later learn that—seemingly arbitrarily—Cincinnati held the dubious record for issuing more jaywalking tickets than any other city in the United States. For some reason, they thought it important to keep the flame alive for that particular violation.

Another new agent and I would laugh about this to no end. Once or twice when there wasn't any traffic or risk, we lured pedestrians into the street by stepping off curbs as though the lights had changed. Everyone would attempt to cross the street following us like sheep to slaughter, and we'd turn back to the curb and watch the confusion as they realized they did not have the light to cross. The crowd would rush back to the curb.

The world was a lot more parochial back then. Once I met with a bank investigator for a 9:00 a.m. meeting at a local bank. The investigator's sleeves were rolled up, his shirt unbuttoned with his tie pulled down as though he just finished a fifteen-hour shift. A gun was attached to his hip, and he pulled out a bottle of Jack Daniels, asking if I wanted coffee, which I politely declined. The next words came out of the investigator's mouth in a slow Kentucky drawl. "Mike Campi. . . . Is that there one of those Italian names?" His pronunciation of the word Italian was with very slow and southern Kentucky "EYETALIAN." I said yes. He then asked, again in a thick Kentucky country accent, "Did anybody ever tell you you talk funny?" My response: "Not yet, you're the first."

I thought the meeting was set up as a prank on "the new agent" by older agents on the squad. But it wasn't a prank. When I shared the story with them, they could not breathe because of how hard they laughed.

* * *

One of my first successful cases was solving a fraud at a clothing manufacturer called Palm Beach Inc. When the company's own accounting showed that something fishy was going on, I helped to uncover a ring of three subjects, one an employee who billed the manufacturer with fraudulent and inflated invoices.

I also got a taste of the kind of action that most people, influenced by television viewing, imagine FBI agents experience all the time. A fellow squad was working on a case that involved stealing from railcars transporting goods through Kentucky and Ohio. There was a section of track where the trains had to slow to about five miles per hour. Criminals would then open the doors and board the train cars, stealing equipment like televisions and appliances. I was invited to come along to assist in making the arrests. I arrived to find other agents at a remote spot where the train normally slowed. The train was completely stopped, and several of the thieves who had been waiting to steal had been arrested. Other thieves had scattered when the agents first arrived, and we thought several were hiding nearby.

I was ordered to help with searching the train cars. I reflected that while there was a chance the criminals could be armed, I felt no fear, only thinking of the task at hand. I climbed to the top of a coal car and, sensing a strong odor of alcohol, found one thief hiding inside. He was overweight, very drunk, and terrified. I took out my small flashlight and drew my .357, privately noting that it was my first time holding my weapon in an authentic law enforcement situation. I placed him under arrest.

As planned, I regularly made trips to visit Nancy at our home in Lansdale, Pennsylvania. Nancy also came to visit me, and the first time she did resulted in my first taste of genuine workplace awkwardness. When I mentioned she was visiting on an upcoming weekend, my supervisor Dave invited us over for dinner. As far as I could tell, the dinner went fine. But after we left Dave's house, Nancy abruptly said she had something important she needed to say.

"There was a moment when I was alone with Dave's wife in the kitchen, when you were in the other room," Nancy told me. "Dave's wife turned really stern, and said something like, 'You need to understand that an FBI agent's job is more important than his wife's job. If you're not prepared to follow Mike as he moves along in his career, you should get out of this marriage now.'"

I was in shock and hoped this was an exception to the rule in terms of the freedom an FBI superior's wife would feel to approach the wife of a colleague about such a personal and private matter. I liked Dave and his support of my criminal investigations.

* * *

After only a little over a year, I was about ready to get out of Cincinnati. Most new agents graduating from the FBI academy were assigned for a minimum of two years in a smaller metro area to enhance their training as new agents. After two years, they would receive orders to one of the top ten offices. Because of this, FBI offices in cities like New York, Chicago, San Francisco, or Philadelphia were composed primarily of more senior agents. I requested a transfer along the Eastern Seaboard, and didn't know that the door to New York was opened a crack because the New York office had an incredible burnout rate. Agents were then paid the same in Alabama and other places as they were in New York, which had a significantly higher cost of living. So, in addition to considerations like commute and other stressors, this all contributed to agents leaving New York. It was also by far the largest office in the country and new agents were always needed.

I had not really wanted orders to New Jersey—even though it would have been a way to be closer to Nancy—because I had the sense that there would be something strange about working "too close to home." Investigations involving criminals in your own former backyard could pose strange conflicts. Some of them might be guys you grew up with or around.

I received a letter saying that I was being transferred to New York City. Immediately after receiving this news, Dave approached me, asking what my preference was for my new assignment. Was there a type of squad or investigative unit that particularly interested me?

In a decision that would profoundly impact the rest of my professional life, I responded, "Organized Crime." I'm not terribly sure why that was my answer. It could have related to persistent table discussions about the mob's reach when I was growing up. It could also in part have related to significant media attention at the time indicating that prosecutions against the mob in New York were starting to gel, with the famous commission indictment and arrests, charging the highest levels of each crime family with multiple crimes. Nancy and I had never discussed the possibility that I might pursue the mob. However, I knew, without it needing to be said, that Nancy greatly preferred my assignment to tackle the much more staid world of white-collar corporate crime. Who could blame her?

As I shared with Nancy the good news of my relocation back East, I decided not to be too explicit about what I had requested. But once I reached the Big Apple, I received confirmation that my new assignment would be the Organized Crime Branch, Squad C-5.

CHAPTER FIVE

FIRST CRIPPLING BLOW
TO THE GENOVESE

"I've just been visited by an FBI agent named Mike Campi."
"Hire an attorney and plead guilty. Now!"

When I joined Squad C-5 of the FBI's Organized Crime Branch at the New York office, I began doing the kind of work I had dreamed about. Squad C-5 was the labor racketeering squad.

One of the highlights of my new post was befriending another new agent named Mike Luzzo. We became such a pair that our supervisor Dennis often confused us. Both of us were named Mike, although we looked different. I always corrected Dennis, but he remained confused. Once, Dennis called me into his office, "Close the door. *Sotto voce,*" meaning we should speak quietly and secretly.

Dennis continued, "First of all, whatever you do, don't tell Campi, but . . ."

I did not cut him off for some time. But after he finished, I said, "Boss, I'm Campi."

The other agents and I had a good laugh about it later.

Luzzo and I used to have laughs. Once, we were getting ready to make pitches seeking cooperators and conducting surveillance before approaching these people. One was an Italian contractor. We parked on the side of the street near his house, with me laying down in the back seat with a camera to take a photo. Luzzo suddenly said, "We've been spotted," because the wife was pointing at us while the contractor ran to his car. I think he may have thought we were connected to the corrupt labor union and had been sent there to intimidate him. Luzzo drove away, while I asked, "Why are we running? It looks like *we're* the bad guys." Luzzo was having a blast, saying, "You'll never catch me, coppers." Meanwhile I kept asking him, "What are you concerned about?" At one point we drove into a dead-end street, and the contractor passed the street. As he was back-tracking, Luzzo turned our car toward the contractor and drove by him, with Luzzo saying, "See ya, copper!" as he passed the other way. Even with all this, the contractor ended up cooperating.

I learned early on the extent to which the mob world and my own private world could become intertwined. For example, Nancy signed us up to help with baby baptisms at our church. The first time I showed up for this, I realized the baby being baptized was the granddaughter of a powerful Gambino capo, Danny Marino, who was incarcerated. I did not know at that time his son, Danny Marino, had moved to my town and other neighbors affiliated with him also attended the service. They were shocked to see me greeting them as they entered the church and probably thought I was working.

Some years later, Nancy and I were invited to a Christmas party being thrown by some neighbors. Nancy and the wife were classroom mothers at our children's school and Nancy really liked the wife in that family. A lot of people were there, including some who were prominent. At one point several people were standing in a circle, me included. A party guest made a crack like, "I'm the only legit guy at this fucking party." This guest did not know that I was an FBI agent. The party host suddenly looked right at me. Nothing was said, but it was clear they knew who I was, just as I knew who they were.

I eventually told Nancy she had to end the friendship once it was confirmed that her husband was associated with the Gambino family. To this day, she wishes they could have remained friends.

One somewhat comical investigation from this period involved several arrests related to the extortion of Russians who co-owned Concord

Limousines. The defendants were named D'Agostino, Romeo, and Tanzi. Among other things, the Russian victims were fascinated with the quality of FBI bulletproof vests, asking how much they cost. They mentioned how they paid $500 each for a vest that was clearly of inferior quality.

I made consensual recordings with the Russian victims to capture the evidence of extortion. The Russians placed calls to D'Agostino to address the issues. D'Agostino put Romeo on the telephone call with the Russian. Romeo, in response to a Russian victim asking the caller who he was, responded, "I'm the fucking devil! If my cousin doesn't get his money today, up pops the devil." He then screamed at the top of his lungs how he would kill them all, and then hung up. We arranged a meeting at a diner, and we arrested them in the parking lot. Each was armed. D'Agostino had a temporary colostomy bag, and his weapon was a cocked semiautomatic, safety off, with a round in the chamber. This could have accidentally gone off as it was in the front area of his slacks pointing down at his groin. Not the brightest light bulb in the pack.

As for Tanzi, he was one of the dumbest guys I ever arrested. He was also so big that when we cuffed him and put him in the back seat, his head was practically in the front seat. The ride to Manhattan took a while and upon arriving in the FBI garage, as we removed him from the back seat, his hands were discolored from the lack of blood circulation. He could not feel his hands but never mentioned any discomfort. He mentioned how he had previously been knocked out by Gerry Cooney, the professional heavyweight boxer, at a Long Island bar as we passed it driving back to the office.

For his part, even as we arrested them D'Agostino commented how he wanted to kill the Russians: "I am going to kill those motherfuckers." He observed that he and I were both Italian, as though this was justification to kill them. I provided details of his statements to the prosecutor and the magistrate judge at D'Agostino's detention hearing. Nevertheless, D'Agostino appeared to like me, and he stepped around the back of his defense attorney to again let me know how he hates "these motherfucking Russians." His attorney placed his hand on D'Agostino's head to motion him back, while saying, "Will you *please* stop talking to him." They all ended up pleading guilty.

After about four years, our squad was retasked with investigating the Colombo LCN family. My new supervisor was an agent named Dave Stone. Dave was the case agent on my squad when our focus was labor racketeering. He developed a case against Bonanno boss Phil Rastelli, and the future boss Joe Massino, in a labor racketeering case. Rastelli was indicted in the commission case but was severed from this prosecution and convicted along with the acting street boss, Joe Massino, at Dave's trial in the EDNY. Joe Pistone testified at both the commission trial in the SDNY and in Stone's EDNY trial charging Rastelli, Massino, and others.

Stone was a good agent who I liked and who was underappreciated by FBI management. That said, Stone had briefly quit the FBI for a couple of weeks to take a job in private industry. He did this primarily for his wife and family and their quality of life. About two weeks into the new job, he contacted the FBI to share that he'd learned that a major trucking business—that did business with his new employer—was affiliated with organized crime. When Dave took this information to his new civilian bosses, they screamed at him, "You no longer work for the FBI!" Essentially, he was reprimanded to look the other way, bury his head in the sand, mind his own business.

At that point, Dave called the FBI office in New York to see whether he could get his old job back. He didn't want to work for a place that tolerated corruption. Fortunately, the FBI had not finished processing his retirement papers. Sadly, Dave lost a lot of money leaving (the new job had been in Ohio), and then returning to New York—with an additional loss of money from extricating himself from the pending sale of his residence. Dave's determination to remove himself from any world that would make him compromise his principles spoke volumes to me.

Early on, I asked Dave how I could become a case agent and lead my own investigation. Dave replied that I could simply prepare a memo citing potential criminal conduct by the subjects and requesting to open an investigation. Eager to get in the mix, I reviewed the historical control files—source files containing information from informants and cooperators—for the Colombos and opened an investigation on the future consigliere Carmine Sessa and his close friend, soldier Bobby Zambardi. Sessa had risen from associate to soldier to capo in a very small window of time. He ultimately became consigliere during the Colombo War, which was a 1991 attempt by acting boss Victor Orena to violently seize leadership of the family via murder while the true boss, Carmine Persico, was in prison. The resulting infighting lasted two years and left twelve gangsters dead, eighteen "disappeared," and an innocent murdered bystander. About a dozen more made men had had enough, and they chose to cooperate with the FBI and provide evidence against their fellow mobsters.

The war continued until Orena was convicted for racketeering, and his supporters relented. While Persico continued to run things from prison for many years afterward, the Colombos were severely weakened by their internal warfare.

C-5 soon thereafter was repositioned to investigate the Genovese. Three agents from C-5 were reassigned to another squad that jointly investigated the Bonanno and Colombo families. Chris Favo was one of the three, and he was a very capable agent who aggressively pursued his work. From afar and with great satisfaction, I saw that he continued to conduct this investigation successfully, eventually having Sessa, Zambardi, and others arrested. Sessa became yet another high-level defector, a cooperating witness. Because he had been consigliere, Sessa was able to provide devastating information and testimony for the FBI in multiple trials.

At his own sentencing, Sessa stated in open court, "I hate everything about the life I led, and I hope that it ends soon because it keeps destroying families and kids who are infatuated with it and can't wait to be 'goodfellas.' I wish I could tell them what it really is."

For his part, Zambardi received a life sentence and later died in prison.

Although another agent had the honor of performing the investigation, I felt that my instincts were validated, that Sessa was the correct person to focus on to try to impose significant damage on the Colombos. I had developed that belief based on the source information I reviewed: Sessa was a rising star in the Colombo family who had been promoted quickly from associate to soldier to capo, and later, consigliere. Based on this I expected that he would be very active. His multitasking as consigliere exposed him because many Colombos had information against him, as did high-ranking members from other families.

Coming full circle, Sessa ended up being an important witness in my later case against Genovese consigliere Jimmy Ida.

* * *

Developing sources often involved hard work, tracking down leads, pursuing possibilities. They in turn could lead to investigations, cases, and prosecutions. And sometimes it all just falls into your lap. But you have to put in the effort, even if you are not sure it will conclude with success. Lazy agents—and there were too many of them—just didn't get it. Here's one experience that illustrates the point. A buddy at the time asked me to join him on a trip to Rikers Island prison to meet with an inmate who contacted the FBI. The premise was his interest in cooperating on a matter related to organized crime.

Our first impression wasn't very positive. The inmate appeared to be sick, an individual who abused narcotics, and may have had AIDS. He was primarily interested in having an FBI agent look into his sentence to determine when he would be released. The inmate did not know anything about the mob. He was your typical West Village street drug addict.

The inmate explained, however, how he would vouch for us to a second inmate who was seeking an opportunity to cooperate with a trustworthy FBI agent. This second inmate had shared some details with him about organized crime figures he was affiliated with. The names he brought up included a Greek mafia boss named Big Spyros from Queens and some Italian organized crime figures, such as "a guy named Ralphie Bones."

As we sat there listening, the inmate shared additional details about what the second inmate, also named Spyros, shared with him. My then-buddy did not take a single note during this entire meeting and appeared anxious to leave. He restlessly sat and listened while I asked questions. As we ended the interview, the inmate requested that we review his sentence and bring him cigarettes, if we could, the next time we visited. I gave him my name and a telephone number so that he could call collect in about a week. This would allow me time to check on the details he provided and any FBI interest in future investigations. It would also give me some time to check on his status as an inmate and the details about his sentence and potential release date.

As we left the prison, my buddy laughed and said, "Campi, you're crazy for giving this guy your contact information." He believed the inmate was a junkie and not credible. I agreed he was a junkie. However, it really wasn't difficult checking the details and determining the potential cooperation from this other inmate, Spyros. If the inmate was of no use, I would simply not accept any future calls.

I learned the inmate was arrested for a minor burglary and was to be released in about eight weeks. He called me as directed and I told him what I'd found out. The inmate perceived this as great news, as if I'd helped him get out. As promised, he then vouched for me and I met with Spyros, who was Spyredon "Little Spyros" Fioravantes, an associate of Gambino capo Ralphie "Bones" Mosca. I debriefed Spyros, who was looking for a deal since he was serving a lengthy sentence for heroin dealing. He provided me with numerous historical details on both the Gambinos and Greek organized crime figures. I prepared a report based on this information, and gladly shared it with the two squads who had investigative interests.

But there was more. Little Spyros ended up becoming a cooperating witness and subsequently testified as a principal witness in the EDNY against Spyredon "Big Spyros" Velentzas. Big Spyros was considered the Godfather of the Greek mafia, affiliated with the Luccheses. He was convicted on multiple counts regarding his role leading a gang of more than thirty criminal associates. Little Spyros also testified at trial against John Gotti. And, based in part on his information, Ralphie Bones was indicted for operating a massive gambling business.

Had the lazy, complacent attitude of my buddy prevailed, none of this would have happened, and it required almost no effort. He discounted valuable information solely based on the inmate's appearance and circumstances. Prejudging someone without fact-checking is a waste of taxpayer money and it is reckless. This was supposed to be his interview.

Shortly after this initial meeting with the drug-addicted inmate, I jokingly hung up on my buddy when he called over the next couple of weeks.

It was as though he was a waste of my time, and we had a few laughs about this.

Do I need to add that, with work instincts like these, the buddy became my squad's supervisor several years later? Another empty suit who never should have been assigned as a squad supervisor.

Newly focusing on the Genovese required me to become familiar with them, and then pivot to finding a subject to investigate. Little did I know at the time, but the Genovese comprised the most important and consequential cases of my career.

The Genovese are regarded as the Rolls-Royce of the crime groups. They are the most powerful, most secretive, and most financially successful. Founded by Lucky Luciano in 1931, in 1957 it was renamed for Vito Genovese. Though the family would be named after him, as alluded to before, things did not go smoothly for Vito from there on out.

Seeking to solidify his new position atop this organized crime family, in 1957, Genovese convened a summit of mob leaders in Apalachin, New York—a small town west of Binghamton. He scheduled this meeting because of the recent murder of Albert Anastasia—as was confirmed to me by Genovese soldier George Barone, a very credible member of Vito Genovese's crew back then.

The Apalachin meeting was meant to address Anastasia's murder and violation of commission rules by violently seizing control of his own crime family, and to install Carlo Gambino as the new official boss.

The resulting fiasco would forever after be known as the infamous "Apalachin meeting." Approximately one hundred representatives from all the country's mafia families arrived at a home owned by mobster Joe "the Barber" Barbara. However, they did almost nothing to conceal their arrival, and Barbara's house was already under surveillance by local state troopers for possible criminal connections. Spotting this enormous gathering, the local troopers called in reinforcements and blocked the roads leading away.

Vito Genovese had barely gotten the proceedings underway when word arrived that the place was surrounded. The gangsters made a break for it in all directions, but about half of them were caught. Law enforcement discounted their prearranged story that they'd heard Barbara had been sick, and this was a collective pilgrimage to wish him well. Even though all the mobsters' convictions for minor offenses were eventually overturned, the episode frustrated and humiliated the mob, and led to a new focus against them. For years, FBI boss J. Edgar Hoover had frivolously insisted that the mafia did not exist in any real sense as an organized collective group of criminal entities. The truth revealed by the Apalachin meeting not only proved Hoover dead wrong, but forced the FBI to take powerful new measures to combat the mafia.

Two years after the Apalachin fiasco, Genovese got hit with a narcotics charge that led to his fifteen-year sentence. It was never proven, but some believe that leaders from the other families conspired against him to orchestrate his arrest. This would not have been done as part of any grand conspiracy against Vito, but simply arising from petty and treacherous jealousies that abound within the mob.

With their namesake leader behind bars, high-ranking Genovese for a time established an unconventional triumvirate to run the family. When Genovese died in jail in 1969, two of the three from this triumvirate became boss. Jerry Catena followed Genovese as boss. Philip Lombardo, a.k.a. "Benny Squint," replaced Catena in this capacity as boss. Both Catena and Lombardo were low key, and their official role was not clearly known by law enforcement at that time. Law enforcement did know them as powerful members of the Genovese family but not their role as boss. Lombardo retired in poor health in 1981, paving the way for the rise of the Chin.

With the exception of informants covertly providing information, the Genovese have had unique and historic success in minimizing cooperators from their own family who testify against them. Unlike the Gambinos (e.g., underboss Gravano), Colombos (e.g., consigliere Sessa), Luccheses (e.g., acting boss D'Arco), and the Bonannos (later, e.g., boss Joe Massino), the Genovese—to this day—have never suffered such high-level defectors. Moreover, up until I helped secure soldier George Barone's cooperation (we discuss how this came about in chapter 11), not even one single Genovese made member fully cooperated since Joe Valachi way back in the 1960s. Pete Savino, a Genovese associate, provided significant cooperation in the past. Vincent "Fish" Cafaro did technically cooperate and assist law enforcement, but he also minimized the information he was willing to provide to protect his own son, Tommy, who was still with the Genovese. As a result, Fish held back information about others, including acting boss Barney Bellomo, which ended up impacting my investigation of Jimmy Ida (discussed later in this chapter). It was Fish Cafaro who sponsored Bellomo to be a made member of the Genovese family. Bellomo is currently the official Genovese boss.

After I reviewed his prior interview reports, I did not view Fish Cafaro as a witness I could use. He was not a true fully cooperating witness but another pathetic example of the hypocrisy of "the life." So while the Gambino, Colombo, Lucchese, and Bonanno families all had ample numbers of made men—some of them extremely high level—who cooperated with the authorities, the Genovese in contrast successfully closed ranks for decades, preventing critically damaging internal spillage.

As an agent I could never be sure where the evidence would lead but I tried to pursue every possible avenue. When the Robert De Niro film *A Bronx Tale* premiered, De Niro held a celebratory dinner at TriBeca Grill, a bar and restaurant he owned. Unconfirmed rumors had long circulated that the mob reached out, or had attempted to reach out, to help De Niro in large and small ways with his film career. Given this, I wondered if Genovese members might show up. It was a fact of life that most gangsters desperately wanted to be "down" with a guy like De Niro. Money, women, and associating with famous people are the trifecta for many mobsters.

I managed to inveigle my way into the party, along with a handful of other agents. We hung out inside for about an hour, enjoying free drinks and waiting to see who might show up from the mob.

One of the agents accompanying me was Gary Uher, who somehow managed to get his way inside the VIP area. While I stood adjacent alongside the bar with my back to the VIP section, Gary stood next to someone who looked like he was out of mafia central casting. And in fact, he was. Not an actor, but Genovese capo Pasquale "Patsy" Parrello, who operated from his historic Bronx restaurant, Rigolettos.

Gary called out to me, "Hey, is this anybody?" I shook my head in the affirmative.

With his best effort at a De Niro impression, Gary for some reason addressed Patsy directly, "Somebody knows you." Patsy laughed in return.

I waved Gary back over, and we all left soon after. There was no further point to it, since the Genovese now knew we were there.

Patsy was an important member of the Genovese. Just a few years later, our squad, working with an NYPD undercover detective, arrested and convicted him for assorted crimes.

Nancy didn't have any concerns about my working mafia cases until an incident involving one of my sources. This was funny to me because it involved my Irish mother breaking into a telephone call while I was on the phone with a source. An FBI operator had patched the source through to my home telephone. As we spoke, the operator interrupted the call as though my mother had an emergency, stating "Mary Campi would like to break into this telephone number 973–7- . . . do you approve? The source remarked, "I shouldn't have heard that," because he had just heard the operator recite my home phone number. My mother, being a stubborn Irish woman, with an impatient personality, did not have an emergency. She just didn't like waiting.

Months later, this same source asked if I was afraid to meet with him alone and what I would do if I saw him in my town. I replied "No, I would shoot you in the head. I wouldn't miss, it is the size of a watermelon."

But I never feared for my family. I had confidence in my knowledge of "the life" and sources. I believed I could locate any gangster and develop sufficient evidence to change their life if there was any threat to my family. I would find that person and tell him to his face.

I did this once when I heard that my brother, who operated a bar in Hoboken, might have a problem due to a girl who came to the bar and liked him. An Italian guy who was supposedly connected apparently also liked her and threatened my brother as a result. I heard about this and called the guy up, letting him know who I was and what I did for a living. I told him if my brother was hurt, I would drop what I was doing and focus every ounce of my attention on him. The guy's life would change dramatically all because he wanted to bang a girl. I did this without my brother's knowledge. When I later asked my brother if the guy ever came to the bar anymore, he said no. He mentioned the girl also had two NY Giants as friends, Jumbo Elliott and Steve DeOssie, who as I understand it, also spoke to the guy.

My now-Genovese squad initially focused on a small group. It appeared there was an interest in pursuing narcotics cases, so after a review of the Genovese Control File, I identified capo Sally "Dogs" Lombardi as a focus. Later, I targeted soldier Nicky "the Blond" Frustaci as a key figure, since he was respected by Chin, the uptown crew, and the Brooklyn factions. Chin also placed him with Chin's own consigliere, Jimmy Ida, to oversee Ida's conduct. Gigante trusted Frustaci more than he trusted Ida.

To make inroads, we focused on the use of confidential informants. A confidential informant is someone who secretly provides useful information, and their identity is not publicly disclosed. Their motivations for doing so can run the gamut and include hoping to get a lesser sentence if ever prosecuted, receiving small payments for their information, hurting a rival, settling a beef, and hoping to keep the agent's focus off of their own criminal activity.

The idea was for us to establish a rapport with figures connected in some way to the Genovese who might become privy to useful information. It could be something big, like plans to commit a crime, or it could be a small detail, like a mobster was moving apartments and here was his new home address. A large amount of information regarding middling white-collar crimes also came through this way. The most helpful informants could also introduce undercover agents to members of a mafia family. That could result in a grand slam—the most well-known example of which was FBI agent Joe Pistone, also known as "Donny Brasco," who was able to infiltrate and devastate the Bonannos. In addition to Pistone, Jack Garcia, one of the most prolific FBI undercover agents infiltrated the Gambino family. He was being proposed for induction into this LCN family by Greg DePalma, a historic capo with this family.

My philosophy in life is—and always has been—to treat people like you would want to be treated. When it came to gangsters, I applied this approach as well—but with caution. I learned early on how important it was to be genuine and open with informants. They need to trust you, and this relationship can develop to where they come to like you. I can be a very approachable and friendly guy, and I learned the importance of keeping my word. Whatever you really thought of an informant, the important thing was to keep your word to one another. This included my verbal caution that if a source lied to me, I would do what I could to ensure prison for him.

I worked alongside an agent named Bob Doherty and two hardworking NYPD Detectives, Pat Maggiore and Joe Simone. While beginning to work on the Genovese cases, I had arrested someone based on information provided by a cooperating witness. This person himself became a confidential source, and he was productive and facilitated numerous arrests. Despite this, over time Doherty's Irish bluntness provided the source with the impression Doherty didn't like him . . . and that was correct. This led to a funny exchange.

One day, while all of us sat in a car, the source asked me why Doherty hated him so much.

Doherty responded, "Because you're a no-good rotten piece of shit who'd whack his own mother to make a score. That's why I hate you."

I added, "If it makes you feel a little better, Doherty treats you better than he treats me."

Doherty immediately responded, "And fuck you too, Campi." Both Doherty and I laughed while the source appeared confused.

Though Doherty and I joked around, we also would have taken a bullet for one another.

As I began to develop and work my own sources, it seemed I was often close to dark connections. One of my sources began feeding me information about another individual who was around two Bonanno associates, Gus and Dominick Farace. Notoriously, the Faraces later set up a drug deal with an undercover DEA Agent named Everett Hatcher. During the meetup, Hatcher lost contact with his support team. Then the worst thing possible happened. Somehow, with details only known to those who were there, the Faraces began to suspect that Everett might be law enforcement. Gus Farace shot and killed him.

The rule all crime families abide by is that you don't kill law enforcement—ever—not out of a sense of decency, but because it is counterproductive to business and brings on too much heat. Law enforcement will get its revenge if its own members are killed off just doing their honest jobs.

So when Hatcher was killed, law enforcement openly approached mobsters at their social clubs and put them on notice. They needed to turn over Gus Farace. If they didn't, law enforcement harassment would be continual and relentless. For example, the small-time Italian social club operations that would normally be ignored—such as poker games and gambling—would be endlessly raided until Gus was turned over. These raids could lead to parole violations and weapons seized. It would disrupt business and the smooth evergreen moneymakers on which so many gangsters rely.

When the mob did not immediately produce results, we were as good as our word. In addition to busts, there was open surveillance that mobsters viewed as general harassment. As just one example, Bonanno capo Anthony Graziano lived on a cul-de-sac in Staten Island. Law enforcement placed cars on his street and would slowly follow him while he walked his dog—calling, "Where's Gus?" out the window.

The tactic worked. Mobsters scoured their ranks for someone who knew where Farace was hiding. Lucchese acting boss Al D'Arco, who later became a cooperating witness, explained how they learned that a friend was hiding Gus from both organized crime and law enforcement. D'Arco himself knocked on the friend's door at midnight. When the friend answered, D'Arco handed him a gun.

"We know you're hiding Gus," he said. "Kill him, or kill yourself." D'Arco walked away.

Not long after, Gus Farace turned up dead. He was executed as he sat in a parked car in Brooklyn. Since my source was aware of this criminal who had a prior relationship with Gus Farace, he became a focus of mine and subsequently became a source.

As noted above, my pursuit of the Genovese included capo Sally "Dogs" Lombardi. Sally Dogs was known to be heavily involved in narcotics. One of my trusted informants confirmed that Sally Dogs was dealing in heroin, even though this went against the official mob rules prohibiting dealing drugs due to the heavy sentences and possible cooperation that could result.

When Sally Dogs was eventually picked up on a drug charge by another law enforcement agency, I quickly went to visit him at Rikers Island. Word on the street was that Chin was salivating to pay Sally Dogs's bail as quickly as possible . . . so that he could kill him. Chin was incensed: (1) that Sally Dogs was involved with drugs; and (2) that he had been stupid enough to get caught. Another blatant example of mafia hypocrisy and treachery at several levels, since both Chin and Vito Genovese had themselves done each of those things and had been convicted for it.

When the FBI gets a threat (in this case that Sally Dogs's life was at risk), we respond. There is only upside in going to see a wiseguy. It gives you a sense of the person, whether they may someday cooperate or become an informant, and whether they're the kind of person who will report a law enforcement visit up the chain. I knew that Sally Dogs was a reckless, treacherous, evil guy because I had a reliable source who knew him well.

I visited him in a secluded area in the prison. Lombardi made clear he had no interest in speaking with me. However, just before leaving I told him, "If you feel that an authentic threat exists in prison, you can contact the FBI, and ask for the squad that investigates the Genovese family. I'm on the Genovese squad. Ask for Campi."

Referring to Vito, Sally Dogs walked away, giggling, and said, "Genovese? I thought he was dead."

* * *

Oftentimes, in targeting a high-level figure such as Lombardi, one has to "work their way up the food chain"—build a case against a lower-level figure, who may then cooperate to save himself time in jail. Sally Dogs was the ultimate target, but I had to work my way up to him. Prior to Lombardi's arrest, based on informant information, I had caught an associate named Romano bringing in two kilos of heroin from Italy. The FBI bureaucracy took the evidence I had acquired and removed it from me, providing it instead to a narcotics squad. Romano pleaded guilty.

The next guy to pop up was named Michael "Bootsy" Booth. A source informed me how Bootsy was going to travel to Italy under a fictitious name to obtain heroin from Sally Dogs's supplier. Building cases takes hard work—there is no substitute—and a bunch of us (me, NYPD Detectives Pat Maggiore and Joe Simone, and my FBI partner Bob Doherty) immediately reviewed more than twenty boxes of U.S. passport applications to successfully identify Bootsy's fictitious identity. We were very passionate in this review. As I recall, Maggiore identified Bootsy's photo.

Based on this corroboration of source information, I contacted the FBI in Italy and obtained authorization to travel. My purpose was to conduct surveillance of Bootsy's meetings that may have included Sally Dogs. Doing so would enable me to provide surveillance photos not only of them, but also to identify their criminal associates and to possibly gather evidence to criminally charge Lombardi as well. Also, this would permit me to identify Bootsy's return flight so that we could search his luggage for the drugs. My Assistant Special Agent in Charge, or ASAC (essentially the FBI deputy to the highest-ranking criminal investigator in each region), approved the request. But at the last minute, he canceled it because a lazy narcotics squad agent convinced him to do so. They were shooting for the "easy arrest" that did not require such effort, believing that Bootsy would behave similarly to Romano. Instead, Bootsy slipped through their fingers. He was not convicted until years later, by another agency which secured photos of Bootsy with Sally Dogs in Italy.

The same narcotics squad agent that interfered also later became one of my supervisors—an empty suit who was promoted time and again, even all the way to an ASAC position in the Intelligence Division. Another example of his ineptitude concerned a cooperating witness who was willing to introduce an undercover FBI agent to Billy Romano, a close associate of Sally Dogs's narcotics operation. The narcotics agent for some reason did not want to take advantage of this opportunity. There's an old FBI adage that we street agents use to describe our generally empty suit management: "I understand how he became an ASAC. What I don't understand is how he became an agent." There is a reason for this accepted wisdom.

Too many of them apply for a promotion as an agent to a management position without having the foundation as a successful case agent.

My work did lead additionally to arrests of mafia associates. We also arrested a corrupt customs agent, a young man who had been approved for NYPD officer training, a Dominican supplier, and others. The toughest person in this entire group appeared to be the customs agent's sister, who was the Dominican's girlfriend.

After my significant frustrations with the above investigations, it was clearly time to focus on other important targets. I again consulted the Genovese control file, looking for the most appropriate target for further investigation. By looking at the FBI's historical records, I paid special attention to who were the most important players, how they had risen to their positions of power, and who stood to replace them if and when they fell. I homed in on respected longtime soldier Nicky "the Blond" Frustaci, consigliere Jimmy Ida, and others. The Ida investigation, prosecution, and conviction is the one I am most proud of to this day. Jim Bucknam had been the AUSA for a previous successful investigation of mine of mafia associates in another crime family. He subsequently became the Chief of the SDNY's Organized Crime Unit and assigned Nelson Boxer as the AUSA for my Ida investigation. Jim was another favorite aggressive prosecutor who we thoroughly enjoyed working with.

Ida was born into the world of the mob in 1940. The son of immigrants from Northern Italy, he grew up in Little Italy. Ida was proposed for induction by Ciro Perrone, a powerful soldier at that time in Matty "the Horse" Ianniello's crew. Ianniello was a powerful capo who was respected by both Vincent "Chin" Gigante and Fat Tony Salerno. Ida became Ianniello's driver. Ianniello's family restaurant, Umberto's Clam House was where "Crazy" Joe Gallo of the Colombo family was famously killed in 1972.

After being inducted, Ida's rise was swift. He was tapped as someone with managerial potential, he handled money collections for the Genovese, and soon coordinated these operations. He made sure small businesses paid "tribute" when it was due. He gradually worked his way up within the Genovese ranks, having been battlefield-promoted to consigliere in

1991 when Louis Manna, the previous consigliere, was convicted on racketeering charges that included conspiring to kill Gambino boss John Gotti. Agent Doherty worked with Jack Mullane and Kevin O'Grady to help secure Manna's conviction.

As for Frustaci, he grew up at 200 First Avenue, in a neighborhood that had been Lucky Luciano's old stomping ground. Nicky wasn't the brightest guy, but he was loyal. He and Chin had been boxers and were close to each other through that bond. It is likely due to this that Chin placed Nicky as his eyes and ears to keep an eye on Ida.

The route getting me into Ida was quite indirect. I began by investigating Nicky the Blond's gambling operation. Gambling crimes do not generally receive significant prison sentences, so they are usually not an efficient use of time. But I follow my subjects and identify those they meet with to begin to determine the scope of potential additional criminal charges. Reviewing Nicky's parking violations led me to his gambling location, and I saw him enter a building. I had a hunch this would be fruitful, and I could identify criminal associates. Nicky had converted the top floor of a three-floor walk-up in Lower Manhattan into a gambling den. My team and I began surveillance of the spot. There was a building located catty-corner to the gambling operation, with a billboard on the roof. It was easy for me to view Frustaci's gambling traffic from the roof and take photos of the men entering and leaving the establishment. Some nights I'd try a different tactic, posing as a pedestrian and walking on the sidewalk just behind groups of men leaving the location. Invariably, they'd be talking about how much they had won or lost that night. Eventually, I managed to develop a rapport with an associate who frequented the den and who later provided me with information about Hickey DiLorenzo's murder, which I would later charge Ida with. The source also provided details about Ida's club, the Little Italy Social Club at 171 Mulberry Street, which ended up being very fruitful. Doing a little research told me that this location was a gathering spot for Genovese major players.

My surveillance of Frustaci's gambling operation also led to an absolutely bizarre intersection with my family's own history. One day I surveilled the gambling operation from the back seat of a van. A black

Cadillac with tinted windows rolled up to the location, but the driver simply sat in the car and waited. This was odd, and so I kept an eye on the guy. Moments later, the driver walked toward Nicky's gambling establishment—all the while keeping an eye on my van as though he knew he was being watched—which he was. To my shock, I immediately recognized him from my past. Many years before, my father abruptly sold his beauty shop business to that same man after taking him in as a partner. This man had caused aggravation because he would not show up for work, etc. It was clear to me that somehow bad blood surrounded the deal and may have been an extortion.

What was more, I had heard rumors from a very credible longtime informant how Frustaci had a guy around him from New Jersey. The informant also believed that the Jersey guy was somehow connected to the mafia and noted that he recently shaved his mustache. Since the mafia does not permit facial hair among its made members, the inference was that he was possibly inducted. Now, here—so many years later—it seemed that there was a basis for these rumors. I had a difficult time believing this because in my eyes, the partner was a pathetic candy-ass. I thought the shaved mustache was most likely related to his vanity.

Once I saw the partner at Nicky's, I realized maybe, as an associate of Frustaci, he extorted my dad and forced him to sell, a standard mobster ploy. I did not want to make my investigation a personal matter. However, if Frustaci decided to later cooperate, this matter would be addressed.

I saw this former partner one other time. I pulled into a gas station one day and he in turn saw me and took off.

One day during surveillance, I saw Frustaci in a heated argument with Bonanno capo Anthony Graziano as they walked down 10th Street and First Avenue in Manhattan. The two seemed to somehow be having a disagreement about an unknown third man walking behind them. Curious about what they were discussing, I later identified him as Dominic Grimaldi, who was on parole after his recent release from prison. Grimaldi had been incarcerated for a murder. While in prison, he met with and developed a relationship with Bonanno boss Joseph Massino. Upon Grimaldi's release, Massino had placed him with Graziano.

I reached out to Grimaldi's parole officer, Vinny Defillippis, and learned that Grimaldi had recently requested permission to travel to South America for his honeymoon. I asked the parole officer to deny the request, because I knew from an informant that Dom would go anyway. I hoped that Grimaldi might discreetly cooperate once arrested for parole violation upon reentry to the country, as the travel would be a violation of his parole. I also suspected that drug trafficking would somehow be involved in the trip, given his determination to travel. As it turned out, my instinct was correct.

After U.S. Customs alerted me that Dom was on his way back to the United States, Defilippis and I headed to the airport. I had U.S. Customs discreetly pull Grimaldi from the customs line and into an office outside anyone else's view, as though it were a random check. There, we introduced ourselves and explained how Dom had violated his parole and would face significant time as a result. In addition to doing five years for his parole violations, I would investigate and charge him with crimes related to supplying cocaine. Dominic Farace, who became a cooperating witness after his cousin's murder for killing DEA Agent Everett Hatcher, had told me that Grimaldi supplied Gus, Dom, and others, including Graziano, with cocaine.

"Now's the time to cooperate because nobody knows we are here with you," I urged Dom. "If you are ever going to, *now* is the time."

Dom acted nervously and said he needed to talk to his new wife, who was outside the office in the customs line. So we brought her inside the office. When she saw us all, she burst into tears. They began hugging and shouting, "I love you." As Grimaldi kissed her all over her face, he pulled her close with both hands on her ass. Then he told her, "Don't talk on the phone. Don't talk on the phone. I love you. They are listening."

Dom then turned to us confidently and said, "I'll never rat. I'd rather die in prison like my old man did." I replied, "I didn't know your father died in prison. Let's go." And with that, we cuffed him and took him into custody.

As we entered the airport's public area, Grimaldi's family and his new wife's family were waiting to greet them. The new wife ran out into this area crying and screaming, "I love you. I love you." Dominic responded in the same manner. The families had no idea what was going on and looked so confused. Defillipis turned to me and said, "I love these organized crime cases." He grew up in the 1st Avenue neighborhood and knew of Frustaci and others. Though Dom's emotions were high, both he and I preserved the unspoken rule that none of this was personal.

Dominic Farace testified at Grimaldi's parole violation hearing. For security, this New York State parole hearing was held in a federal courthouse. He testified about how Grimaldi supplied Farace and his brother with the cocaine they sold. As defense lawyers always do, Grimaldi's attorney attempted to portray Farace as a liar who was trying to save himself from a significant federal sentence. Farace responded in a typical genuine organized crime manner, citing how he liked Grimaldi, but that Grimaldi and the mob wanted to kill him, and the feds wanted to put him in jail for life. To help himself, as his cooperation agreement required, the only way to do so was to tell the truth.

I later learned that the meeting between Graziano and Frustaci did not concern the drug deal, but instead concerned Grimaldi's new wife. She had previously been married to someone aligned with Frustaci. She worked for the telephone company and met Grimaldi while connecting his collect calls from prison. She found his sense of humor in their brief conversations hilarious. So the heated meeting between Graziano and Frustaci which led me to investigate Grimaldi was not necessarily about drugs after all. Instead, the primary purpose of the meeting was because the new wife's former husband wanted to retaliate against Grimaldi for her divorcing him and marrying Grimaldi.

* * *

Although Grimaldi didn't cooperate, we made major headway in the Frustaci/Ida investigation by persuading a federal judge that informant information combined with overhears about bank robberies and surveillance justified placing a listening bug, also known as a wiretap or T-III, in Ida's club at 171 Mulberry Street. Among many other things, what we heard as a result made us privy to information that many in law enforcement—and many regular New Yorkers—often conjectured about but had never known for sure. Namely, the extent of the mob's involvement with the very popular Feast of San Gennaro festival, held each fall in Little Italy.

The Feast of San Gennaro has been a popular New York City tradition for decades. It's an eleven-day event with booths and stands where vendors operate games or sell food. The Feast was purportedly operated by an organization called the "Society Saint Gennaro Naples and Suburbs, Inc," consisting of laypersons and not part of or affiliated with any church. Nevertheless, the Society received tax-exempt status as a charitable organization. While on paper the feast was sponsored and operated by the Society, in fact it was controlled by and a money-generating vehicle for the Genovese family. Ida had overseen the operation since around 1988.

Overhears from our wiretaps made clear that the Genovese maintained strict control. For example, we heard soldier Tommy "Gigali" Cestaro describe how he controlled stand locations, and the fees charged. If you wanted a booth at the festival, you had to go through the Genovese. The street lighting for the festival and booths were also controlled by the Genovese. What made this all the more repulsive was that festival profits were *supposed* to go to charitable causes, to provide aid and support for those in need. But the mafia doesn't care who they steal from, and it was clear that the Genovese were taking a huge skim. They also forced each vendor to fudge their tax paperwork, reporting that the cost of their booth or stand was far less than it actually was, so that less money would be taxable by the city. Who cares if streets aren't paved, garbage isn't collected, water isn't clean, or the police force has to be cut due to inadequate tax revenue? Certainly not the mob.

The amount of the fraud was substantial. The majority of the rent the vendors paid went directly to Genovese gangsters. The city was defrauded, the IRS was defrauded, the intended charitable recipients, and the patrons of the feast were defrauded. The public had the impression that churches and charities benefited from the festival, as everyone thought they received the income generated by this event. In terms of hard numbers, while the Society publicly reported a total of $250,000 in vendor income (resulting in a New York City permit fee of $50,000), in reality the total vendor rent was conservatively estimated at $1,400,000, meaning the proper New

York City fee paid should have been about $280,000, therefore costing the city $230,000 each year in lost revenue. Note that this is for just one festival, while there are numerous such feasts throughout the city under mob control that almost certainly also avoid paying the proper fees.

And while the public thought that churches and charities were the beneficiaries, in reality about $5,000 each year was donated. The mob took everything else for themselves.

We wanted to see if we could get some of the vendors to flip on the mob. We initially served grand jury subpoenas on some vendors, anticipating that they would report this to Gigali and that we would capture the resulting criminal conversations at the club. This was a long shot, but worth trying. So I talked to the vendors at the festival. I knew they had been pressured, and many of them were obviously very scared. Nevertheless, I provided them with my name, business card, and subpoena. When I left, as expected, many vendors told the mobsters that an FBI agent named Mike Campi had come around asking how things worked. I didn't know it at the time, but this turned out to be a major contributor toward my name circulating among the mob.

We also served subpoenas on vendors to tickle the wire (meaning, encourage mobsters to discuss the subpoenas so that we could listen to their conversations about it) at 171 Mulberry Street, and we eventually arrested some vendors for perjury in their grand jury testimony. This helped other vendors realize the potential impact on them for lying about what they paid for their booths. I explained how the criminals involved in the fraud didn't expect the vendors to go to jail for them, and that if we immunized them, they only had to answer honestly because we had seized the records that identified the amounts paid.

The most approachable vendors were full-time carnival people who traveled between festivals and fairs year-round. They had no special experience with the Genovese. One of my tactics was to try to talk to vendors in front of their wives. I observed that wives for some reason tended to be more open to disassociating from criminals, so I wanted them to be around for these talks. From the games to the food to the electricity that powered the festival itself, I gathered solid accounts that almost everything was controlled by the Genovese. This information was haunting, because the festival in some sense represented a microcosm of the entire city. This kind of corruption—stealing money from honest workers, creating a climate of fear and terror, depriving the city of needed revenue to provide services, even breaking people's morale and core belief in a fair society run by fair laws—was simply everywhere.

One haunting example in particular of how the mob lack any sense of humanity always stood out to me. A Catholic priest on Broome Street near the festival had publicly remarked that he did not think San Gennaro (or Saint Januarius) met the true qualifications for Catholic sainthood, and that holding a festival in his name was inappropriate. After making this simple and innocent statement based on his sincerely held religious beliefs and his exercise of free speech, the Genovese did not engage him in debate. Instead, they threatened to kill him. This man of the cloth saw no option but to flee from the United States to South America just to stay alive.

And I met with another priest who refused to talk to me because he was so scared.

We used events like the San Gennaro vendor interviews to build a case against Ida. However, this was just one piece of a larger mosaic of crime, violence, and corruption that could be used to charge him and others. The bug at 171 Mulberry Street continued to provide tremendous amounts of useful information and evidence. However, disaster soon threatened to strike these inroads because we overheard that Tommy Cestaro, also known as "Gigali," planned to renovate the club's interior. Whatever contractor they used would surely find our bug. We needed to remove it, and fast.

I sent team members on several late-night break-in attempts, but they did not succeed, either being unable to discreetly gain entrance, or there were still Genovese inside the club when they showed up.

With time running out, I thought I had no option but to come up with an alternative plan that, in my humble opinion, was fairly creative.

The FBI is required to notify anybody, even including mafia members, of any credible threat on their lives. The reason for this is we can't, and shouldn't, arbitrarily decide whose lives should be protected. Mob members knew this, and FBI visits for these purposes were not entirely rare events.

But nothing prevented us from also using this moral obligation to our advantage—to protect the public from the mafia. So just before the renovation was scheduled to begin, we showed up at the club, identified ourselves as FBI, and told them there was a credible threat that an explosive device had been placed inside their club. We were there to find it. Assisting us in this ruse, at the time Tommy Gigali and the Genovese were in the middle of a beef with an Asian gang from Chinatown (which abuts Little Italy in New York City), so this was not entirely out of the realm of believability.

Fortunately, the plan worked. With many agents and NYPD fanning out inside 171 Mulberry Street, one of them was able to discreetly grab and disable the bug when no mobsters were present. In a humorous epilogue to this vignette, we then learned that the Genovese did not even believe that we were really FBI agents. Instead, they believed that we had been NYPD officers posing as FBI, just to harass them in their club. They were partially correct, since my squad was a combination of FBI agents and NYPD detectives.

After the renovations were complete, we were able to covertly reinstall our listening device. But this did not go smoothly. I heard Gigali's brother-in-law, Michael Autori, discuss with Anthony "Tits" Coiro that a device had been installed in the club. They mentioned how they had read the FBI is great at discreetly installing bugs and how the NYPD can't do it quietly, so they concluded that it must have been the NYPD installing a bug the other night since they made so much noise. But in fact, it was us, the FBI.

I visited our surveillance operations team to ask how the installation had gone. They proudly responded that there were no problems. I then played the tape for them, and they looked so embarrassed. Unfortunately, this investigation experienced several other failed attempts by the FBI and NYPD teams to install listening devices in locations where I had obtained T-III court orders authorizing their installation. My wife thought it had to be corruption because how could they be so incompetent? She would stress this while urging me to move to white-collar crime investigations.

I explained how it is clearly a difficult process to discreetly install bugs in organized crime social clubs.

Prior to getting caught, this club was frequented by gangsters from all five mob families. That changed. Mob members from other New York families began to drop by the club far less frequently. Really important meetings began to take place at other locations.

Years later, after "Cookie" D'Urso cooperated and we began working together, I learned that D'Urso was the one who had actually caught the FBI breaking in to install the listening device that night. Here's what happened: Driving by the club, D'Urso saw the lights on and the shades down. He assumed a mobster was inside with a woman and knocked on the door, observing people running around inside. No one answered the door, and then he noticed a car parked nearby and asked the driver what he was doing. The agent responded how he was waiting for a friend. D'Urso asked who the friend was, and the agent, unable to name anyone living on Mulberry Street, provided an evasive response. D'Urso did the math and figured out what was going on. He told Gigali, Aparo, and his friends and decided never to return to the club. D'Urso messed up an important aspect of my Ida investigation. Beginning with chapter 8, you'll learn how he more than made up for it.

Observing that 171 Mulberry Street was now being made less use of, I noticed Gigali routinely left the club on Monday evenings at about 9:00 p.m. I discreetly followed him to a meeting with Ida, Frustaci, and other mobsters. This clearly was a weekly crew meeting. I began to tail guys from the club to different locations uptown. Eventually, I had raids conducted on three of their lucrative gambling locations. I anticipated that in response Ida would want to meet with others to discuss this, and it turned out I was correct. He made two calls on the same day after the execution of the search warrants. In the first, he spoke to somebody who warned him to stay out of New York City. In the second, a Genovese soldier told Ida that Gigali wanted to meet with him. Ida responded to meet at an Upper East Side restaurant, without identifying which one. But a subsequent beeper exchange between them listed "3" and "62." I thought about it . . . and realized this wasn't a partial call with only three numbers but was instead the intersection of the Avenue (3rd) and the Street (62nd) where the unnamed restaurant was located. It was the trendy Mulholland Drive restaurant where Ida held other meetings with his crew. So now I knew where they were going.

Ida sent instructions for Gigali to take two taxi cabs to the restaurant and to look out the back window to make sure he wasn't followed. No need—because I knew where they were headed. I parked outside the restaurant prior to anyone arriving.

I staked out the cafe in a Range Rover that the FBI had previously seized. Range Rovers were good cover because nobody expects law enforcement to have one. I watched the mob guys enter and leave the cafe and made videos of all of this. Ida was the only gangster canny enough to look suspiciously at my vehicle, and I videotaped him staring directly into my camera as he passed by and into the cafe.

In addition to the club recordings, I also obtained judicial approval to install a T-III on Ida's cell phone conversations, which is how I was able to learn about the meeting referenced above. Through surveillance, we identified the residence Ida lived at in Bedford, New York, a multimillion-dollar, ten-acre ranch with a listed owner as James Hickey. Hickey was a multimillionaire and associate of Ida's and was the nominal owner to help conceal Ida's illicit financial gains. The recordings we took from the tap—in which Ida often freely discussed criminal activity—proved to be another nail in the coffin. Incidentally, Ida maintained a vehicle on the property which was registered to Genovese associate Jack Gordon—La Toya Jackson's husband. In fact, I conducted surveillances where Ida and Gordon met.

As a general matter, Ida was extremely cautious about being tailed. But surveillance was crucial to help build the case. I persuaded my supervisor to greenlight my getting a hack license, and the FBI built a custom "taxi" for me to drive. I got the license in my mother's maiden name on the off chance that someone would recognize my name.

The ploy was effective. As one example, I was able to discreetly follow soldier Cestaro from the social club on Monday nights to late-night meetings with Ida and other associated mobsters. These meetings were held at pool halls, diners, and restaurants located across Manhattan. And because of this, in turn, several of my applications to install listening devices in these locations were approved. Moreover, because Ida frequently changed the locations for these meetings, we obtained approval for the first ever "roving" T-III wiretap. This meant that the court approved our installing a wiretap in *any* location where the group met.

I would also return to the office after conducting the surveillance and attempt to identify unknown males who'd participated in the meetings, to identify the scope of the enterprise. Identifying them involved a variety of methods including checking DMV records, consulting informants, and talking to Kenny McCabe, a retired NYPD detective working for the SDNY U.S. Attorney's Office.[11] Kenny had an encyclopedic knowledge of gangsters and helped identify some of the unknown males. He also valued the additional details that we were obtaining.

All of this not only helped the investigation, it also brought some comical moments. Nancy and I had recently moved, and she was less than thrilled that the new neighbors would think she'd married a cabbie when I parked the taxi in our driveway every night. I didn't care what the neighbors thought, I just cared about the case. Also, some Realtors who knew about my position as an FBI agent most likely shared that information.

My colleagues in law enforcement joked that I could make extra money working as a cabbie off the books. And in fact, once I forgot to turn on the "Off Duty" light when driving down Hudson Street. A random guy jumped in the back while I stopped at a light. It was lightly raining at that time but about to pour. The guy was an arrogant Wolf of Wall Street banker type, who demanded I drive him uptown even when I claimed to be off for the night. The banker became abusive and raised his voice, saying he would pay me double, calling me lazy. It was by now pouring rain, so I drove the guy to a spot on Canal Street just before the Holland Tunnel where there was no shelter from the storm. Then I pulled over, flashed my FBI badge, and stated, "I am not a cabbie—get the fuck out."

---

11 SDNY refers to the Southern District of New York, which is a federal jurisdiction that covers Manhattan, the Bronx, and some counties north of New York City.

The surveillance also often meant I kept extremely late hours in the cab, circulating among drunk drivers and joy riders. One night (or morning), at about 4 a.m., I was coming out of the Holland Tunnel when a car full of teenagers ran a red light. Slamming on the brakes, I could not avoid T-boning them into a streetlight that was set into a concrete stanchion. Thankfully, nobody was killed, but it took Emergency Services around twenty minutes to cut the kids out. The local police were there immediately and described how they'd been discreetly following this vehicle and had watched them run the red light. I was unhurt but stayed around to make sure they were okay.

At one point, a young guy pulled up on a Harley motorcycle to see what had happened. He chatted with me and agent Gary Uher, who had pulled over when he saw the accident. The Harley guy asked where the driver of the cab was, and I replied, "that's me." The guy revealed that he also drove a cab, adding, "I thought I was the only white cabdriver in Manhattan."

"You are," Gary replied, disclosing nothing more.

I eventually replaced the cab with other vehicles so as not to draw undue suspicion, even once using a Rolls-Royce.

A murder we eventually charged was the murder of Anthony "Hickey" DiLorenzo. Ida, in his capacity as consigliere, met with and told Lucchese acting boss Al D'Arco to have his crew cease associating with Hickey because they were going to kill him. A few days later, Hickey was killed. Part of the evidence concerned my obtaining a court order for a blood sample from Ida's brother Joey, a Genovese capo. I suspected Joey may have actually been the individual who shot Hickey, but we didn't have sufficient evidence to charge Joey as the shooter.

Bob Doherty and I met with Joey and his attorney at the Beekman Hospital in lower Manhattan to take the blood. I anticipated Joey would report back to his brother about what happened, so I had a surveillance team on Jimmy while Doherty and I secured Joey's blood sample. The surveillance team reported to me that Jimmy drove to a parking garage practically adjacent to the hospital, confirming that my suspicion was correct. The surveillance team remained outside the garage.

Doherty and I then drove Joey and his lawyer over the Brooklyn Bridge to where their cars were parked. We asked Joey what he was going to do the rest of the day, and he replied that he'd go home to Staten Island to handle his homing pigeons. As we returned to Manhattan over the Brooklyn Bridge, a source informed me that Jimmy was meeting with Nicky the Blond by Nicky's residence in downtown Manhattan. It became clear Jimmy—always alert—had spotted the surveillance and left, avoiding them when he left the parking garage and taking a subway or cab uptown to Nicky.

Doherty and I were stoked. We were convinced that Joey was at that meeting as well. As we got to Nicky's street, we didn't see any sign of a meeting. We went to Veniero's Bakery, knowing Frustaci often spent time there. We also went to DiRoberti's Bakery and walked directly to the back area. No luck at either place. However, we did pass Genovese member Red Hot Gentile, who had a unique look with a protruding forehead similar to a Neanderthal. As we did so, Doherty asked me, "Who the fuck is that?" And I responded, "That's Red Hot. He's nobody." I could feel Red Hot's glare of hatred as we walked by and prepared myself for a confrontation that did not occur. Red Hot was a treacherous Genovese soldier who hated law enforcement. I had a very reliable source who was reporting on him from this neighborhood.

As we got ready to leave, we made one more pass by Nicky's gambling club, and parked to look around. To our amazement, parked literally right next to us sat Jimmy, Joey, and Nicky. Joey was in the driver's seat, with Jimmy beside him and Nicky in the back. My vehicle was so close to theirs that Joey couldn't even open his door. They didn't notice us as Doherty began to take photos. Doherty and I enjoyed ourselves immensely. As Jimmy leaned over to hug and kiss Joey, he stared into Doherty's camera and saw us both sitting there, smiling. Jimmy then just bolted from the car, walking briskly away and turning down 1st Avenue. I immediately followed him, leaving my car on a one-way street, which blocked any traffic from passing.

As I followed immediately behind Jimmy, I sarcastically remarked how funny it is that Jimmy just happened to be meeting with his brother Joey—right after we had seized Joey's blood in relation to Hickey's murder.

"Joey was going home to fly his pigeons. Funny how he came to meet you instead." Jimmy's anger and frustration at having been caught in such a compromising moment was palpable. He stopped walking, turned back toward me with his head down, raised his head, and told me to speak to his attorney, Jeff Hoffman.

At that moment, Doherty called out to me because I had the keys to the vehicle blocking traffic. Doherty then followed Jimmy as I got back to the car. There, I met with both Joey and Nicky to try to spur conversation for further evidence on this murder. The first thing I said to Joey was how I thought he was going home to Staten Island. I also made a comment to Nicky, who was clearly embarrassed since it happened in his neighborhood.

As Doherty followed Jimmy, Jimmy crossed west then back east as he headed south on 1st Avenue. Being the blunt ball-breaker he was, Doherty sang the Dean Martin song lyrics, "When the moon hits the sky like a big pizza pie, that's amore." At some point, Doherty asked Jimmy if they would walk all the way back to the parking garage by the hospital. That's when Jimmy realized he had been followed all day. He just waved a cab down at that point.

When we got back to the office from this productive day, which would prove very useful for evidence at trial, a prominent defense attorney, not Hoffman, called me, saying he understood I'd arrested his client Jimmy Ida. In response, I explained that Jimmy was not arrested but may be drinking heavily somewhere, having had such a bad day. The last we saw Jimmy was him getting into a cab while cursing. The defense attorney burst out laughing as he hung up, thanking me for the details.

The main proof concerning Ida's role in DiLorenzo's murder came from D'Arco. D'Arco explained how Ida told him about real concerns whether DiLorenzo had all his mental faculties. DiLorenzo displayed signs of instability and it was also feared he could be a possible confidential source for law enforcement. While serving a prison sentence, he openly spoke about narcotics trafficking and hung out with a known informant. D'Arco also cited how after DiLorenzo was released from prison, he continued to act in a manner consistent with being viewed as an informant, openly proposing narcotics deals while among made members from multiple crime families, and discussing the criminal activities of others. Hickey also began openly saying Chin's name aloud—which was forbidden—instead of touching his own chin. The Genovese also were concerned that Hickey might start spilling their secrets to the Luccheses, or mob secrets to law enforcement. Based on this and similar behavior, Ida informed D'Arco that he and other Genovese (all murders being approved foremost by the boss, Chin), decided to kill Hickey. The irony of killing DiLorenzo for being actually crazy while the boss, Chin, claimed to be crazy and used this ploy to stay out of jail is almost too much to believe.

We also charged Ida, acting boss Barney Bellomo, acting underboss Mickey Generoso, and Genovese associate Louis Ruggiero Sr., with their role in the murder of Ralph DeSimone, who had been proposed for Genovese membership. Again, key witnesses included D'Arco along with Carmine Sessa. D'Arco related how Ida had provided him with a list of names of people who were being proposed for membership in the Genovese family, including DeSimone, and that Lucchese acting boss Anthony Baratta informed D'Arco that DeSimone was a government informant, and had previously testified in a narcotics case.

Baratta raised the question of Desimone's status at a meeting with the Genovese acting administration. Baratta added that he could obtain the transcript of Desimone's testimony to support his allegation. Generoso then stepped forward, made a gesture as if he were pulling a trigger of a gun and stated, "We'll take care of it," while Ida said, "Yeah," and Ida and Barney nodded their heads in agreement.

The evidence at trial established how this murder happened in the basement of Ruggiero's home. In further evidence of the treachery embedded into the mob's DNA, Ruggiero was selected to kill DeSimone because they were friends, which would relax DeSimone's guard. The evidence also showed Ruggiero had lunch with DeSimone around one hour prior to DeSimone's murder. There was additional damning evidence against Ruggiero, and it seemed close to airtight. However, Ruggiero spent the entire trial reading a newspaper until the murder evidence was provided, as though he hadn't a care in the world. It was as though he had a juror in his pocket.

What became a comfort to me was the specific details from the United States Court of Appeals for the Second Circuit provided to me by Nelson

Boxer. The defendants filed appeals in the fall after a nine-week trial of Ida, Frustace, and Ruggiero. This appeal argument by AUSA Nelson Boxer, captured trial details that rejected Ida's appeal. In Ida's appeal, his attorneys argued how "there was insufficient evidence that Ruggiero conspired to and murdered DeSimone. As the district court found, there was overwhelming evidence that Ruggiero killed DeSimone in the basement of Ruggiero's home."

DeSimone died on June 12, 1991, approximately an hour after eating lunch with Ruggiero. That same day, Ruggiero placed a rush order for carpet installation. In the late afternoon, a ransom call demanded $150,000 for DeSimone's return. That night, Ruggiero appeared at the car wash, where family members were waiting for more calls from the purported kidnapper (although none came), and Ruggiero told DeSimone's family that they were "crazy" to call the police. He made inconsistent statements to family members regarding DeSimone's whereabouts and further contradicted himself the next day, when he showed up unsolicited at the police station. Apparently, after receiving a telephone message from the police, Ruggiero did not want to chance their arrival at his house, where an irregularly shaped portion of the carpeting had been ripped up and the padding was stained, supposedly from a mystery flood of unknown origin. That morning, Ruggiero had negotiated with the carpet company to tile the portion of the basement where the carpeting had been ripped up, caring less about the floor covering than about the speed with which the damage could be concealed. By the time the worker arrived the next day to tile the area where the carpet had been ripped up, the stained padding had also been removed.

Ruggiero's primary concern again was the speed with which the job could be accomplished. By the time the police searched Ruggiero's house on June 20, the carpeting on the steps leading up from the basement to the next level had been ripped up, leaving only the padding. Forensic tests subsequently revealed that a carpet fiber seized from Ruggiero's matched a fiber found on DeSimone's body; and a trash bag seized from the house was consistent with the bags that had covered DeSimone's head. This evidence was more than sufficient to demonstrate Ruggiero's involvement in DeSimone's homicide and to furnish the requisite overt act required to sustain Ida's conviction on Racketeering Act 2 (a). Racketeering Act 2 charged Ida, Generoso, and codefendant Bellomo with conspiring to and aiding and abetting the murder of Ralph DeSimone. Bellomo and Generoso avoided this trial by pleading guilty to labor racketeering charges.

A murder conspiracy we charged Ida with was a plot to kill Dominic Tucci. A Genovese associate, John Schenone, requested Ida's approval because Tucci had an affair with Schenone's girlfriend. I used cooperator Richard Sprague, a criminal associate of Schenone's, to help build this charge.

Schenone had told Sprague he needed to meet with "Little Jimmy" to get approval to kill Tucci, and Sprague drove him to this meeting. It was Ida's role as the consigliere to address these types of requests. Although initially reluctant to provide approval due to Tucci's blood relationship to Genovese soldier Michael Bove, over time and after several meetings, Ida eventually agreed. Because Schenone asked Sprague to help him, Sprague decided to cooperate with the FBI. Sprague's cooperation led to some entertaining recorded conversations with Schenone. In one, as instructed, Sprague told Schenone he couldn't provide Schenone's guns because they had been removed from his truck when his truck was towed. Schenone exploded furiously, "That's impossible! If they took that out of there, you'd be fuckin pinched. That's bullshit. I want my fuckin gun, Richie. That's my personal motherfuckin gun." The next day, Sprague refused to meet with Schenone, which prompted this response: "Whatever I got to wait, I don't care where you are, I'll find you."

By the way, small world story. After a college rugby game, my friends and I visited the San Gennaro feast. At one point, we stepped over a railing at Umberto's. Schenone came out and said that place was reserved for "the family." Schenone told us we could finish eating but then we'd have to go.

My squad was the first FBI joint organized crime task force, meaning that we partnered with the NYPD. Of our thirty-six people assigned, about half were detectives and half agents. Given the large number of law enforcement, and aware that the environment was potentially not always secure, I had my sources use nicknames whenever they called in. It was fun to create code names for them. The names I chose could relate to their personality or a characteristic, or just to be extremely protective and confusing to mobsters if there was a leak. So a rip artist might be "Alibaba," or "Dimples" might be a name for somebody who enjoyed golf. The benefit of this name, which I used later as you will read in chapter 7, was that if there was a leak then mobsters might instead try to incorrectly identify somebody with dimpled cheeks.

At one point two NYPD detectives, Joe Simone and Pat Maggiore, asked me where I went every day. My response was, "I follow wiseguys. I haven't seen one come through the squad." They laughed, we hit it off, and they asked if they could join me. I developed a tighter relationship with them and became closer with them than with most of my fellow agents at that time, although shortly thereafter Bob Doherty came aboard, and we became very close. In general, I worked well with the NYPD and any law enforcement who actually worked.

Joe and Pat knew many of my sources and shared "war stories" from their time tailing mobsters. But they also made arrests. During the Colombo war, both detectives were assigned to assist the Colombo squad. Information that my sources provided often placed mobsters in certain locations with illegal guns. As I received this information during the war, I'd share it with Pat and Joe, who then made car stops and arrests. Pat and Joe did excellent work during the Colombo war. Among other things, they were introduced to a Colombo member's nephew that resulted in a multi-kilo narcotics arrest. They also arrested Colombo soldier John Rosatti with a gun. Rosatti appreciated Pat as an honest detective going forward.

Seemingly out of the blue, in December 1993, Joe was arrested for providing information to the Colombo family. This completely devastated me. What happened was Pat went to make a copy of a document, and he found an internal document that had been left on the copier. The document related to an internal FBI investigation on Joe based on a source who stated that Joe provided information to the Colombo family in return for money.

Pat brought the communication to my supervisor, who, ironically, had himself stupidly left the copy on the machine. Pat and I then went for a long walk. He was understandably stressed out and upset. He and Joe had such a long and close relationship. Pat was concerned that others at the FBI would think he was also corrupt even while the investigation was being conducted.

For my part, I was confused and in complete shock. I knew Pat was honest, as among other things he had testified several times regarding Colombo weapons hearings. Joe and Pat both also knew my source who identified weapons for car stops and arrests. This one source was alive and well. If Joe was on the Colombo payroll, why wasn't the source killed? It all made no sense. Plus, they arrested no fewer than twenty guys with guns during the Colombo war.

An emergency squad meeting was called a few hours later. The ASAC advised that Joe had, in fact, been on the Colombo payroll for years. He was arrested soon thereafter. Crushed, Pat retired soon after. At that time, prior to his arrest, Joe was reassigned to One Police Plaza as he awaited his retirement based on a disability.

In hindsight, I believe I may have been used unknowingly to assist the internal investigation on Simone, to help determine whether he was in fact corrupt. As I mentioned earlier, Chris Favo, the case agent, was a competent agent who played a key role in building cases to help decimate the Colombos. He had previously been on my squad, with Pat and Joe, and they assisted Chris with making arrests. One day, a white-collar crime supervisory agent came to my desk with Favo to ask me a question related to the Colombos. I provided them with responsive details. In hindsight it appears the purpose was to have Simone, sitting within earshot, hear this information and see whether he responded in a manner as corrupt law enforcement would—sharing the details with the Colombos.

From what I understood, agents followed Joe when he left the office that day. My supervisor, who lacked credibility, described how Joe appeared to drive in a manner to "clean" himself, consistent with ensuring he wasn't followed. Doing so would help him identify any trailing cars. But it didn't work, and he was seen driving to Colombo associate Armando "Chips" De Costanza's house.

Simone contested the charges and took his case to trial. It turned out that he had coached a football team, and one of his players was De Costanza's nephew. It is unfortunately not uncommon for someone who lives in Staten Island or New Jersey to have children who play sports with the children of parents affiliated with organized crime. My and my wife's social lives were greatly limited based on this hard truth.

There were also law enforcement recordings that apparently involved Colombo members discussing how they could bribe Joe in exchange for information. When Simone went to visit Chip's nephew to discuss the team, Colombo capo Sal Miciotta was there with De Constanza. Unbeknownst to either Simone or De Costanza, Miciotta was cooperating with the FBI. Miciotta later claimed that they discussed bribes in exchange for information at this meeting. However, Miciotta turned off a tape recorder that would have documented the conversation. In my experience, combined with common sense, this strongly suggested that Miciotta was not being fully truthful. As I recall, the trial also included evidence of recordings made by Miciotta indicating that Joe had previously turned down money offered by the Colombos. This meant our ASAC and squad supervisor lied to us about money they claimed Simone received. There wasn't any money.

Stone and Doherty also testified as defense witnesses for Joe's character. All of the evidence left me with significant doubts as to his corruption. This truly bothers me even to this day. I am still in touch with Pat, who should have been promoted to 1st grade detective, the highest rank at the NYPD.

There was also evidence that others, not Joe, may have been the source of leaks. Colombo member Greg Scarpa was a longtime FBI informant, and his handling agent at this time was Lindley DeVecchio, the supervisor of the FBI squad investigating the Colombo family. Favo and others believed DeVecchio may have been manipulated by Greg Scarpa. He was indicted but found not guilty at a Brooklyn state trial. Nevertheless, because the government alleged DeVecchio's corruption, nineteen soldiers from the Vic Orena Colombo family faction had their convictions reversed or thrown out.

Gun to my head, I feel strongly that Joe Simone was not corrupt. In any event, the jury agreed and found Simone not guilty. However, he was then subjected to an NYPD departmental administrative trial, at which he was found guilty. He lost his job and pension. Joe has since passed away.

I feel extremely sad when I think of the stress and shame his family may have felt at that time and hope this brings closure and pride to them, knowing the confidence and trust Pat, Bob Doherty, Dave Stone, and I all had in Joe.

Back to the Ida case. When I presented the accumulated evidence to SDNY prosecutor Nelson Boxer—one of three prosecutors who eventually worked on the case—he immediately agreed to move forward. In addition to focusing on Ida and Frustaci, I had also built strong cases against Bellomo and Generoso. Not only was there evidence of their participation in Desimone's murder, but I also had evidence concerning their involvement in the extortion of Local 46 of the Mason Tenders Union. A previous investigation by my squad (conducted by agents Paul Meyer and John Pistole and prosecuted by AUSU Jim Bucknam) focused on capo Jimmy Messera. I was aware that recordings from that investigation captured meetings that also implicated Ida, Frustaci, Bellomo, and Generoso. Combined with the information D'Arco made available after he cooperated, there was now enough evidence to indict these other powerful leaders of the Genovese along with others.

The evidence we accumulated was against so many mobsters that at one point Nelson told me, "We're done at this point, because we won't be able to fit any more suspects in the courtroom." Maria Barton and Barbara Ward were the two other prosecutors.

All of this work culminated in the June 1996 arrest of nineteen gangsters, including the entire Genovese administration (with the exception of their boss Chin): acting boss Barney Bellomo, acting underboss Mickey "Dimino" Generoso, and consigliere Ida.

Collectively, the charges included murders, a murder conspiracy, extortion, labor racketeering, thefts, the San Gennaro scheme, illegal gambling, and tax violations. Bringing this case down against such powerful and respected leaders represented a devastating blow to the Genovese.

This had been a massive and difficult investigation that presented many obstacles, including Simone's arrest. It also included the loss of two valued partners prior to the indictment: Agent Doherty (he left organized crime due to his frustrations with the dysfunctional leadership and asked to be reassigned to the Fugitive Task Force), and Maggiore, and the reassignment of my most supportive supervisor, Dave Stone. Stone was my favorite supervisor, so of course the incompetent ASAC replaced him with somebody else who was fired a couple of years later.

Another major benefit of the Ida investigation was that it somewhat randomly—but powerfully—led to evidence in another case against a crew of violent bank robbers. Not only was this of high value to protecting the public, but some of the bank robbers would themselves play a critical role in my next major investigation, involving Mike "Cookie" D'Urso. And it also bizarrely all related to why D'Urso was shot in the first place and why his cousin Tino Lombardi was murdered. That's a big mouthful, so let me begin to spell some of it out for you, and I'll elaborate further in chapter 6 and 7.

Early on in the Ida investigation, I was conducting surveillance at 171 Mulberry, trying to obtain evidence to support an application for a bug/wire. On Monday nights during football season, the club operated high-stakes gambling, with guys routinely staying until 4:00 a.m. I was in a construction-type van right outside the club, trying to obtain overhears. Genovese associates "Baby Carmine" Russo, Elio "Chinatown" Albanese, and Tommy Barrett came out of the club and stood right next to the van. They then actually discussed their bank robberies, specifically an armored car robbery, while they leaned on my van. While they did so, I wrote down, verbatim, what they said. They even referenced the actual van I was sitting inside: "We need a van like this, we pull up on the armored car and slide open the door. . . . I've been in shoot-outs before. . . . We need an insider." Needless to say, these details helped me obtain authority to install a wiretap (critical to building a case against Ida and the others), and also provided strong evidence in their eventual prosecution.

These guys were part of a crew under Genovese capo Allie "Shades" Malangone that included "Fat Gerry" Guadagno, Russo, Albanese, Barrett, and others. Carmine Polito was frequently observed with them as well, and appeared to be an associate aligned with this crew. However, he was actually an associate of Tino Lombardi's and D'Urso, who were part of capo Ross Gangi's crew. Polito later organized a hit on both Lombardi and D'Urso in large part because Lombardi would not "release" Polito to the bank robbery crew.

But my fortuitous van episode was not the only bit of good fortune in bringing them to justice. As with all of life, hard work is indispensable, but good luck (which often flows from the hard work) can carry you a long way as well. A few weeks later, I parked my bureau car near the Tribeca Grill. As I approached Hudson Street, I saw Bonanno soldier John "Boobie" Cerasani (who played a prominent role in undercover FBI agent Joe "Donny Brasco" Pistone's undercover operations many years before), nearby. I knew Boobie was going to prison on a guilty plea in the next few weeks. Nevertheless, he was watching an armored car delivery at a bank, and I watched him as he watched the armored car.

Returning to the office, I shared this info with the Bonanno squad, who told me agent Jim Kossler made a similar observation, seeing Boobie with others. Kossler didn't know the names but did know their faces. When I showed him photos of guys from Ida's club, he picked out Russo, Barrett, and Albanese.

We coordinated with the bank robbery squad and bank security for the next big money armored car delivery. Our team was out there, with SWAT—the robbery crew was known to be heavily armed with AK-47s, and based on source information, they were armed that day with fully automatic weapons. We were prepared for a shooting.

We observed Barrett driving a *New York Post* truck as a safety valve, a "crash car" to protect fleeing bank robbers. The *New York Post* operation was adjacent to a Genovese social club frequented by Barrett and controlled by Ross Gangi, capo. I sat in a truck with five other agents, parked across the street from the bank and the armored delivery car. All the bank robbers were spotted in the area. We may have been overaggressive with the surveillance, however, and were most likely detected. They didn't attempt the robbery that day. But this attempt was still later charged as a bank robbery conspiracy.

The bank robbery crew was quite active and made use of contacts embedded deeply within the banks. For instance, they robbed a Chemical Bank located near to Rockefeller Center of $1.5 million a few days before Christmas 1993 (police recovered around $500,000 of this from the getaway van). The vault attendant, Alfred Driano, was a longtime friend of Mario Fortunato, who also later participated in the plot to kill Lombardi and D'Urso. Fortunato introduced Driano to Polito, but Driano refused to assist them with this robbery. He was later paid to keep quiet.

Likewise, they robbed a bank where "Fat Gerry's" daughter-in-law worked. She left the teller's cage door ajar after the armored car delivery. Barrett was caught clearly by the bank's camera view. And Tino Lombardi got himself hired as an armored car driver. He allowed it to be robbed, cuffing himself to the steering wheel to make it appear as though he was a victim. Unfortunately for him and the rest of them, my surveillances showing that he and the other bank robbers were close associates undermined this effort at a defense.

They also robbed a bank next to Polito's pizzeria, hence his nickname "Carmine Pizza." Polito was identified by an agent as a witness until I explained that he was one of the bank robbers, not a witness.

The bank robbery arrests contained some strangely humorous moments. They suspected arrests were coming, so Baby Carmine actually asked me for a courtesy heads-up—he was worried that his mother would find out. This was insane on multiple levels, including that of course she would eventually find out because he would be arrested and charged and convicted and go to prison. But in addition, I told him, "Are you *nuts*? Your mother was already arrested because she worked at the courthouse and passed on a fake indictment in a sting operation." Carmine said he knew, but she was old. I agreed.

On the day of the arrest, I called Carmine and said, "We're here." Carmine thanked me. "Campi, I'll be right down." Agent Gary Uher had been racking his shotgun prior to the arrest while we were standing outside Carmine's Mulberry Street residence.

We also arrested Fat Gerry. As noted above, his daughter-in-law aided the bank robbers. She had just had her first baby, so I explained the situation to Fat Gerry's wife: He was going to jail, her daughter-in-law was also going away, and her son too. "There was no way your daughter-in-law participated in this bank robbery without your son's participation. They'll all be arrested, and you'll be alone with the baby, so you should be open to everybody cooperating." She heard me out and then called to her husband, "Did you hear what he said?" Fat Gerry responded, "That's Campi. He's crazy." We all laughed as we cuffed Fat Gerry.

In 1995, Polito and six others pleaded guilty to the bank robberies and were incarcerated for several years. One went to trial and was convicted.

Special Agent Mike Sharkey was the case agent, with Nelson Boxer the prosecutor. We had great evidence, including bank camera footage during some of the robberies and surveillance on the aborted attempt. For some reason the AUSAs chose not to charge Fortunato even though he played a role in the historic relationship with Driano, and his business card had been found in the van used in the Chemical Bank robbery. On July 14, 1998, just a few weeks after D'Urso's cooperation began, he recorded a conversation with Aparo citing details of this bank robbery and how he was asked to participate. The details include how Polito met with Fortunato's friend, Alfred Driano, the bank's vault attendant. Barrett slapped Polito after he learned Polito did not pay Driano for this bank robbery.

Back to Ida again. In the face of the accumulated evidence, almost everyone charged in the case chose to plead guilty, including Bellomo, who agreed to a ten-year sentence.

Three took their chances at trial—Ida, Frustaci, and Ruggiero. The judge, the Honorable Lewis A. Kaplan, impressed me with his grasp, knowledge, and memory of the details of the evidence.

After a lengthy trial, Ida and Frustaci were convicted. The evidence consisted mainly of testimony from myself, D'Arco, Sessa, and others, along with numerous tapes, surveillance, and cryptic conversations to avoid law enforcement scrutiny that were captured on T-IIIs. FBI Agents Craig Donlon and Glenn Muenzer were significant assets during the investigation and subsequent trial. Glenn reviewed the T-III conversations daily as they were happening. They were also team leaders on arrest teams.

Ida received a life sentence. As noted above, Ruggiero appeared quite relaxed throughout the trial. He was somehow found not guilty despite overwhelming evidence against him. It would not surprise me to learn about a corrupt juror. A few weeks later, Ruggiero was observed in a meeting with a powerful member of Chin's crew.

The United States attorney for the Southern District of New York cited my tireless efforts, perseverance, and dedication as a model of law enforcement in the unprecedented conviction of seventeen Genovese members and associates, including their ruling administration. I also received a

Tribute to Valor Award from the New York State Bar Association in recognition of bravery, leadership, dedication, and exemplary service to the public. In typical fashion, nothing from the FBI.

I rarely view these awards, having placed them in a room I almost never enter.

But I was sure of one thing: some of the lazy and useless managers who were impediments to my investigation would cite the Ida case as a prominent personal success on their applications for future promotions. They had absolutely no role in this investigation's success.

After all of the guilty pleas and the trial convictions, I indirectly learned the extent to which I was now a fixture on the Genovese radar due to the sheer scope of the investigation and its severe impact on them. An officer who had until recently worked at the Federal Bureau of Prisons was assigned to a joint task force adjacent to my squad. When we were introduced, he declared, "*You're* Mike Campi? You wouldn't *believe* how many times I've heard your name." He went on to explain, "One of my jobs was to monitor calls coming to and from the prison. Your name came up a lot, the wiseguys discussed you so much. I will never forget, one time a mobster told another 'I've just been visited by an FBI agent named Mike Campi.'" The officer then affected a mafia-type accent, supplying the other guy's response, "Hire an attorney and plead guilty. Now!'"

Even years later, as you will read below, I remained firmly on their radar. Acting boss Barney Bellomo made that clear by talking about me in an extremely ironic comment to a criminal confederate during my next investigation into the Genovese (see chapter 10).

* * *

Although we had taken down the Genovese administration, at the end of the day I felt a bit of a letdown and was listless. I enjoyed going out with the trial team to celebrate. However, I also had an empty feeling, as I mostly thought about Bob Doherty, Dave Stone, and Detective Pat Maggiore, who were there from the beginning with Joe Simone. I called Pat from the bar and told him about the convictions—thanking him for his work. We hadn't spoken since the day he retired, and Pat knew the obstacles I had to overcome. I let him know that the supervisor who left the communication on the Xerox machine was subsequently fired for lying—or what's called "a lack of candor" in our business. As for Doherty and Stone, both of them had issues with the then-ASAC, and both of them were enjoying their new positions more than when they worked organized crime.

I joined a gym and decided to take a few months to determine whether to refocus on white-collar crime or to stick with organized crime Shortly thereafter, Mike Sharkey, the case agent on the overlapping bank robberies, was transferred to my squad. That was good news. There were also some new agents who graduated from the FBI and were assigned to C-5. This new group was anxious to get involved in organized crime investigations.

Then I received a call related to Cookie D'Urso, and a new opportunity presented itself. It was off to the races again. But this time I'd be operating from directly *inside* the Genovese family.

Years later, fellow agent George Khousami asked me to join him to approach Joey Ida about possible cooperation. Joey's wife answered the door. "He's not here and I don't know when I'll fucking see him again." When I said my name, Joey appeared from inside the house. "Mike Campi, I got a bone to pick with you." We talked for nearly a half hour while George watched, fascinated. Joey claimed I had fixed his brother's trial. I explained how I did not fix the case, and explained who the witnesses were, and the overwhelming evidence that the jury considered to secure his conviction. The details included Jimmy Ida's role as consigliere facilitating DiLorenzo's murder. I did have two suspects, Joey being one of them.

I always suspected Joey may have played a role in DiLorenzo's murders, for which his brother was convicted. I told Joey that if he knew details of the murder, and was interested in cooperation, I was always available to discuss. Joey laughed and remained silent.

Another interesting postscript came around a decade after the convictions. I was driving to a retirement luncheon with a younger FBI agent, Tim Flannelly. Nicky Frustaci had been recently released from prison for my case, and I saw him walking down the street. I pulled the car over to speak with him. Nicky looked like a deer in the headlights when he recognized me—as though he expected me to arrest him again. When he realized that was not the case, we had a nice chat, just shooting the breeze. It was a "When did you get out? You look great. Best of luck going straight," type of thing. Nicky became comfortable, smiled, and engaged in easy banter with me.

When I returned to the car, Flannelly asked, "Was that your uncle?" He was so surprised when I explained who Nicky was, and how we could treat each other with respect. Our prior interactions had been all business, nothing personal.

CHAPTER SIX

COOKIE

While I was beginning to build cases against the Colombos and then the Genovese, Genovese associate Mike "Cookie" D'Urso was working hard on the other side of the law, gaining the respect of certain very powerful Genovese gangsters. Events would eventually bring D'Urso and me together, presenting another massive opportunity to take down the Genovese and others.

To understand how we got there, it all began when D'Urso fell victim to some of the treachery embedded in the mafia's very DNA—and nearly paid for it with his life. At the time, from my perspective it seemed like just another random, treacherous mob hit gone wrong.

On that day in November 1994, D'Urso went to the San Giuseppe social club in Brooklyn to meet up with his cousin Tino Lombardi and some friends to hang out and play cards. Still in his mid-twenties, D'Urso was a mafioso on the rise. Machiavelli famously commented on the qualities of a lion and a fox. One could succeed in the world by being like a lion—tough and feared, and always bringing the prospect of violence. Or one could succeed by being like a fox—that is, being clever enough to set tricks and traps, and canny enough never to fall into a trap oneself. The Genovese valued D'Urso because he embodied that rare combination, the best of both.

He was muscular and intimidating and didn't hesitate to use his physical powers to get his way. By his late teens, with the assistance of steroids, he could bench-press over four hundred pounds. He first drew the mob's attention when, as only a teenager, D'Urso was arrested for running a massive check-cashing scheme. It made millions, and when the arrests finally came, it also was splashed across the headlines of the New York papers.

Over time, he also became exceedingly talented at devising other clever schemes to make money. His crimes ranged the gamut, from credit card fraud to counterfeiting valuable baseball cards, to more traditional mob staples like loan-sharking. D'Urso could both design the scam and then also act as enforcer when someone involved needed the fear of God put into them.

Back to 1994. On November 30, D'Urso was with his beloved cousin Tino and some good friends—or so he thought. D'Urso regularly played cards with "Carmine Pizza" Polito and Mario Fortunato, who you may recall from the bank robbery discussion in chapter 5. They had each attended D'Urso's wedding only months before. Although D'Urso had troubles with Fortunato in the past, they had set their differences aside (again, or so he thought). Also present were Polito's cousins John "Gingale" Imbrieco and Anthony Cerasulo, a.k.a. "Rookie." Later, Anthony Bruno arrived at the club. Bruno was a local drug addict who was previously assaulted by D'Urso. Cerasulo and Imbrieco knew Bruno from the neighborhood.

Not long into the game, D'Urso felt what he would later describe as like being hit in the back of the head with a baseball bat. He fell to the floor, where he heard gunshots. When he was eventually able to open his eyes, he saw Tino lying in a pool of blood. Everyone else was gone. Another stark illustration of the betrayal and utter hypocrisy of the mafia. In what real family would one's friends lure you to your death?

As D'Urso stumbled to the nearby residence of a friend to call emergency services, he realized that he had not been hit with a bat as he thought, but rather had been shot in the back of the head. The gun had been placed directly against D'Urso's skull when the trigger was pulled. This is actually what saved his life. Had it been held just an inch or so away, the projectile would have gained adequate speed to pierce his skull and kill him. Even so, the head of the bullet went down into D'Urso's neck, and he would have portions of that bullet embedded in his neck for the rest of his life. Tino had no such luck, as he was now dead.

D'Urso's shooting resembled many similar shootings in organized crime, such as Joe Valachi, who was shot in the head as he sat in a car with friends and left for dead. He too survived.

The majority of genuine gangsters do not cooperate with the authorities under any circumstances, so when the police arrived, he told them pure nonsense.

D'Urso gradually gathered through the gangster grapevine that the hit was about money and politics. Bruno had shot D'Urso, while Imbrieco and Polito shot and killed Tino. Polito, a degenerate gambler with continual financial woes, had organized the hit. He owed Tino $50,000 on a loan. Polito chose to kill his friend rather than pay back the money. Polito also owed D'Urso about another $10,000. Killing both friends was easier than paying them back. It was also prudent to kill D'Urso first, since Polito knew D'Urso would seek revenge against Tino's killers.

As an interesting sidenote, days after the shooting, as part of the Ida investigations, I surveilled the Genovese acting hierarchy: acting boss Barney Bellomo, acting underboss Mickey "Dimino" Generoso, and consigliere Jimmy Ida. They met with two capos. One capo was Ross Gangi; D'Urso and Lombardi were in his crew. The other was a powerful capo Allie "Shades" Malangone, who had a close relationship with Bellomo. This meeting clearly concerned the shootings. When the participants left the meeting, they became aware of our presence, and they all fled in a panic. The surveillance included photos of this meeting.

Malangone was involved due to the politics part. Polito had been "under" Tino. But Polito wanted to switch to the crew that did bank robberies, the same crew that I helped convict as part of the Ida case, and Tino opposed this move. The bank robbery crew reported to Malangone. Because of this, Malangone may have obtained authorization sanctioning the hit, and in fact recordings we made later indicated that, in all probability, he obtained authorization to do so. Another example of treachery and violation of mob rules. Since Ida was consigliere, and Bellomo was the acting boss, they most likely also played a role in the prior decision to kill D'Urso and Lombardi. Malangone was closely aligned with Bellomo at the time due to the Genovese control in the corrupt carting business. This meeting would also address D'Urso's request to retaliate. The request was denied.

During D'Urso's cooperation with me, he made a number of recordings addressing Polito. On September 1, 1998, D'Urso recorded his meeting with Sammy Aparo. One of the topics discussed involved Carmine Polito. Polito was telling people he was going to be "straightened out soon." This is a term used to identify one's induction into an organized crime family. Aparo agreed that if Polito is to be "made" then Alley Shades Malangone previously obtained the sanction to D'Urso and Lombardi's shootings. They also discussed how Baby Carmine Russo and Elio Albanese, a.k.a. "Chinatown," wanted to kill Polito after the bank robberies. I understand from law enforcement who maintain contact with me, Polito is currently the capo of a crew having Russo and Albanese as soldiers.

D'Urso decided to settle the matter himself, and he expected that his mob superiors would let him get his revenge. Gangi made this request to the Genovese administration, which everyone thought would be quickly granted. In yet another example of mob treachery, permission was denied. As noted above, this may have been because the hit was sanctioned. More powerful than Gangi, Malangone might have persuaded the powers to quietly authorize the assassination. This authorization may have included details of a previous beating D'Urso participated in of a bouncer for a high-profile nightclub controlled by Bellomo. This prior incident could influence Bellomo to side with Malangone.

But even if the hit was not authorized, another reason why D'Urso's request may have been denied is because all organized crime faced tremendous pressure from law enforcement during this time. In a historic event, D'Arco had cooperated a few years earlier because he feared that his own crime family was plotting to kill him. Pete Chiodo had cooperated as well, after his own crime family had tried to kill him, threatened to kill his father, and also shot his sister in a failed effort to assassinate her. There was also Gravano, who cooperated after learning that his boss, John Gotti, was likely setting him up to take a fall. Layers and layers of betrayals within a criminal organization whose crime family is supposed to come before a blood family.

As an FBI agent who has worked on these types of investigations, I could understand both sides of the argument, D'Urso's and his superiors. The Genovese wanted to insulate itself from law enforcement capitalizing on murder retaliations, as the mob was suffering from real turmoil at the time. Therefore, many made members cooperated. (Some cooperated prior to D'Urso's cooperation and many after his cooperation.) In addition to those listed above, for the Luccheses there was underboss Anthony "Gaspipe" Casso, capo Anthony Accetturo, soldier Frankie Gioia, and others. Colombo defectors included consigliere Carmine Sessa, capo Salvatore Miciotta, capo Anthony Russo, and others, not to mention the revelation that capo Greg Scarpa was a longtime FBI informant. The Gambinos included underboss Sammy Gravano, capo Mikey "Scars" DiLeonardo, soldier Dominic Borghese, and many others. Each of these powerful mafiosi became government witnesses, which had a seismic and catastrophic impact on the mob. And it posed a clear threat to the overall survival of the mafia, as their collective example paved the path for future potential cooperators who sought to get out from under this hypocritical life.

The Genovese administration may have concluded that even a warranted vendetta could result in unwanted law enforcement attention and the type of cooperation that plagued the other crime families, from which they had so far been spared. And what if D'Urso's retaliation didn't succeed, just like the hit on D'Urso had failed? Then Polito or others might become witnesses and help bring down Malangone and others. So, I understood the decision to postpone any murders until the heat calmed down over time.

Whatever the reason, D'Urso was crushed. Tino had been like a brother to him, and he needed revenge no matter what he was told. D'Urso was strong-willed and somewhat reckless, and he ignored the warning not to retaliate, gathered others, and went out "hunting" for revenge. Eventually an associate of his, John Kirby, shot at Polito with a silenced gun but missed. Gangi then gave D'Urso a message from Bellomo that if they found out D'Urso was responsible, they would kill him. As former Colombo capo Franzese has explained, "The guys that [are] ready to kill, they don't last. They don't last because people say I'm not going to worry about that guy.

He's too quick with the trigger." I was aware of many young associates who behaved similarly to D'Urso and were killed for a lack of discipline and self-control. Being directed not to retaliate also tested one's loyalty to the mob, and an ability to follow orders. Those who can't follow orders will not be inducted and may be killed due to their reckless nature and the risks this presents to the mob. D'Urso did have many powerful allies, though, who saw his potential.

In the weeks and months that followed, D'Urso continued to throw caution to the wind as he sought revenge anyway. And although he had told Kirby to drop his own efforts because Kirby was not reliable, Kirby shot Polito in the head. Like D'Urso, Polito survived. Rather than face prison time, when law enforcement attempted to arrest him, Kirby ran out into the street and shot himself dead. He had told D'Urso he would never go back to prison, and he kept his word.

Incidentally, remember when I wrote earlier about pursuing Polito and others for bank robberies? It was around this time that Kirby shot him. Not knowing at the time of D'Urso's involvement, I assumed Polito's shooting was related to the bank robberies. My working theory was that fellow crew members shot him because they viewed him as the weak link and considered him likely to turn into a witness, so they may as well eliminate him. How's that for loyalty? The mob has a long history of shooting first and asking questions second, so this made sense. I went to visit Polito in the hospital with agent Uher, and suggested that Polito consider working with me. His wife was in a panic and his brother was a police officer. I asked Carmine, "Is it really worth it?" but he wasn't interested. I imagine Polito informed Genovese higher-ups about my meeting with him at the hospital.

I later learned that although Polito had not been shot to silence him, my instincts were nevertheless spot-on. I say that because Genovese acting capo Sammy Aparo was later recorded stating that two of Polito's fellow bank robbers, Carmine Russo and Elio "Chinatown" Albanese, considered killing Polito because they were concerned he was "going to go bad" (cooperate).

Eventually, to outside observers, D'Urso seemed to move on with his life. He used large amounts of his ill-gotten mob earnings to form a construction and renovation company and bought and rehabbed properties in the New York area. He would drink and play golf in his spare time. He never sold drugs, but very occasionally he'd rob drug dealers for sport.

Yet beneath his smooth and intimidating mob exterior, D'Urso was often close to the breaking point. He understandably never got over the fact that gangsters killed his cousin and had come within a literal inch of killing him, and yet he had been told that if he obtained revenge he would be killed.

The facade had been ripped off, and the underlying raw hypocrisy and treachery woven into the very fabric of "the life" was undeniably on full display. D'Urso and Tino had done nothing wrong, and yet their "friends" assassinated one and nearly killed the other and were now being forcefully protected by the Genovese powers. What "values," "loyalty," and "honor" did this display? None. What "family" engages in this type of barbarism? None. What true friend tries to kill you? None. For D'Urso, who had previously fully bought into the mafia's public relations sales pitch hook, line, and sinker, it was hard not to recognize that "the life" was in fact about absolutely nothing of value. There were no sacred systems of honor. That was a con and a lie. Getting ahead, even just surviving, was all about who you knew, what you could do for them, and who had power.

The mob was only about this obsession with raw power and constantly watching your back: your "friends" might well be the ones who stabbed you there. Mob history is replete with multiple other instances of this type of treachery.

Although D'Urso nevertheless remained completely loyal to "the life," these internal tensions and realizations were cracking his armor. When he discussed this general topic with other mobsters with whom he was close, in a case of surprising self-awareness, they had similar insights. D'Arco, Chiodo, Gravano, and others' recent cooperation was prominently on their collective minds. As D'Urso's mentor Sammy "Meatballs" Aparo often told him, these mobsters defected because they had been abused by other mobsters, and their cooperation was completely understandable.

How could D'Urso not apply this same logic to himself? Who had been abused worse than him? Eventually, he would turn the corner and come to me.

CHAPTER SEVEN

COOKIE BECOMES DIMPLES

"Another takedown and this life is over."

As the Ida case concluded, I was not sure what to do next and was feeling a bit aimless. Then I received a phone call in 1998 which reignited the fire and changed absolutely everything.

D'Urso was the catalyst for these changes, so let's briefly bring you a bit more up to date on him.

By 1997, D'Urso seemed, in all outward appearances, to have cooled since the attack. He was an active and well-respected member of acting capo Aparo's crew. Like all eligible associates, D'Urso still dreamed of becoming a made man. He had actually been proposed for membership more than once in the early 1990s, but the "books" had been "closed" for some time due to a variety of factors such as D'Arco, Chiodo, and Gravano becoming witnesses, other internal turbulence, and the ranks not being significantly depleted by murders or natural deaths. By rule, the original structure of each crime family has to be maintained in the identical proportions to when originally created. Men considered to fill these vacated spots typically perform in some manner to be viewed as worthy, although some people pay to get made or are made due to a blood relationship with someone with pull. More hypocrisy. Quality control also requires that the name of a deceased member is provided along with the name of the proposed member who will replace them. On occasion a crime family may attempt to use a deceased member's name on multiple occasions so that they can enlarge the size of their gang. If caught, they act as though this was a mistake. Sometimes, too, a family may "sneak" members in. All of them being criminals and liars by nature, this is something they always have to be on the lookout for, and it makes them perpetually paranoid.

There were also others whose sponsors may have been more respected than D'Urso's sponsor, Genovese acting capo Sammy "Meatballs" Aparo. This was due to Aparo's prior history where his capo slapped Chin's father-in-law when Chin was still a soldier, causing Gigante to also resent Aparo. The capo was killed, but it is not known if his murder was related to the slap.

Also, mobsters who disliked D'Urso had put a quash on proposing him because of his reputation as a hotheaded guy who at times was thought to have stepped out of line. Nevertheless, he always dreamed of being made, and felt as though it was long overdue. As a factual matter, many get inducted at a later stage of life. D'Arco, for instance, wasn't inducted until he was fifty.

In any event, in D'Urso's case—given what happened to him and his cousin and like others who are not easily controlled—beneath his cool facade he remained a simmering cauldron of anger and resentment.

Johnny Zero was a low-level clerk in a small-time illegal gambling office. D'Urso and Zero had an arrangement where D'Urso provided bettors to place bets, with D'Urso receiving a portion of the money from the bets that were placed.

Without telling D'Urso, Zero engaged in shenanigans with three especially desperate losers who gambled through D'Urso's book. Zero was required to record their bets like any other, but he did not do so. Instead, he secretly placed their bets to the side in anticipation of keeping their money all to himself. This meant that he was essentially stealing from the betting office he worked for, which was headed by a guy named Castellano.

One day, disaster struck for Zero when all of these desperate bettors won. D'Urso came to collect for them and Zero was forced to explain what happened and reveal he didn't have the money to cover the bets. Because he was a street guy himself, and was friends with Zero and understood

Zero's scheme, D'Urso gave Zero a week to pay him. But instead, Zero doubled down. He figured there was no way they would hit two weeks in a row and planned to get their money by once again holding the bets himself. However, they each hit. Suddenly, Zero owed D'Urso $70,000. When D'Urso went to collect, Zero tried to put D'Urso on the phone with Castellano.

D'Urso assumed Castellano was with the Gambinos because Castellano was the last name of former Gambino boss Paul Castellano (murdered by John Gotti to seize power). D'Urso gave Zero a beating, figuring that since the Gambinos were in the wrong, this would force a sit-down between the Genovese and the Gambinos, at which the Gambinos would be forced to admit this. D'Urso was showing strength on behalf of the Genovese and their interests, just as he was supposed to do.

D'Urso and Zero designed a scheme to expedite the payment of the money owed. They had Zero call Castellano and act as though D'Urso was going to give Zero another beating. Castellano instructed D'Urso to come to his marina to obtain a partial payment of $10,000. This marina was located off the Cross Island Parkway in the vicinity of Whitestone, Queens.

Later that day, D'Urso received a call on his cell phone from an unknown number. When he picked up, a mysterious voice began to berate him for having beaten up Zero. The man claimed to be Castellano's boss and stated that Zero was protected. He also stated, "You want to hurt my clerk? You threaten my clerk? You don't know who you're dealing with." The unknown caller turned out to be Serpico, and he instructed D'Urso to "have his Uncle Sammy go to a restaurant on 82nd and 2nd Avenue. . . . "If you know what's good for you, you'll stay away." Then the mystery caller hung up.

Incensed, D'Urso got in his car and went directly back to Zero. Then he redialed the mystery number and when the same man picked up, D'Urso stated, "I can't beat Zero?" Then he beat Johnny over the head with the phone while screaming things like, "You think you can tell me who I can hit and who I can't? If a guy owes me money and doesn't pay, he gets beat. I don't care who doesn't like it. I'll rip *your* fucking heart out and eat it too."

What D'Urso didn't know was that the man on the other end of the line was not with the Gambinos. Unbeknownst to him, D'Urso was talking directly to Frank "Farby" Serpico, a powerful Genovese who had been promoted to acting boss while Bellomo served his prison sentence in my Ida case. In other words, Serpico was the boss of D'Urso's boss—directly below Chin. And D'Urso had just threatened to kill him, to rip his heart out and eat it.

Farby immediately reached out to Genovese acting capo Alan Longo. Longo was being utilized as a messenger for the acting administration of the Genovese family to insulate and protect them from law enforcement scrutiny. Farby was furious at D'Urso's behavior and wanted him immediately killed. He instructed Longo to take it up with Sammy "Meatballs" Aparo, who was responsible for D'Urso. Longo explained to Sammy that Farby had become the acting boss, a secret to which even most Genovese were not privy. So in this instance, their renowned secrecy intended to insulate them actually backfired—had D'Urso known, he would never have addressed Farby in this manner. And I would never have had a chance to take them all down again due to what happened next.

Sammy Meatballs spoke up for D'Urso as did others, such as powerful Genovese soldier Joe Zito, who liked and respected D'Urso. Zito also had a close relationship with Chin. D'Urso's allies argued forcefully to Serpico that D'Urso should be given another chance, as he had no idea who he was talking to. He had actually thought he was standing up for the Genovese against the Gambinos. Only by interceding did his friends save D'Urso's life, because Farby eventually relented and agreed on a six-month probation. If D'Urso disobeyed any order or stepped out of line in any way in the next six months, he would be killed.

Sammy informed D'Urso of the outcome. D'Urso was angry more than he was horrified, to learn that he'd inadvertently threatened the new boss. Why would the acting boss not identify himself, and why would he intervene on behalf of a low-level bookie? It was also ridiculous for the acting boss to call D'Urso on a phone so recklessly: What if there had been an FBI wire up on the call? If anyone was at fault for this incident, it was clearly Serpico.

Nevertheless, Sammy Meatballs ended the conversation with tears falling from his eyes, chilling D'Urso to the core: "If I call for you, don't come."

Sammy's meaning was crystal clear. He was like a father to D'Urso. In the mob's twisted value system premised on betrayal, if the decision came down to kill D'Urso, Aparo would be the one assigned to set him up. Who would expect their father to kill them? Sammy might not be the one to pull the trigger, but he would lure D'Urso to his death. This is another prime example of both the hypocrisy and treachery of the mob. What "family" would require a father to set up his son for murder? Particularly when the son had done nothing wrong, and the father knew it. This was another example of how there is no honor, loyalty, or family in "the life."

At this moment the path forward crystallized in D'Urso's mind. Not only was he facing possible death at the hands of the gang to which he had been so loyal, but he had not too long before participated in a murder. Two of D'Urso's friends and fellow gangsters, Vito Guzzo and Anthony Tabbita, wanted to kill John Borelli for personal reasons, and D'Urso had agreed to help. Borelli was associated with Charles Carneglia, a high-ranking Gambino capo now doing life in prison. Guzzo told Carneglia he wouldn't kill Borelli, and then immediately told D'Urso that they would have to do the murder quickly. I believe D'Urso more or less knew he would soon be arrested for the murder, as law enforcement was asking lots of questions and clearly circling round to move in.

Given all of this, D'Urso concluded he could no longer serve the mob. They had killed his cousin and tried to kill him, forbidden him from taking the rightful revenge he was due. Now his own stand-in father might possibly be ordered to take D'Urso's life over a misunderstanding in which D'Urso and many others believed he'd done the right thing.

The Genovese had further damaged a promising young associate. They also ironically laid the groundwork for the FBI to create a relationship with yet another man spurned by and furious with the hypocrisy of "the life." All on their own, the Genovese internally created a new powerful enemy, and law enforcement, namely me, would soon have yet another useful tool.

D'Urso acted carefully. At the time, he was building a house in south Florida. He enjoyed warm weather and golf. As he began to seriously think about cooperating, the idea of having a home base in Florida felt safer too, permitting him to better control risk. Many mobsters had homes in Florida, so this would raise no eyebrows. He could still collect money from debtors, run schemes and scams, and generally stay on top of all his criminal rackets while frequently being out of state.

On one of his trips back to New York, D'Urso checked in with Sammy Meatballs at Florio's Restaurant, located on Grand Street in Little Italy. Aparo seemed distracted and not his usual self.

He told D'Urso that I had just paid him a visit.

D'Urso asked whether this was because I was on the mob's payroll.

"No, he's not corrupt, he's an honest agent," Sammy responded. "His name is Campi. He's the agent who put Barney, Jimmy, and Mickey away. And he just informed me about a threat on my life." Aparo likely thought the threat came from Farby due to the dispute over D'Urso—in fact, the threat was not related to Farby.

As noted before, when an FBI agent receives information involving a direct threat to someone's life, we always provide the person threatened with some kind of notification. We don't disclose the specific person who presents the potential threat. One reason for this is the mobster may simply go out and kill the person who is thinking of killing him. Since I had information of this sort concerning Sammy, I had informed him of a possible threat to his life.

That got D'Urso thinking. . . . If he were to cooperate, I was the agent he wanted to cooperate with. He was attracted to the idea of connecting with the FBI agent who had delivered the head shot, building a winning case against and arresting the Genovese active administration—their street boss, underboss, and consigliere.

D'Urso made note of my name.

I knew of D'Urso as well, at least a little bit. This was because he often hung out at Ida's social club and was photographed with Polito, Russo, Albanese, his cousin Tino, and other criminals involved in stock fraud schemes. My focus, however, was on Ida and other higher-level mobsters. D'Urso was among the low-level associates who I did not target. My sources had also mentioned D'Urso to me before, but usually as a side character in their narrative. One source described him as "treacherous." At the time, I viewed him as another wannabe youngster who hung out.

In the days following his conversation with Sammy, D'Urso moved closer to flipping. More encounters gave him an additional ominous feeling that it was time to make his move.

Mob rules prohibit all gangsters from carrying firearms unless explicitly permitted to do so, for instance on a hit or a robbery. This is because having a weapon can lead to bad outcomes. Law enforcement might recognize a concealed weapon, and a subsequent arrest may take place in the presence of other wiseguys, in turn causing their potential arrest for charges such as possession of narcotics or parole violations. Convicted felons caught with a gun also face a statutory minimum of five years incarceration. Such arrests are also useful to law enforcement at future trials, because they can identify mob members as "associated" with an arrested person.

Because he was willful, difficult to control, and had been shot in the head and threatened again, D'Urso started openly disobeying this standing order for his own protection. D'Urso brought his .357 Magnum whenever he went for a meeting. This is of course further evidence of the mob's hypocrisy, treachery, and ever-present betrayal—that a valued gangster felt the need to carry a gun when meeting with fellow "brothers" to protect himself against their own potential attack.

At one such meeting, his own captain Ross Gangi, accompanied by vicious Bonanno soldier John "Boobie" Cerasani (as described by undercover FBI agent Joe "Donnie Brasco" Pistone), confronted him about this. D'Urso responded, "Look, I'll come when I'm called, but I'm bringing my gun. If you don't want me to show up with a gun, don't call me." This response cut in two directions. It confirmed his reputation as the ultimate tough guy, fearless and ballsy, who could prove very useful to the mob. On the other hand, it also demonstrated open disobedience, a lack of control and respect for mob authority—and even worse, to his own crew's capo. It was a disrespectful statement in a culture obsessed with respect. Being so confrontational with Gangi and Cerasani could theoretically justify D'Urso's murder on that basis alone.

Around the same time, D'Urso noticed that Gangi appeared to be "feeling him out" in a strange way. For example, Gangi asked D'Urso to meet with him another time, and Cerasani was once again present. At this meeting, Gangi asked D'Urso for a loan of a modest amount of money. Having firsthand knowledge and experience with his cousin Tino having been killed in part over a loan, D'Urso knew that some gangsters were killed over this, because a dead guy can't collect. Gangi could theoretically even kill D'Urso the same day of the loan and claim he never received the money, that whoever killed D'Urso probably robbed him.

In a bind, because after all this was his own captain requesting the money, D'Urso said that he wanted to run the loan by Sammy.

Boobie applied more pressure, replying that this made no sense. Gangi was Sammy's capo. Why would D'Urso have to separately talk to Sammy? D'Urso said he simply wanted to put it on record with Sammy, since D'Urso reported directly to him.

Gangi pressed D'Urso further, asking, "What if I asked you to *kill* Sammy? What would you do then?"

D'Urso was cornered. If he replied no, then this was direct insubordination, which would justify killing him. If he replied yes, then would he now be sent to kill his father figure? But D'Urso's street skills were finely honed. He replied carefully, "Are you asking me *asking* me, or is this a hypothetical question?" he managed.

"I'm asking hypothetically," Gangi claimed.

"Then hypothetically," D'Urso replied in his typical straightforward and ballsy manner, "if a day comes when you really do want Sammy killed, you come to me, and I'll give you my answer on that day. I don't do hypotheticals." His reply made clear that he was formidable, a true street guy with backbone—backbone enough to not react with fear or to bend to this pressure.

Leaving this encounter, D'Urso felt like the walls were closing in even tighter. It was now or never.

D'Urso went directly to Sammy. "We have to kill Rossi," D'Urso told him, and said he would go do it. He explained how Rossi asked him if he were willing to kill Aparo. Sammy appreciated D'Urso's offer to kill Gangi for him, but told D'Urso to hold off while Aparo looked into it. Interestingly, D'Urso connected his exchange with Gangi to my conversation with Aparo, believing that when I warned Aparo about a threat to his life, the threat I referred to was the one possibly posed by Gangi (it wasn't).

D'Urso then also spoke with his close friend Vito Guzzo. Guzzo was always hell-bent on violence, and always saw violence as the first and best option. He suggested that they assemble others, kill Gangi and Cerasani, and go to war. D'Urso declined this offer.

All mob families have their own cadre of lawyers who serve the family, and the Genovese are no exception. Those lawyers would never help a mobster client flip. Instead, they would immediately relay this information up the gangster chain and tell them about their client's desire to provide information against them. That spells certain death. All gangsters know this, and for this reason D'Urso knew that if he wanted to cooperate, he'd have to find a lawyer without any mob ties. He'd previously hired mob lawyer Gerry Shargel to help him with some matters but there was no way on earth he would ask for Shargel's help—he might as well tell the Genovese administration himself.

But this presented a big problem—who could he trust? It's not like he could ask any of his mobster friends for a lawyer recommendation. D'Urso caught a lucky break while walking down the street in Lower Manhattan. He ran into the lawyer who prosecuted him when he was arrested a decade earlier on the check-cashing scheme.

D'Urso remembered the former prosecutor as fair, capable, and effective, and she was now in private practice. She was not a mob lawyer, and he felt he could trust her. At a nightclub, he also bumped into the former NYPD cop who had arrested him in the check-cashing case and who now worked in private security.

D'Urso explained his situation to both of them, and they immediately confirmed they would help. I should note that the circumstances of D'Urso initially coming forward are *extraordinarily* rare. He had not been arrested. He had not been convicted. He had not just been shot. He was not serving a lengthy sentence which he hoped to reduce. And although he did have reason to be concerned about his welfare and safety, he had powerful allies in the mob (such as Joe Zito) who were working hard to ensure he stayed alive and well and eventually inducted. For all these reasons, the Genovese had no reason whatsoever to suspect D'Urso would flip either. Advantage, FBI.

D'Urso asked his lawyer to go to the guy Sammy Meatballs told him about—me, Mike Campi. Instead, she reached out where she already had contacts—the Organized Crime Section of the Eastern District of New York, because she had been an assistant district attorney with prosecutors who were now there. She set up a meeting with the chief of the unit, Mark Feldman. After a couple of introductory meetings for D'Urso and the prosecutors to feel each other out and develop a level of comfort, they scheduled a more in-depth talk in which D'Urso would be prepared to "give them the goods."

The Phone Call

Mark Feldman called me in the late spring of 1998. He identified himself as the chief of the Organized Crime unit in the EDNY. Mark didn't provide any particular context but asked what I knew about Cookie D'Urso. I provided him with what details I knew: D'Urso was a tough kid associated with Genovese member Sammy "Meatballs" Aparo and had frequented Tommy "Gigali" Cestaro's Mulberry Street social club.

Feldman told me he'd heard I didn't work in the EDNY, and I responded, "You heard wrong. I work in Brooklyn, Staten Island, Bronx, Queens, Long Island, wherever crime occurs and I have a prosecutor. I stopped crossing the Brooklyn Bridge to work in the Eastern District because I didn't get a quality job. If I wanted to get a hand job, it was easier to cross the street to the Southern District of New York than get into a car and get another parking ticket to cross the bridge." I had some prior bad experiences with EDNY AUSAs whose performances left me unimpressed, to put it mildly, but I was always willing to keep an open mind. Back in 1985, I enjoyed working in the EDNY on the Labor Racketeering cases with prosecutors Anthony Siano and Patrick Cotter. Feldman asked me if I would attend a meeting with someone, my purpose being to validate information that would be provided in a meeting that was about D'Urso.

Mark didn't tell me that the meeting would be with D'Urso. He kept this information close to his vest for the time being, since he didn't yet know me and had some reservation about whether I'd be willing to work with his office. My reputation was that I only worked with the SDNY in Manhattan. Eventually, though, he told me we'd be meeting with D'Urso.

I didn't yet know it, but this wasn't the first meeting. D'Urso and his lawyer had met with Mark and other AUSAs on a couple of other occasions to explore D'Urso's potential cooperation.

And I learned D'Urso had requested my presence even though we had never met.

On the day of D'Urso's next scheduled meeting—the one I'd be present at—D'Urso's lawyer called him and told him not to show up, and to go home. The EDNY changed the location for the meeting at the last minute, which, his lawyer told him, never happens. She told D'Urso that this was giving her bad vibes and she'd try to figure out what was going on.

Because of an open investigation on Sammy Meatballs, I happened to be watching through a concealed camera showing the street outside of Florio's restaurant in downtown Manhattan. I watched D'Urso and his wife appear, and then turn around and head home.

When D'Urso and his wife got home, multiple FBI agents emerged with their guns drawn and took him into custody. They charged him with John Borelli's murder. The FBI team that investigated Vito Guzzo and the Borelli homicide did a thorough investigation with an aggressive prosecutor, Jim Walden.

D'Urso had no idea what was happening. After all, he was headed to a voluntary meeting with prosecutors to discuss cooperating with them, and he felt certain that he had somehow been betrayed.

He was taken to the U.S. Attorney's Office, where I waited along with a number of other FBI agents.

The circumstances of D'Urso both coming to meet with prosecutors to discuss and disclose his crimes—and also being arrested for murder on his way to that meeting—were viewed by D'Urso as beyond strange. I wasn't privy to the reasons for this because, at that time, I was not even aware that D'Urso was meeting with AUSAs. My educated guess is that there were two camps at the U.S. Attorney's Office. One camp was working hard to develop evidence to arrest all of those who participated in Borelli's murder. They had developed enough evidence to arrest D'Urso and put him away for life, and they wanted their pound of flesh. The other camp wanted to continue to meet with him to assess his possible use as a cooperating witness. Apparently, a bizarre resolution was reached where he would both be arrested and then brought to the prescheduled meeting with the prosecutors.

This may have destroyed the entire opportunity from the outset, because if anybody saw his public and splashy arrest for murder and reported it "up the chain" in the mob, D'Urso would be quickly killed if he was suddenly back out on the street. The mob would know the only logical explanation for his freedom would be that he was working for the FBI.

D'Urso didn't know who to trust at this point, but he was especially thankful that I was in the room and directed a lot of his comments to me. I didn't really care which way the meeting went. I was there to assess his credibility, as measured by his response to the questions he was asked to see if he could be usable as a cooperator. I did not anticipate that he would ask to work with me. D'Urso passed the test, appearing to be honest and forthright and admitting his role in multiple crimes, including the Borelli murder. Although he was thrown by his arrest earlier that day, he said he would plead guilty and wanted to work with me.

Asked why he wanted to cooperate, D'Urso replied that he wanted to "get" the people who had participated in his cousin's murder and his own attempted murder. Feldman and I believed D'Urso, and we agreed to work with him. In my experience, it's very difficult to predict which gangsters are going to flip/cooperate. That is because cooperating requires somebody either extremely weak or extremely strong. In a lot of instances, you think you've got him, but they don't have the nerve. On the other hand, sometimes their flip comes as a complete shock, like with Gravano or D'Arco. And sometimes you think a guy is about to be killed and will flip, like Polito, but you get turned down. It's certainly not an exact science.

I felt that D'Urso searching me out and specifically requesting to cooperate with "Campi" was divine intervention and part of my destiny. I knew his friends had shot him in his head and killed his cousin Tino.

Likewise, I had an uncle who was also shot by his friend. I never wanted to make it personal. Otherwise, I would have requested a transfer to the Newark Division, where my uncle's shooter was located. I imagine my uncle knew about his friend's criminal life. I learned about my uncle's shooting while I attended a friend's wedding. I had no idea my uncle was shot, and believed his injury was related to his prior military service during WW II.

During Christmas each year I watch my favorite movie, *It's a Wonderful Life*, and try to get my children to watch it with me. The movie has had a very positive impact on my life, especially as an FBI agent. I firmly believe that a single person can make a huge difference in another person's life without ever knowing the impact. When I arrested anyone, especially an organized crime figure, I felt good knowing I protect others from murders and other serious crimes that can devastate a family, community, and/or country.

I also had empathy for someone in "the life" who may want to cooperate. That person's internal struggle with this decision could relate to many things, perhaps a father who had been mistreated by former law enforcement. Sometimes, this decision was too difficult for them to cross that bridge. But D'Urso had decided to come aboard.

The initial plan for D'Urso's cooperation was primarily to address his cousin's murder along with the bank robbery in which Fortunato and others participated in and/or assisted. We anticipated that this would take several months and that we'd wrap up before the end of the year.

D'Urso and his wife spent the night in a hotel on Long Island with me and several other agents posted as security. The next day he appeared before the Honorable Sterling Johnson. In a small-world irony, Judge Johnson had been the district attorney in charge of the office that prosecuted D'Urso years before for his check-cashing scheme. In a sealed courtroom a secret deal was struck. D'Urso pled guilty to murder for his role in the Borelli murder, in addition to various other, lesser crimes including multiple murder conspiracies. Judge Johnson made clear to D'Urso that if he did not cooperate, all bets were off, and his role in the Borelli hit meant that he was eligible for the death penalty.

D'Urso walked out of the courtroom and into a brand-new under-cover life. His deal, as outlined in his written cooperation agreement, was to provide any and all assistance law enforcement sought, and to always tell the truth. Violation of any of these rules would end in his agreement being torn to shreds and him being stuck with his guilty plea to murder. Nevertheless, keep in mind that D'Urso initially approached law enforcement voluntarily, and he remained intent on wreaking revenge against the hypocrisy and treachery that plagued him despite his loyalty to "the life."

I would be the case agent creating the strategies to make the best possible use of him. We now had a man on the inside, our own Trojan Horse.

"I'll Call You after This Meeting. If I Don't Come Back, You Know What Happened."

There were suspenseful moments right out of the box. Lurking in the background we didn't know whether anyone had seen D'Urso's public arrest for murder. Just as we were setting the mob up to have D'Urso record their conversations, they might be setting him up to lure him to his death. The only real choice we had was to put him out there, have his back to protect him as best we could, and find out.

I put D'Urso to work that very same day.

"We're gonna call you Dimples," I pronounced as we met.

"Why 'Dimples'?" D'Urso asked. "I understand that I have to have a new nickname, but?"

"Two reasons," I replied. "One, you told me you like to play golf, and a golf ball has dimples. Two, you don't actually have any dimples, so if somebody in the mob ever hears us talking about a cooperator named 'Dimples' they're not going to think it's you. They'll think it's somebody with dimples." I further pointed out that if a gangster with dimples was killed, it could signal that the mob knew they had a cooperator in their midst and were trying to kill him. This could also give us notice of a threat to his life and the existence of a mole in law enforcement. I also knew well about former corrupt murderous NYPD detectives Louis Eppolito and Stephen Carracappa, who worked in the city's Organized Crime Unit. They had been on Gaspipe Casso's payroll with the Lucheses for many years, and their sharing of confidential information led to several murders. They also participated in murdering informants and killed rival gangsters. And there had been others, such as the trial of FBI agent Lynn DeVecchio, who was alleged to have corruptly favored one side in the murderous Colombo wars. I'd also had prior experience arresting corrupt law enforcement to include NYPD. We needed to take every possible precaution.

I required everyone in the tight group who would work with D'Urso to only refer to him as Dimples. Nobody else would know his real name. I then wasted no time and began taking D'Urso through the ins-and-outs of wearing a wire, beginning that very first afternoon. The "wire" devices used by the FBI in the late 1990s fit snugly "underneath the wearer's clothes, in a way unlikely to reveal its presence even during a pat down." The likelihood of him being patted down in the first place was minimal. The mobsters had never patted him down before. Why would they begin now? Unless they knew he was cooperating, in which case they would kill him anyway.

Paul Weinstein, a senior EDNY AUSA, was assigned to be my liaison in the prosecutor's office. I'd periodically check in with him and keep him up to date on the evidence we had obtained.

At this initial stage, I didn't anticipate how much value D'Urso could bring. After all, he was an associate in a crew that was not particularly well regarded. My best-case hope was D'Urso would capture conversations related to homicides, bank robberies, illegal gambling, and other potential crime. That first day, I sent him out to meet with, and record, his boss Sammy Meatballs.

In a fascinating irony, in that very first recorded conversation, Aparo directly referenced the Ida prosecution and convictions which I had orchestrated, "We can't take another hit like that. If we have another takedown, this life is over."

This comment set the table perfectly for what we were just now beginning to do: build exactly that next takedown. With any luck, it would further devastate the Genovese, and Aparo's warning would become a reality.

The recording with Sammy was clear, and nothing indicated any suspicion of D'Urso. Although having literally just the day before been arrested for murder, pleading guilty to murder, and now facing the death penalty, D'Urso was the picture of cool, and he gave nothing away. We were off to a very good start.

His only comment on our debriefing concerned the recording device itself. D'Urso let me know that the battery on the device burned his skin. I was able to locate an alternative device and we provided this new technology to D'Urso, a few weeks later. ███████████████████ ██

D'Urso was an active participant, wanting to do as much as he could to assist me in my work.

One critical piece of advice I passed on to D'Urso early in our collaboration, "*Always* tell the truth. *Always* tell the truth about what you saw, and what's going on. You never know who else from these meetings might cooperate one day. We may get more than one perspective on things. Lies are hard to keep straight, but the truth never changes." Many years later, D'Urso often repeated these words as the best and most important advice I *ever* gave him.

We settled into a regular pattern, often reconnoitering under the Williamsburg Bridge, and then driving into Little Italy. D'Urso would drive while I gave him talking points for that day's recording—questions to ask, and topics to bring up. These topics came from my review of his recent conversations, or my interest in a criminal topic that I was familiar with and wanted to explore and secure evidence. Many of these subjects came from my understanding of the mob and their criminal business.

We also talked at night, while I walked the family dog. We'd map out the next day's recordings after I reviewed the details of the recorded crimes already discussed. As one example, we used D'Urso's murdered cousin Tino to our advantage, to generate discussions about past crimes. For instance, one time, D'Urso was around 1st Avenue and 11th Street, in Nicky the Blond and Enrico "Red Hot" Gentile's neighborhood. I'd have D'Urso raise conversation about Red Hot, by fictitiously stating that Tino mentioned a Red Hot Gentile. Since Tino was dead there was no way for this to be challenged. This would open the door for Sammy Meatballs to then discuss the topic, and provide details about Gentile, who I had been unable to include in the Ida case. Sammy described him as a treacherous killer and was about to describe one of the victims, when he changed the subject.

Sammy was an old-timer, and we even once recorded him describing corrupt NYPD back in the day, and his own role in the infamous French Connection heroin case that became a movie of that title, starring Gene Hackman in 1971. Aparo described how the mob's rules changed in 1957: "No more junk, no more counterfeiting, no bonds. If you have anything in the works, finish it up." He explained that a corrupt NYPD officer removed the seized heroin from the French Connection arrests under the guise it was needed for evidentiary purposes and replaced it with another substance like flour. Aparo described how the corrupt police, after taking the heroin from evidence, "sold it to us." He claimed that he never was punished for his role because the judge was "connected" and Aparo knew someone very close to the judge. Aparo cited how his photo was on the front page of the *Daily News* for this arrest.[12] According to Aparo's recorded statement, the judge instructed someone to have Aparo's attorney submit a motion to dismiss the case against him, and the judge supported the motion.

D'Urso made most of his recordings in clubs, bars, restaurants, and on walks and talks. I would be nearby both for security and surveillance purposes. Often, I would sit outside the restaurants and clubs. It was also very common for the mobsters to do a "walk and talk" around the streets of Little Italy. They considered this safer than talking indoors because it would be nearly impossible for law enforcement to record an outdoor conversation. Of course, since D'Urso was wearing a wire while engaging in these walk-talks, these precautions were useless.

I also used walk-talks to my advantage. For instance, whenever D'Urso spoke with someone whose identity I wanted to verify, I'd call his cell. This would cue him to suggest a "walk-talk" because it was "safer." That would, of course, serve them up so I could get incriminating pictures. In one memorable instance, an elderly lady joined me on a bench outside a popular deli on Grand Street, down the corner from Tommy Cestaro's

---

12 It was on page 2 of this newspaper dated Thursday, February 4, 1965.

social club. The lady commented on my photography. I told her I was a graduate student in architecture and was including Little Italy as part of a paper I was working on. The explanation worked like a charm.

D'Urso and I were learning to trust one another during this period. From his very first recordings, he proved himself quite skillful, productive, and capable. He needed to just be himself, participating in criminal conversations just like always. The only difference was that now he did not seek to commit those crimes and was recording them for the FBI. My focus was to obtain evidence through him to convict as many organized crime figures as possible.

We would also always address any loose ends, issues that required follow-up after I reviewed the day's recordings. Closure would help ensure convictions down the road, because it is very difficult for a defense lawyer to cross-examine his client's recorded admission of criminal activity.

D'Urso also trusted me not to place him in a situation where his life would be in any more peril than it was inherently. Nevertheless, there were highly suspenseful moments. Soon after beginning to cooperate, on July 13, 1998, Sammy called D'Urso at 1:00 a.m., saying his son Vinny needed something, and D'Urso should go straight to his house. This call screamed red flags. Sammy almost never called D'Urso at this late hour, much less to send him off somewhere. D'Urso had no alternative but to respond he was on his way. He immediately called me, stating that he thought they may know about his relationship with the FBI and would kill him. This belief was aggravated by his ongoing concern that he had been spotted when he was initially arrested by the FBI—possibly by a neighbor—and then quickly released. There was also the ever-present possibility that a corrupt member of law enforcement learned details of this new cooperator.

Sammy's call and order to D'Urso could mean his death. I offered to immediately drive to Vinny Aparo's residence, but D'Urso did not want to delay his trip. The problem was I lived much farther away from his home than did D'Urso, who would arrive before I could even get halfway there. It also would look highly suspicious if D'Urso tarried. One rule known by all gangsters is when you are summoned, no matter what time of day or personal circumstances, you must go, even if your mother is on her deathbed.

In the end, it was his call and D'Urso made the decision to go. There is no other word to describe this choice than courageous, since there were good reasons to think this was a set-up and because I was unable to be there to provide any security. D'Urso certainly faced pressure on the other end, because if he refused to go or went late, then they would suspect or know he was cooperating. Then they might kill him, or we would pull him off the street, and his cooperation would be virtually worthless. He'd be facing a death sentence due to his guilty plea, with very little to point toward mitigating it. But still, to travel directly into the perceived face of death is not a choice that most would or could make.

"I'll call you after this meeting. If I don't come back, you know what happened," he said and then hung up the phone. I sat up, tensely waiting for his call.

Fortunately, it turned out that our fears were misplaced. Vinny wanted to unload some illegal guns and silencers he had been keeping. The urgency stemmed from Vinny's receiving a tip his house might get raided, and he of course wanted to avoid their discovery. This tip was based on a meeting Sammy had with Ernest "Butch" Montevecchi, a Genovese soldier, who provided documents that identified bugs placed in Florios naming Vinny, Sammy, and D'Urso as subjects of an FBI investigation.

Relieved, D'Urso took the guns and turned them over to me. This was a huge emotional turning point for D'Urso. When he surrendered the guns, this meant that he was "all in" with the undercover operation. He had just given up both his father figure and his father figure's son. There was no turning back, and Sammy and Vinny both now faced serious charges. Of course, D'Urso's guilty plea to murder did not provide him with the option of deciding whether or not he was "all in," but at an emotional level this served as his tipping point.

This also goes to show how luck-dependent are operations of this sort. ███ ███ ████████████████████████████ Creativity and spontaneous solutions are constantly needed to address cooperating witnesses who are embedded with criminals. ███████████████████████████████

██

████████████████████████████

Jane

Another extremely puzzling potential blow to my investigation took place early on. But this one was internal—it originated from within the FBI.

Jane was a female agent on my squad. She joined our team because she had been working on another investigation with overlapping targets that were to be prosecuted in the Southern District of New York. I had noted numerous odd things about her, but it wasn't my call. D'Urso's guilty plea was in the EDNY while the SDNY had this other investigation addressing Sammy Meatballs's and the Dacunto brothers' criminal activities. I agreed to provide both the EDNY and SDNY with copies of all FD-302 reports involving D'Urso's recordings. Jane would deliver the SDNY reports to the SDNY.

Just a couple of weeks after beginning to work with D'Urso, our dysfunctional and lazy supervisor, Prince (we had a prior run-in when working on narcotics cases), inexplicably attempted to remove me from handling D'Urso. This in and of itself was lunatic. But on top of it all— he wanted to substitute Jane of all people in my place. Prince did this completely out of the blue one day while all of us were sitting in his office. The ASAC passed by and stuck his head in to ask how everything was going with D'Urso. Prince responded that they were going to replace me with Jane, because I was "too busy."

For so many reasons this statement made no sense and left me baffled until after I retired when I learned something that likely explained it, as you'll read much later. I immediately responded that I was not busy, had no other assignment, and had given my word to D'Urso and the EDNY prosecutors that I would work with him. The ASAC directed Prince to keep me on the investigation. Why Prince would make this comment to our ASAC without even discussing this with me was reckless and crazy. Prince was clearly pissed off that I responded in this manner.

Some years earlier, when Jane was a relatively new agent just out of the FBI Academy and assigned to an Organized Crime Squad on my floor in the New York Division, she reacted to my involvement in an incident involving another female agent.

I was working on a shared computer in a squad area. As I attempted to complete a simple report that was about one or two paragraphs, an agent approached and asked about my knowledge of a gangster. I stopped typing and responded with a few details about this individual. As I resumed typing, another agent approached and asked how long I would be at this computer, and I replied, "just a few minutes." This agent sat near the computer and watched as I responded to the other agent's work-related question. The agent who asked me how long I'd be there wanted to use the computer and she became agitated, stating that I was clearly taking longer than a few minutes. My response was, "If you just let me finish typing without interrupting, I would be done, you moron."

The agent stormed off while Jane came running up to me. "You are my hero." I did not know Jane nor care to meet her; I just wanted to finish typing my report. Jane then described how the other agent always got her way with the agents on her squad. Agent Bernie Kane approached as Jane was talking. He was currently assigned to the same squad as Jane. Both Jane and Bernie were recruited as new agents by the FBI Philadelphia Division. I previously worked with Bernie in the Cincinnati division. He then related a story about Jane as she proudly stood there, listening.

Bernie said that while Jane was undergoing new agent training in Quantico, she dated a high school boy. She laughed when Bernie concluded but did not deny the story. It appeared as though her laughter was confirming the story. This struck me as a red flag that Jane was just a bizarre character.

As time went by, though, I heard further stories about her. One was that she and another agent had sex in a car while they were on surveillance. Jane was said to hope this agent would divorce his wife to be with her, and when this didn't immediately happen, she publicly confronted him at a bar, punching him and threatening to tell his wife. This assault was observed by other agents and FBI staff.

Once we began working with D'Urso, I also noticed that Jane began to wear sundresses to work. I never really noticed any other agents dressed in this manner. I didn't think much about it at that time because she really didn't provide any input during meetings, just staying quiet and out of the way. Her role in the case was to obtain each investigative report (FD-302) for her Dacunto brothers investigation and provide them to the SDNY AUSA. The Dacuntos were rarely, if ever, a discussed topic. I have no recollection of Jane asking a question of D'Urso to address this investigation.

I had also noticed that Jane made mistakes that seemed to indicate a fundamental misunderstanding of how to prepare FBI paperwork, specifically an interview report. We use this form to report information to prosecutors that may one day become testimony. Among other things, the report identifies the agents involved, details of the topics discussed during the recording if there is one, surveillance observations, the name of the agent who prepared the report, and any other agents involved with this meeting. The agents and detective(s) who participated in the recording review the report for accuracy before signing off on it.

During the D'Urso investigation, Jane initially rarely prepared one of these reports. However, I noticed that she misidentified a person's true name by a nickname mentioned during the recording. This was early in the investigation. The true name would typically be identified after the nickname if you are quoting a portion of the recording. And although she reviewed the recording, she did not interview D'Urso to discuss the details. Instead of asking D'Urso who was being discussed, she used the name from a prior report I prepared—believing it to be the same person. That would be similar to hearing someone speak about "Mike (D'Urso) and Jane," and, without confirming which Mike it was, preparing a report citing "Mike (Campi)" in the report. I had to explain to her how to prepare such a report. That kind of sloppiness can kill a prosecutor's case, because defense attorneys zero in on such errors, "Your report said that Campi was present, not D'Urso!"

She also attempted to use information from my reports, "repurposing" the information, instead of trying to confirm it with D'Urso herself through a post-recording interview. Such sloppiness and inattention to detail was also a red flag because only direct interviews provide agents with the exact details a cooperating witness will testify to on the stand one day. Otherwise, there is ample room for error that defense lawyers love to

Salvatore "Sammy Meatballs" Aparo's arrest in the historic French Connection investigation, February 4, 1965. (source: *New York Daily News*)

Surveillance Photos

Jimmy Ida and Barney Bellomo meeting with Mario Gigante (capo and Chin's brother), November 4, 1992.

Jimmy Ida after meeting with Frank "Farby" Serpico, November 16, 1994.

Liborio "Barney" Bellomo and Michele "Mickey Dimino" Generoso, September 12, 1991.

Jimmy Ida, Nicky "the Blond" Frustaci, and Barney Bellomo going to a meeting to address a dispute involving the Lucchese family, July 11, 1989.

John "Jackie" DeRoss
Underboss, Colombo family

Pasquale "Patty" Falcetti
Capo, Genovese family

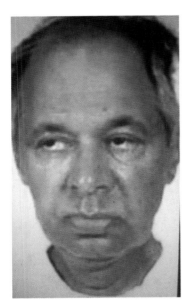

Frank "Farby" Serpico
Acting boss, Genovese family

Dominick "Quiet Dom" Cirillo
Acting boss, Genovese family

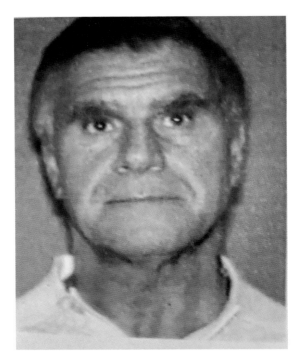

Pasquale "Patsy" Parrello
Capo, Genovese family

Tommy Cafaro
Associate, Genovese family

capitalize on to attack the credibility of witnesses and give the prosecutors migraine headaches.

I realized this most likely was due to her inexperience and provided her with instructions on how to improve. If I had any questions as to details in a report, as I told her, I would call D'Urso to ensure accuracy before signing off.

In sum, a swirling bizarreness surrounded Jane. But my focus was on D'Urso and the investigation, so I didn't pay her too much mind. None of this impacted my investigation in a material way—or so I thought.

Much more on Jane later . . .

Back to the Investigation

As the months went by, D'Urso's value increased exponentially as he delivered useful recordings on a near daily basis. By the end of his work, he had generated the second-largest number of interview reports of a cooperating witness in the *history* of the FBI's investigation of the New York mafia. Only Al D'Arco has more documented FD-302s. D'Arco was about sixty years old when he came to cooperate with the FBI, so he had decades of history to relate and was also a former acting boss, which would make him privy to a ton of useful information about all of the five crime families. D'Arco had many years of crime with the mob to refer back to, including murders and interfamily disputes.

In contrast, D'Urso was an associate and less than half that age, only in his late twenties. D'Urso did all of his work in just a three-year period of time. Nevertheless, as you'll read, the results were absolutely devastating. More importantly, D'Urso's reports concerned contemporaneous consensual recordings he made with powerful members of all five New York-based crime families. D'Arco by comparison came off the streets and provided the details of crimes that had been committed in the past.

Remarkably, while he was working as a quasi-undercover FBI agent, the mob was nevertheless so impressed by D'Urso that they began to groom him for future leadership. Stop and think about that for a minute.

This heightened view of D'Urso, combined with the complete lack of suspicion, permitted me to use him to record a litany of criminal acts, way more than I ever expected initially. But our huge break—what converted

my use of D'Urso from an excellent and useful cooperator into a staggering, truly historic one—arrived as a gift in late 1999, when D'Urso was
invited to a holiday party in Florida. This is what began to break the case
wide open and gave me access to the upper echelons of the Genovese.

It all stemmed from the Genovese wanting to groom D'Urso after
identifying him as a future leader. Because of this, they let him in on some
of their closely guarded secrets and cultivated his relationships with their
powers.

On December 12, 1999, D'Urso contacted me and told me that he had
attended John Albanese's Christmas party the night before. We were a
year and a half into the investigation. Joe Zito invited D'Urso to attend
a Christmas party in Ft. Lauderdale at a restaurant owned by Albanese,
a.k.a. "Johnny Meatballs," a Springfield, Massachusetts–based Genovese
associate.

Zito was D'Urso's original employer when D'Urso worked as a busboy
at Zito's restaurant, Ruggiero's, located on Grand Street in the Little Italy
section of lower Manhattan. Over time, Zito became his mentor. As previously noted, Zito was highly respected by Chin and others in the administration, and his words carried weight. After his acquittal in the infamous
Windows case, Zito remained in the Bronx and was a respected soldier,
having passed on the capo role due to his concern that the government
would focus on him since he was acquitted.

Zito told D'Urso he would meet the Genovese "power base" at the
party. He introduced D'Urso to "Patty, a kid from the Bronx"—the seat of
the Genovese's active power. Patty and D'Urso immediately hit it off, and
Patty told D'Urso he'd like him to meet a friend of his, "Tommy," who
also lived in Florida.

The following morning, D'Urso called me and described what had
happened. Patty was described as about forty years old, dark hair combed
back, about two hundred and twenty pounds, having a muscular build.
Patty further described how he was originally around Fat Tony Salerno.
They discussed the dispute between D'Urso and Frank Serpico. Patty
agreed D'Urso did nothing wrong. Patty cited how he would speak to
Ernie Muscarella about D'Urso and cited how "Ernie would love a guy

like you." Patty provided D'Urso with all his contact information: cellular, beeper, and home phone numbers.

Based on D'Urso's description, I believed that "Patty" was likely the powerful and trusted Genovese capo Patty Falcetti because Falcetti was from the Bronx, and Zito had said he was introducing D'Urso to "the power base" and "a kid from the Bronx." From the Windows case, I knew that Zito was close with the Genovese hierarchy, and I also knew the strength that the Bronx faction carried. For instance, future acting boss Ernie Muscarella was also a Bronx guy, and I knew he was aligned with then-acting boss Barney Bellomo.

I faxed D'Urso a photo of Falcetti. D'Urso confirmed this was the "Patty" he had met. My suspicions confirmed, I additionally expected that "Tommy" would turn out to be "Fish" Cafaro's son. I concluded this both because Tommy lived in Florida after being released from prison on a prior case, and he had also been captured in surveillance in the Bronx accompanied by both Falcetti and Bellomo. I also knew Tommy was "with" Barney, which could prove very fruitful, because Tommy's father Fish protected Bellomo during his cooperation, meaning Bellomo would have every reason to trust Tommy. Fish proposed Barney for induction into the Genovese family.

The Genovese were always the most secretive of the mob clans, and in the late 1990s were also clearly still the most powerful. The fact that D'Urso—while working directly for us, no less!—was apparently being moved deeper and deeper into the uppermost layers of the Genovese circle of trust simply exhilarated me and my fellow agents. This development was absolutely extraordinary.

At the same time, I remained cautious as always. Were the Genovese simply erecting an elaborate trap to lure D'Urso to his death? There was no way to be sure. In operating D'Urso, not only was there the ever-present risk of a leak, but I was also acutely aware of reasons they might have to kill him even if they didn't suspect he was working with me. D'Urso was a hothead who, as noted above, had tried to kill Polito and others although explicitly directed not to do so. He had engaged in other reckless activity over the years, such as assaulting a bouncer at the China Club, which, according to recordings made by D'Urso, was controlled by Bellomo.

Bellomo had apparently tasked Muscarella with beating D'Urso and others in retaliation. But D'Urso stayed away from the club and the tensions eventually appeared to dissipate. These and other examples would be considered unfavorable marks against D'Urso's character that could warrant his murder. And then there was the ever-present treachery in the mob. Were other crew members secretly hostile to D'Urso and envious of his quick ascent? Might they seek to eliminate him?

I flew to Florida to facilitate recordings and provide security if it turned out this was a trap.

Getting access to Patty, who was close to Bellomo and to Cafaro (who himself met directly with Bellomo, who was incarcerated from the Ida case), was a massive breakthrough. Getting Tommy to potentially share details of his meetings with Bellomo would provide evidence usable in future cases against Bellomo, not to mention against Cafaro, Falcetti, and others.

Based on Patty's desire that they meet, Cafaro invited D'Urso to join him at his gym. This meeting happened in January 2000, after the holidays. As was my practice, I slipped into the background to perform surveillance. My hope was that Cafaro would provide useful information to D'Urso. As it turned out, Cafaro needed very little prodding.

Their meeting lasted several hours. It was clear that Cafaro was intent on impressing D'Urso with his knowledge and his connections. It became almost comical. Cafaro almost literally wouldn't shut up about his relationship with Bellomo and other high-ranking Genovese.

There were only two plausible explanations for what I witnessed. The first and most likely was confirmation that D'Urso had been identified as a potential future power, and Tommy was following instructions to begin the priming and grooming process for an eventual position of power; to let him in on secrets, to understand how those in power worked and operated. The only other plausible scenario for Tommy to talk to D'Urso in this way, although much less likely, was to make him comfortable enough to kill him.

Among other things, Cafaro shared that he was one of only two people Bellomo permitted to visit him while incarcerated. The other was Genovese attorney Pete Peluso, who himself later cooperated as discussed in chapter

16. During this initial meeting, Cafaro was recorded describing numerous topics. How Cafaro owns a building on First Avenue near RAO's restaurant. That he wants half a million for it, and he was sixteen years old when the buildings were bought. Cafaro described how he pays tax on his corporate and personal income. How he created a company in the Bahamas, and he buys stocks with it and has a credit card with this business. That he has a meeting Tuesday night with a tax guy (Peter Tarangelo—the "Tax Doctor"). Cafaro described how this is Barney's guy handled by Cafaro. Cafaro described how Barney doesn't want anyone from the LCN to meet the Tax Doctor. Similar to the check-cashing scheme, I created a scenario to meet the Tax Doctor and record his role in these money-laundering crimes. Cafaro and Falcetti violated Barney's request based on their comfort with D'Urso and our future FBI scheme. D'Urso also recorded Patty describing how he has a bookmaker, a travel agent, how he's trying to get into recycling, and that he has an air conditioning and refrigeration company in New York that he is trying to promote. Patty had not told Ernie yet that he met D'Urso. They discuss the incident at the China Club and Frank Serpico.

During another meeting, I instructed D'Urso to conduct a "walk-talk" in the parking lot after their workout. My goal was to corroborate their meeting with photographs and video. The scene, which I caught on film, was right out of a movie. Like all compliant mob members, Cafaro touched his chin whenever he meant to invoke Chin Gigante, or he simply said, "this guy," while doing so. He used code to refer to others as well. For instance, Cafaro puffed out his pecs to reference capo Ernie "the Bear" Muscarella, to simulate a muscular "bear" physique. Likewise, Cafaro placed his finger to his lips when referencing Genovese administration member "Quiet" Dom Cirillo. He pointed to his ears to invoke the legally deaf legendary Genovese soldier George Barone.

I captured it all on video and D'Urso captured it all on audio. Layering the two together was extraordinary, as you could simultaneously hear Cafaro's words combined with his matching gestures. Topics Cafaro discussed ranged from Barone's historic role in furthering the Genovese's control of the powerful International Longshoremen's Association (ILA), to an insult Barone made to Chin and Andrew Gigante that would lead to a hit being placed on

Barone, to Peluso's role carrying messages to and from Bellomo. Cafaro also described how Florida law enforcement had no idea about him. He liked to stay low key. "These guys don't know me at all. I was making my little moves. You know with businesses. We got the kids with mortgages, we got the kid with financials, we make money with commissions." This mode, remaining behind the shadows, was important. He cited the Genovese boss prior to Chin, Philip "Benny Squint" Lombardo: "All those years nobody knew who Ben was, nobody knew who he was."

Cafaro also told D'Urso how he navigated the hazardous waters surrounding his father "Fish's" cooperation. Even though Fish may not have fully cooperated in order to protect his son, he did inflict some damage on some Genovese members he hated. To ensure he would not be killed for his father's actions (another example of embedded mafia treachery), Tommy said he worked hard to demonstrate his loyalty to the Genovese. Cafaro taped conversations between him, his father, and his father's lawyer talking on the phone and provided these tapes to the Genovese. He also "took my [four-year-old] son to court every day when my father was on the stand" to pressure his father. Cafaro also explained how he taped his mother and sister's conversations with Fish without their knowledge and also provided these tapes to "the guys" so they would know he wasn't hiding anything from them.

A few days later, Cafaro took D'Urso to the pool. In this encounter, as though it were even possible, Cafaro became more forthcoming. With D'Urso recording every word, Cafaro discussed the entire Genovese power structure. Listening in, I couldn't help but smile and think that these were the topics I'd want Cafaro to discuss if Cafaro had called me up directly completely out of the blue and requested a formal meeting to provide me the Genovese's innermost secrets. Here he was, just handing the information over directly to D'Urso (and me), someone he met only days before but clearly wanted to impress. I was essentially witness to the mob's version of an accelerated leadership apprenticeship.

It was apparent that Bellomo (based on recommendations from powerful and well-respected D'Urso allies such as Zito, capo Alan Longo, and others), had directed Cafaro to begin to fast-track D'Urso up the Genovese ladder. D'Urso's humor and charismatic personality helped to further develop the relationship. D'Urso, Falcetti, and Cafaro established a comfort zone, and they appeared to empathize with D'Urso's position.

On the other hand, I also considered whether Zito may have wanted the crew affiliated with Muscarella and Bellomo to get a sense about D'Urso and his character before finalizing any decision about his murder. If they decided to kill him, there would also be a comfort zone that may make it easier to do so. Balancing all of this, I still harbored a residue of doubt as to whether Cafaro was just getting D'Urso relaxed and comfortable to ultimately murder him. This concern was greatly reduced as time passed with the significant topics obtained in the recordings secured.

Ironically, at one point, Cafaro and D'Urso discussed how before Gigante was incarcerated the Genovese were at their strongest and life was the best. Cafaro added, *"It's only gonna get worse. It's not gonna get any better."*

He and dozens of others were to eventually find out how prophetic his words were.

CHAPTER EIGHT

EMBEDDED WITH THE GENOVESE

"A lot of treachery and hypocrisy in the life."

Entering 2000 was exhilarating, as D'Urso's introduction to the Bronx power base made clear that the Genovese were intent on elevating D'Urso—all while he was working for me and the FBI. We began to produce tremendous results. The Genovese included D'Urso in more of their criminal schemes and they let him in on more of their secrets, almost to comical effect. Why did these highly suspicious criminals—whose very survival and ability to thrive depend on their suspecting *everyone*—do this, despite the fact that he was our spy? How did they not suspect him, not notice that every day he was gathering and delivering evidence—directly to me—against them?

D'Urso was valued by powerful criminal allies who saw his potential. They also registered that D'Urso had been shot in the head and didn't cooperate. His cousin had been murdered and D'Urso didn't cooperate. D'Urso had a death sentence placed on him by acting boss Farby and (so far as they could see) he didn't cooperate. In their eyes, he had proven that he was hardcore gangster, through and through. In fact, they began to treat him as a made man, introducing him to other crime families as somebody to be treated with that level of respect. They also viewed him, and treated him, as a future leader. It was completely surreal—and I'll provide you with many of those details here.

Perhaps one of the best illustrations occurred after some of D'Urso's fellow crewmembers were inducted into the Genovese. By mafia rule, any discussions concerning induction ceremonies are secretive: disclosing that they are coming up, who will be inducted, the details of the inductions, are all themselves violations of omertà—each technically punishable by death.

Yet the gangsters themselves must view this as a joke. Sammy Aparo spilled everything to D'Urso. Sammy was recorded on February 23, 1999, citing his own historic LCN background. He explained how he was inducted into the Cosa Nostra in 1957. Salvatore Palmieri, a.k.a. "Sally Young," was the capo who proposed Aparo. Aparo described how Chin hated Sally Young because he previously slapped Chin's father-in-law. This was back in time when Chin and Aparo were soldiers. Sally Young put Aparo in a bad position with Chin. Prior to this incident, Aparo was in good standing, having known Chin and his family his entire life. Chin originally grew up on Mott Street across the street from where Aparo lived. Chin was also inducted the same day as Aparo.

Aparo related a recent meeting with Longo whereby Longo described how they were all talking among themselves and [Genovese administration member] Quiet Dom [Cirillo] was telling him,

> We'd better get some fucking young kids. We got nobody. Who we gonna get to shake 'em up. Nobody's got no kids around. . . . They're going to do the induction in a month. He just told me don't tell nobody nothing. He says next week I'm passing the list around to all the families. We wait two weeks for an answer, if they don't answer us we just go ahead and do it. In other words, in case they want to knock a guy down, the other families.

On September 7, 1999, Sammy was recorded telling D'Urso that Muscarella, Larry Dentico, and Danny Leo inducted Vinny Aparo, Frank Demeo, and Bobby Debello the night before. Aparo also described how they conducted the ceremony:

They make you swear by the oath. You can't fuck around with this, that, that, that, that. You get killed. You fuck around with a friend's wife, you get killed. . . . When Vin went in there, they got the gun and the knife covered on the table. So now when they got him, they say "You know why you're here?" He says no. He says [Petey Red] didn't tell you? He said no. They went through the whole ritual thing.

Of course, relating any of this was itself a violation of omertà, punishable by death. Ironically, Aparo added that *nobody* was to be told about the inductions.

Aparo also related how Paul Geraci drove one of the cars used to transport them to this induction, and Geraci added that this was his fifth trip transporting people to inductions that day.

Demeo and Vinny both also blabbed to D'Urso all about it—signifying not only that omertà was a joke but also the fact that they all viewed D'Urso as an equal. Literally just hours after the ceremony, following his father's example, Vinny described the entire process to D'Urso, including all of the closely guarded secrets. Vinny provided a firsthand account for D'Urso to record as though he had been there himself. To D'Urso's amusement, Vinny shared that the inductees were all naked, ironically to ensure that nothing could be recorded. No need, since Vinny himself provided a thorough play-by-play just a few hours later to D'Urso and me:

> Do you know why you are here? I says no. He says Petey didn't have a conversation with you? I says yeah. If he would have said "What was the conversation?" I would have said I'm supposed to be at a certain place at a certain time.

Vinny was also given rules:

> You can't raise your hands to another friend. You can't fuck around with counterfeit money, no drugs . . . you break any of these rules we'll kill you and if we can't get you we'll go after your family.

Vinny also complained that he was provided with almost no information. Hearkening back to the screw-up with Farby Serpico, Vinny noted that he was not told who the Genovese administration was, nor was he even introduced to DeMeo or DeBello as a made guy, "Nobody told me who's who, not for nothing I don't even know who's who. They don't even know themselves who they are."

D'Urso asked if he had any burn marks on his hand, "No, no. They lit a napkin. You know how a napkin burns. It doesn't really burn. It smolders."

In an ironic nod to the mob's symbiotic relationship with Hollywood, Vinny added, *The induction ceremonies depicted in the movies are done better than the real inductions.*"

Vinny also carefully explained to D'Urso that Dentico stated, "You are not to tell anyone you're made" (which is exactly what he just did), except when they were being formally introduced to other made men. Details of who had been made were normally only permitted to be disclosed in an official capacity when there was a mob dispute. When this happened, someone known to all parties in the dispute would introduce the person in question as "a friend of ours" to indicate that he was "made." By contrast, "a friend of mine" means that they are an associate.

Significantly, Vinny also deferred to D'Urso, telling him that D'Urso should have been made instead of Vinny himself. Vinny said that D'Urso had initially been selected but that Farby shot it down, so they put DeMeo in his slot. Vinny assured D'Urso that he would be in the next "class" of inductees so he should not get discouraged.

Sammy Meatballs confirmed that it should have been D'Urso instead of his own son. By this point in time, D'Urso handled practically every significant matter for that crew, so they had a strong incentive to finally reward him—even though he was all along developing evidence for the FBI. Months later capo Longo again violated omertà by telling D'Urso and others about upcoming secret inductions, which were to include Alex Conigliaro.

There were other shocking examples of clear violations of omertà, the sharing of secret mob information, at times revealing a double standard. And we caught much of it on tape. D'Urso routinely saw mobsters spill their guts to impress women or to impress rich and "important" people.

For whatever reason, this blatant violation of mob rules seemed to be tolerated. For example, we recorded Longo, who served as a high-level messenger to and from Chin's crew, describing his then-capo Allie Shades Malangone's attempts to woo an actress. Longo was recorded describing Malangone meeting at Pastels, a Genovese run nightclub in Brooklyn and at Campagnola, an Upper East Side restaurant, with Hugh Grant and Elizabeth Hurley, who were in town to film *Mickey Blue Eyes*, a romantic comedy about the mob. Malangone controlled Pastels, and Grant was spending time with him to conduct research for his part.

We captured Longo and Geraci on tape describing how they and fellow Genovese crew members watched as Malangone tried to impress Hurley. To their amazement, Malangone loudly described the entire structure of the Genovese family to her. He also explained that he was a capo, and what this meant, and gave her the details of the soldiers in his crew. This violated the omertà code at the mafia's very core. These were the exact, specific things you swore—under penalty of *death*—you would never talk about or acknowledge. And yet this high-ranking capo blabbed about it into Hurley's ear, at a table filled with other mob guys, and nobody said anything. And Longo and Geraci, in turn, were violating omertà by blabbing to the uninducted D'Urso and others about what had happened. Longo also described how he and their whole crew hated Malangone because he abused his crew.

The fact that mobsters could be such hypocrites about whom they kept secrets from—and whom they blabbed their asses off to—provides additional evidence of the underlying hypocrisy of "the life." It's not a secret life, it's simply elaborate cover for a life of self-serving greed.

The investigation revealed so many more examples of mob treachery and hypocrisy, and I'll provide a snippet of these immediately below. These recordings are only a small sample of numerous examples of the treachery, hypocrisy, and violations of omertà that are a regular part of mob life, and which are rarely depicted in media or movies. I cannot stress this enough: the mob is a false brotherhood, made up of a treacherous group of egomaniacs. The longer you are involved in this life, the clearer the treachery. I respect former Colombo gangster Michael Franzese's efforts to discourage others from getting involved in this evil life.

Many gangsters know this all to be true. As Tommy Cafaro stated bluntly in one of our recordings, "A *lot of treachery and hypocrisy in the life*."

What follows are some additional examples of omertà violations, lies, hypocrisy, and treachery that we recorded.

Capo Aparo:
- Stated how Gigante's arrest and conviction in 1959 for heroin dealing took place after Chin shot Frank Costello. As I understand, this was a violation of a recently created mafia rule. In 1957, at the infamous Apalachin meeting, dealing in narcotics was now prohibited. Organized crime viewed this as too risky to the health of their personal family members who could get addicted to the drugs. They also viewed it as a powerful tool for law enforcement to facilitate lengthy jail terms and cooperation.
- Aparo described knowing Bonanno boss Massino before he was ever made and stated that the Bonannos have "the only stable crew. . . . They have a boss, they got an underboss, a consigliere, no problem, no rats." Aparo contrasted this to the Genovese secrecy, adding, "*We don't even know who the fuck is there.*" (Meaning boss and other high-level members.) Ironically, shortly after this recording, Massino and his under-boss were arrested, and both cooperated with the FBI, as did numerous other Bonannos, causing massive damage to that family. Massino's cooperation happened after he was con-victed at trial. His brother-in-law, Salvatore Vitale, who was the underboss, testified against Massino at this trial. Vitale real-ized Massino was involved with a plan to murder Vitale. This facilitated Vitale's cooperation. In addition, Massino's coopera-tion included a prison recording he made with the acting boss, Vincent Basciano, involving a murder. Basciano was convicted and is now serving a life in prison without parole.
- Cited a story from former Colombo acting boss Vinny Aloi concerning the murder of underboss "Wild Bill" Cutolo. Colombo gangsters went to Cutulo's wife requesting money "he

had from us." She responded with anger and sarcasm, "When he comes back, I will ask him where the money is to give it back." Aloi also cited how a few years before, they thought Jackie DeRoss was a "rat," but he became the Colombo's "top guy."

- Cited how "I'm going to do a little lying too. You can't ask nobody. You have to take my fucking word for it," regarding an upcoming meeting with Colombo acting boss DeRoss. Aparo intended to tell DeRoss that the murdered Cutolo agreed that a business he controlled owed Aparo $37,000.

- Aparo was recorded citing how he lied to Farby Serpico by denying that he warned D'Urso of Serpico's interest in murdering him.

- He also discussed how major mob figures pay attorney fees for arrested members and associates. Although at first glance this may be viewed as supporting the members, in reality, he explained how it allows leadership to control them: these attorneys ensure any defense doesn't implicate leadership, and they prevent cooperation. The attorney would *never* offer his client's cooperation to law enforcement even if it's in the client's best interest to do so. Aparo described how the attorney also reports back about his interactions with his clients. These details can even include how the figure who provided the money to the underling corroborates with the defense attorney the amount paid to the lawyer—a way to see if the underling is lying and/ or stealing. The defense attorney also provides law enforcement reports and evidence to the mob, who can use this to understand what is known about them, help determine exposure they may face in future arrests, and develop possible defenses.

Capo Longo:
- Although Chin was convicted at trial of conspiring to kill John Gotti, Gotti apparently plotted to kill Chin as well. Longo was recorded describing how Malangone and Gotti planned to murder Chin, but it was prevented because Gaspipe Casso refused to participate. Longo described Gaspipe as loving Gotti but also

being close to Chin.[13] If the murder had taken place, Malangone
(by betraying and killing off his own family boss) would have
become Genovese boss. "John Gotti was taking over. Cause
our friend grew up with him we could make a deal. He [Chin]
was dead. You know who helped him out? Gaspipe himself. If
Gaspipe had been talked into killing our friend, you know who
would have been our boss. Alley Shades. He was up John's ass.
They were making a big move over there. When Gaspipe was
getting started with him, he loved him to death. Loved him."

- Described how capo Danny Pagano told him he doesn't like
  Bellomo.
- Described that Ralph Coppola was killed for speaking badly
  about Farby and Chuckie Tuzzo, since Coppola thought he
  should have been made the acting boss. In the mob, previous
  murders are never to be discussed because this poses the risk
  of evidence being recorded by law enforcement—exactly as
  happened here. "We were at Torre's on Bay Parkway. He was
  bad mouthing everybody and again I just held it in. There
  was nobody else around [except for "Bucky"]. Farby, Chuck
  (Tuzzo) he was bad mouthing. Chuck, Farby 'this fucking guy.'
  Barney was the guy, right. He went to jail [and] they put Farby
  there [as boss]. Very strange kind of guy. 'This guy's the worst
  scumbag in the world,' [you're] not supposed to say that. You
  got to respect where it came from. For you to bad mouth the
  guy that straightened him out, you're bad mouthing the whole
  administration." Longo was citing how Bellomo proposed
  Coppola to be made with the Genovese family. The term to
  "straighten him out" is a reference to becoming an official,
  inducted, member.
- Again directly violating omertà, Longo described why Farby
  Serpico was given the acting boss role. "He was the closest guy
  to Barney in the street. When Barney went to jail they didn't put

---

13 Gaspipe's son-in-law is Paulie Geraci, a member of the Genovese family, specifically, Bellomo's crew.

Ralph [Coppola], they put Farby there. [Chin Gigante's brother] Mario was very close to Farby when Mario went to jail. They put Farby there, that's how he got there."

Capo Falcetti:
- Told D'Urso how "the Bronx guys" hate soldier Butch Monte-vecci (hate can typically lead to murder in their life).
- Cited how he doesn't think that Artie Nigro and Scop (Pasquale DeLuca) belong in "the life." Nigro subsequently became an acting boss and Scop held a powerful position as well.

New England Boss Adolfo Bruno:
- Offered to induct D'Urso into his Massachusetts crew. He also described how he frequently meets with Farby and the Chin and stated that he used to deliver guns for murders to Chin. Bruno was murdered two years later, in 2003, after D'Urso's cooperation became public with the first indictment. I believe this recording may have been the reason he was killed (offering to induct D'Urso on the sly, mentioning Chin, and mentioning assisting Chin with murder). Genovese street boss Artie Nigro was eventually convicted for Bruno's murder and sentenced to life in prison.

Soldier Zito:
- Cited how the Genovese don't demote or break capos, "we kill them." That's why they have so many acting capos, because when you're acting, they can demote you rather than kill you.

Soldier Geraci:
- Cited how he lied to Muscarella and Serpico about an $80,000 dispute with Lucchese acting boss Joe Defede. Defede later coop-erated with the FBI when confronted with the hypocrisy of this life. D'Urso also made numerous recordings with Geraci about

his role in the inductions, who was inducted in the Genovese family when the books were closed.[14]

Associate Cafaro:
- Described how he was one of the few people who could meet with Bellomo in prison. Bellomo did not want him to meet with anyone or be involved criminally with anyone from the mob while Bellomo was in prison. This was so Cafaro could just focus on Bellomo's business. Cafaro stated that he did not comply with Bellomo's instructions, and how he would be in trouble if Bellomo knew about his conduct. Also described how his father, "Fish," proposed Bellomo for induction when Bellomo was nineteen.
- Described how "Scop" (Pasquale DeLuca) and "Farby" Serpico "are no fucking good." Scop and Farby were at the highest ranks—two members of the Genovese acting administration. Cafaro also

---

14 "Made" member of an Italian organized crime family indicates the individual went through an official induction ceremony to become an official member of this crime family. There is a process of being proposed for membership based on one's criminal conduct under the guidance of another made member. This typically involves a lengthy process over years. The individual is considered an "associate" of a made member's crime family. You also must be Italian on your father's side in order to be inducted. This originally required both parents to be Italian but changed over the years to just requiring the father's heritage.

The "books" have to be opened. This means that organized crime families can induct members to replace those members who died. The crime family can only replace the members who have passed unless the crime families agree to a proportionate increase. When a member is proposed for induction, his name is passed from his New York crime family to the other crime families to conduct what I would describe as a "background check." This is to ensure there isn't anything bad in his past criminal conduct. Was he an informant or not trustworthy? Did he demonstrate fear and weakness? If all comes back good, he will be proposed along with the name of the deceased member's name that he is replacing. This is required in order to keep the proportion of each family in place. In the past, some LCN families have attempted to induct members utilizing the same deceased member's name.

When a person is "made," he is initially a "soldier" in the family. This is the lowest rank of a made member. There are numerous terms used by members to describe a made man: "friend of ours," "good fella," "wiseguy," "straightened out," "button," and other terms discussed by gangsters.

described Albert "Chinkie" Facchiano as abusive to him, and that Chinkie thought he should have been boss instead of Chin.

- Described how Colombo boss Carmine Persico killed "the life." Cafaro stated how Persico placed his son as boss; Cafaro didn't understand how he did this since Persico himself received a lifetime prison sentence, exposing his son to the same thing. With the Persico family it appears the biological family came before the mafia family, in violation of the mafia's rules.
- Tried to discourage D'Urso from wanting to be inducted, "stay the way you are, a regular guy."

Associate Frank Campanella a.k.a. Frank Campy (Colombos):
- Told D'Urso the following and told him not to repeat it. It concerned a then-recent dispute between the Colombos and Gambinos. The Colombos had about fifteen guys in cars with weapons outside a meeting Jackie DeRoss attended in Queens. Jackie told them, "If I come out pissed off, you're going in." Campanella explained how they were to kill all the Gambinos who were present. This was obviously a violation of mob rules concerning how to resolve interfamily disputes.

D'Urso attempts to retaliate:
- Even though several years had passed, there were ongoing discussions concerning D'Urso's ability to seek vengeance against Polito. In one, Aparo described why the request was denied— if the murder failed, Polito would have nowhere to go but to the FBI, and he would cooperate. Aparo stated the Genovese administration said, "fuck you, and protect themselves" (ironically, in part because revenge was denied him, D'Urso himself became a cooperating witness):
- Aparo stated: Everybody had the right ear at the time. Even our own friends [were told] "do nothing or you're held responsible." ... Alley [Malangone] had [acting underboss] Mickey's [Generoso's] ear and had Barney [Bellomo], so you could understand there was some truth to that [message] "don't do nothing right now."

I believe that recorded statements like the above are examples of how the mob do not want these details to be seen in the public eye in a trial, and they keep it quiet by insulating themselves with guilty pleas. This also prevents other law enforcement agencies from knowing about the recorded evidence that can be shared with them in their own prosecutions of organized crime. Aparo was also recorded describing how underhanded incidents and backstabbing regularly occur in "the life."

In another conversation, Aparo told D'Urso about a request to align Polito with the Luccheses.

> **Aparo:** You know you're in a bad situation.
> **D'Urso:** Why am I in a bad situation?
> **Aparo:** You're supposed to get straightened out so don't worry about that.

Aparo then told D'Urso and Vinny Aparo about the request.

> **D'Urso:** How do they even ask that? That's a disgusting thing, I got to fucking ask.
> **Vinny:** Can I say something that might be very stupid here. Can't we just do it [kill Polito] and end this stupid fucking thing?
> **Aparo:** They didn't give us permission to get this guy. So now you do anything they might say you were told, and you didn't come and ask [to kill him].
> **D'Urso:** My fucking cousin got fucking killed.
> **Aparo:** No, we know all this, they know all this.
> **D'Urso:** Is this going to lay dormant forever?
> **Aparo:** No.

Longo provided authorization for D'Urso to kill Polito. I imagine Longo would have simply denied this if the murder was unsuccessful and Polito subsequently cooperated.

Numerous recordings address Farbi Serpico's ego, which led him to initially order D'Urso's murder. Months later, Serpico agreed D'Urso could finally collect his money from Johnny Zero (the dispute with Zero was what led to the conflagration between D'Urso and Serpico). Zero had moved to Florida, and I located him there and had D'Urso meet with him to discuss Serpico's authorization for D'Urso to collect the debt. Zero described how he already provided to Serpico the money he owed to D'Urso. This meeting was unannounced and was initiated with a recorded call made by D'Urso on February 22, 1999, to Zero's Florida residence. A female answered the phone with D'Urso requesting to speak with "John." D'Urso told Johnny Zero that he was finally able to locate him in Florida and would like to meet him at a local Dunkin' Donuts. Zero initially cited how he didn't want to come, having other plans. D'Urso explained that he had nothing to worry about. He was grateful that Zero stood up for him with Serpico preventing D'Urso's murder. D'Urso just wanted to go over a couple of things at this meeting.

Zero arrived at Dunkin Donuts located in Spring Hill, Florida. I was again recording this meeting and conducting surveillance as it occurred. Zero arrived at the meeting and hugged D'Urso and discussed the circumstances concerning the gambling debt. Zero was recorded stating he paid this debt to Serpico and Castellano providing them with approximately $65,000. He obtained two separate home equity loans to satisfy this debt. One of the loans for $40,000, concerned his Queens, New York residence. The second loan involved his Florida residence and was in the amount of $25,000. Zero was paying fourteen points in interest on this loan.

Serpico told Zero he had to give him the money so that he could pay "your guys." He described how he received the $40,000 from the Queens house loan and provided it to Serpico that past June or July. He provided Matt Castellano with the $25,000 in July when he was in New York. Zero was insistent that he was telling the truth and described how Serpico and Castellano were there in Florida two weeks earlier.

D'Urso addressed Serpico's intent to murder him over this incident. Zero stated, *"They were going to kill you. I swear to God. . . . If I didn't go that Monday you were gone. . . . He told me point blank, how would you feel if you found out tomorrow this kid was history."*

According to Zero in this recorded conversation, Serpico checked out D'Urso and told Zero that he is no good and that he doesn't listen to anyone. He also cited an incident at the China Club. Zero also met with Matt Castellano to prevent D'Urso's murder. Castellano explained how Zero may also be killed as a result of this issue. Castellano further explained how the money would not be provided to D'Urso but would be provided to D'Urso's people. Serpico also instructed Zero not to speak with D'Urso and that is why he never returned calls from D'Urso.

Serpico attended Zero's daughter's wedding.

I observed Zero's daughter conducting surveillance of her father in this parking lot as it happened. She would drive from one parking spot to another watching D'Urso with her father. She subsequently returned to her residence with D'Urso calling her up and jokingly asked for assistance in obtaining a telephone number for cab service. This was D'Urso's humor to let her know we were aware of her presence. The daughter in an angry tone instructed D'Urso to never call that telephone number again.

Serpico learned about this discussion—he lied to the Genovese administration about receiving the money from Zero. Numerous recordings detailed that everybody knew Serpico was lying. As one example, Cafaro told D'Urso, "You know they took that money from you."

If you want to join this life and you still believe that there is honor, respect, omertà, a band of brothers, loyalty, or anything resembling any of that, then you should go back up and reread the past few pages. There are many more recordings I will share with you in this book and so many more recordings in other investigations.

The drive to induct D'Urso was strong and highly motivated, and it went even beyond what I described above. Powerful Genovese such as Zito and Geraci were captured on D'Urso's recording devices talking about inducting D'Urso "on the sneak"—behind Farby's back. They were willing to consider doing so even though it would have placed their own lives in danger had Farby found out.

The Genovese had previously made soldiers "on the sneak," going behind the backs of other crime families and thereby violating critically important organized crime rules. Geraci described to D'Urso one such instance involving the induction of Joe Dente Jr D'Urso recorded Geraci stating:

> I would have been straightened out a long time ago [but] my father-in-law [Anthony Gaspipe Casso] became a rat.[15] I was getting straightened out. . . . Now Carmine Sessa goes bad [became a witness], the books are closed. They snuck Joe Dente, Bucky in when the books were closed. . . . They would have snuck me in, they held me back. [The risk was] they straighten me out and I tell Gaspipe. God forbid. The books are closed. They were going against the rules, they weren't supposed to be straightening guys out.

Geraci explained how the risks became elevated when Gambino acting boss Peter Gotti asked, "Joe Dente's a wiseguy? When's his name on the list? I would have remembered that name. My brother [John] would have remembered that name." Geraci added "That was back when Mickey [Generoso] and Barney [Bellomo] were there. They snuck those two guys in. They were never on the list. They got straightened out when the books were closed."

"You're Going to Be the Next Gotti"

Aparo also stated on more than one occasion that D'Urso would become eventual Genovese boss. Likewise, Geraci was recorded referring to D'Urso as a future Genovese power.

In one such conversation, Aparo told D'Urso he would "put you in the same class as John Gotti. When I first met him he was nothin . . . a nobody. I said one day you're gonna be the boss. *I'm gonna have to tell that to you now."* Aparo then stated how he believed D'Urso would eventually be involved in running the Genovese. Aparo said he saw Gotti's potential to run a crime family and viewed D'Urso as having that same potential:

> *You're going to be the next Gotti.* I seen him when he started out and I told him, the exact words, I told him, "you'll be there [as boss] one

---

15 In another recording, Geraci stated how, like Tommy Cafaro, Geraci feared he would be killed because his father-in-law cooperated.

day," and sure enough, he was. [Gotti] remembered that I told him. He told me when he got it, he told me, he says "you told it to me a long time ago."

Clearly Aparo's comments were meant as high praise, and D'Urso also admired Gotti. But I thought this comparison was unintentionally an example of complete failure and not something to which any mobster should aspire. Gotti loved media attention, thereby violating omertà, which requires a shadowy presence, and his craving the spotlight and publicly summoning crew members to his social club made him an even easier and more important target for law enforcement. The FBI also had conducted surveillance of Gotti yelling at passing cars, which he believed contained law enforcement, leading him not to observe other vehicles that actually did. Gotti's ego inadvertently greatly assisted law enforcement and destroyed his and others' organized crime life on the streets. Many gangsters share my view. For instance, Genovese capo Angelo Prisco was secretly recorded speaking of John Gotti and his brother Peter, "All of them—I hate them fucking gangsters—they singlehandedly destroyed this whole life. . . . [John Gotti's] downfall was his ego. That was his downfall."

The recognition of efforts on behalf of D'Urso extended beyond New York. Joseph Todaro, the Buffalo family boss, offered to induct him, but he turned them down. The New England Patriarca family also wanted to straighten him out—very discreetly. As noted above, their boss Adolfo Bruno was recorded on tape making this offer. Bruno knew D'Urso was experiencing major problems due to Farby holding things up, so Bruno told Joe Zito that he would make D'Urso in two seconds. He would have quickly elevated D'Urso to his underboss because D'Urso helped his nephew Johnny Meatballs collect from a bettor, an autobody guy who was with the Genovese.

Zito's response to Bruno was to leave D'Urso alone, that the Genovese would make him instead. Zito was certainly in position to know because he regularly met with Quiet Dom Cirillo, who had direct access to, and was a confidante of, Chin and knew his plans. Anybody made was made only with Chin's okay.

D'Urso was frequently assured that his induction was being planned. In one such talk, Aparo advised him that both Muscarella and Longo supported his being made: "Alan even said that they got to do it [induct D'Urso]. Ernie said to us, yes. in other words, we're going to get together with Dom [Cirillo] and everything, set a time and do it." D'Urso expressed surprise that such high-level figures were involved, to which Aparo replied "They have to. Bosses have to sit down, whoever's in charge has to sit down and talk to you. That's why they have to be careful about it: Where you gonna go, who meets, who brings them, everything."

To help further illustrate D'Urso's ever-increasing stature even while he was handcuffed in what he could actually do crime-wise because *he was working with me this entire time*, his capo "Petey Red" DiChiara[16] asked D'Urso to directly send messages to Falcetti instead of doing so himself, captain-to-captain. In essence, the capo (Petey Red) believed that the associate (D'Urso) had enough respect and power that it would be better for D'Urso to talk to the other capo (Falcetti) on his behalf. Sammy let DiChiara know that D'Urso had Falcetti's ear. So Petey Red would ask D'Urso to deliver messages to Patty Falcetti to give to then-Genovese street boss Ernie Muscarella. It should be noted how Muscarella replacing Farby (who was battling cancer) as acting boss was intended to provide additional insulation from law enforcement scrutiny.

Another example illustrates D'Urso's direct path to acting boss Muscarella. D'Urso had a dispute over an accident that took place with one of D'Urso's buildings. The excavator who caused the accident was with the Bonannos. The Bonannos involved in resolving the dispute were Tony Green Urso, who soon became Bonanno underboss and later their boss, and Tommy Defiore, a powerful capo. Tony Green reached out to Genovese acting underboss Little Larry Dentico. Little Larry returned with a resolution that D'Urso didn't find satisfactory. D'Urso knew Petey Red would not take a strong position to support him, so D'Urso instead went to Falcetti, who said he would run the issue by Muscarella. Muscarella sent a message back to D'Urso supporting D'Urso's position.

---

16 DiChiara became capo after Gangi went to prison, and he was eventually elevated to Genovese street boss.

Petey Red was by now uncomfortable with the high-level political maneuvering and potential for discord (since Genovese acting boss Muscarella had overruled Genovese acting underboss, Dentico). So Petey, the capo, then asked D'Urso, the associate, what to do? This further demonstrated the power and respect D'Urso commanded. D'Urso responded, "No disrespect you're my captain, but please let Little Larry know what Ernie decided."

But that did not end the matter. The Bonannos wanted a sit-down, a meeting to resolve differences. D'Urso attended this sit-down with Sammy and Petey Red, who introduced D'Urso as 'he'll get straightened out, so treat him as one of us.' Sammy and Petey Red said nothing, letting D'Urso defend himself and handle the sit-down. So D'Urso as an associate went up against the Bonanno underboss and a high-ranking captain. Things got heated, as the Bonannos raised their voices to him and told him he had to pay the excavator to resolve the dispute. D'Urso responded that he had to relay the Genovese message that if Jesus Christ told him he had to pay he was not to pay, but that if they insisted, then they would need to talk to Muscarella. In essence, D'Urso had the authority, directly from the Genovese acting boss, to invoke his authority against the Bonanno hierarchy, who dropped it from there.

Also, in this general time period, Bonanno captain Louie Restivo invited D'Urso, Zito, Sammy, and Vinny to have lunch with Bonanno boss Joe Massino at Casa Blanca restaurant in Queens. Massino had been recently released from prison. D'Urso was supposed to be introduced to him as proposed for induction. Other than again demonstrating D'Urso's rising and recognized stature to be invited for such an introduction, the underlying larger significance to this meeting is that the Bonannos had been weak for years after the Donnie Brasco/Joe Pistone sting. But by the time of this meeting, they were emerging as a rebuilt, secretive, and stable crime family—as compared to the Gambinos, who were then a mess (Gotti had been convicted in 1992 of killing ex-boss Castellano, and Chin and others tried to kill Gotti in retaliation), while the Colombos and Luccheses were viewed as disoriented and disorganized—they had so many former members who cooperated with the FBI. Ironically, as noted above, both

Massino and his underboss, along with many other Bonannos, ended up cooperating.

An interesting anecdote about Massino further illustrates the mafia's layers of hypocrisy and treachery. "Good Looking Sal" Vitale was Massino's brother-in-law, and a former New York state corrections officer after serving as a U.S. Army paratrooper. Massino later mentored Vitale and proposed him to be made. However, since prior law enforcement service is prohibited by the mafia, other mob families objected to Vitale's induction. Massino addressed this by simply lying, denying Vitale's prior employment. Vitale was not only made but eventually rose to become Massino's underboss.

Based on information and testimony provided by cooperating witnesses, Massino, Vitale, and other Bonannos were charged with murders and murder conspiracies in 2003. Information these witnesses provided details to include Massino's plan to kill Vitale. Reminiscent of so many others, once this treacherous disclosure was made Vitale cooperated himself, providing details concerning approximately a dozen murders, and he testified at trial against Massino.

Facing a death sentence after his conviction, Massino, the boss, was next to cooperate. Massino disclosed how acting boss Vinnie "Gorgeous" Basciano expressed interest in killing his prosecutor. Massino initially had no credibility after his conviction. To address this credibility issue, we had Massino record a prison conversation with Basciano, in which, among other things, Basciano admitted ordering associate Randolph "Randy" Pizzolo's murder, for which Basciano was convicted. He killed Pizzolo in part because Pizzolo had previously insulted some mobsters. Basciano is serving a life sentence in prison now.

I often cite my two degrees of separation from people; I had previously investigated Pizzolo, serving him with a subpoena for handwriting exemplars. Pizzolo appeared in a black tuxedo with a pink bow tie while the other shop stewards, who also had been subpoenaed, wore work boots and construction clothing. When I interviewed Pizzolo, he mentioned he had previously been with the U.S. military. When I asked him what had interested him in joining the military? Pizzolo stated he was drawn to the military because he "liked killing people."

Yet another example of how other gangsters held D'Urso in such high esteem was how they occasionally relied on him to solve their problems. As noted above, his own capo had D'Urso handle meetings, pass messages, and take care of sit-downs on his behalf. But there was more. For instance, some time before Demeo got made, a gangster named Antonucci stole watches belonging to somebody close to Demeo. The Antonuccis were wild—there were several brothers—and Demeo was afraid to try to get the watches back. So he and capo Petey Red came to D'Urso. D'Urso was well respected and well known on the street and Demeo had a problem: Could D'Urso reach out to get the watches back and solve their problem?

This presented an extremely delicate and important problem to solve. I had to figure this out and quick, because otherwise, D'Urso would have to "go to work" on some to get the watches back. Obviously, I couldn't let him do that. But if he didn't do that, then his conduct would be highly suspicious. He would lose status and, more important and dangerous, someone could begin to ask questions about why D'Urso didn't take the obvious gangster steps.

I called the Antonucci brothers' home and ended up speaking with his mother. I discussed the potential threat to her son that I said I received from informants for him stealing a watch from someone connected to powerful gangsters. If the watch was returned, it would prevent her son's possible murder. I strongly warned her to take care of it and have her son call me. By way of thanks, she basically told me to go fuck myself and mentioned how another son was shot and killed in front of her house.

But the watches were returned and potential disaster for my case was averted. This enhanced D'Urso's reputation in the eyes of Petey Red. Having Antonucci, who had a treacherous reputation, return the watch so quickly was impressive.

In light of the elevated status in which the Genovese regarded D'Urso, and creative juggling acts like just described, we were able to continue to build and construct what was turning into an increasingly massive case. This was no several-months-and-wrap-it-up, as I initially envisioned. If the cards continued to fall right, I realized this was going to be really, really big—like Jimmy-Ida-take-down-the-administration-level-once-again big. Maybe even much bigger.

Not everything that took place was serious, though. One time, D'Urso and Sammy were on Grand Street as some of the *Sopranos* cast stood across the street at Ferrara's Bakery. D'Urso asked Sammy, "What do you think they're thinking?" Sammy replied, "They're thinking they're just actors. We're the real deal."

CHAPTER NINE

CONTINUING TO QUIETLY DEVASTATE THE GENOVESE

"Nobody meets him."

As we swung into 2000, I continued to utilize D'Urso to build criminal cases—against dozens of mobsters. And because he was so well regarded, and considered a rising star, we were able to implicate criminals in *each* of the five crime families, eventually disrupting operations for all of them. But the path again was not smooth. I faced continuing hazards within the investigation itself, along with new and more difficult obstacles presented by FBI bureaucracy. Fortunately, I was able to navigate around them.

There were also some interesting developments. D'Urso's intention to gain revenge against Polito remained an open issue, even years later. Polito attempted to land with the Luccheses for a while, moving over from the Genovese. This came from a relationship Polito developed while in prison with other members of the Lucchese family. And when he did, the Luccheses attempted to broker a peace. But even though D'Urso was working for me, he had to retain his gangster credentials and he turned them down. The Luccheses proposed that the matter should be put to rest, since both D'Urso and Polito were shot in the head. D'Urso responded that his cousin Tino was dead. He told the Luccheses to have Polito bring his closest cousin, Gingale Imbrieco, to D'Urso. D'Urso would kill him, and they could bury the hatchet. They did not take him up on this offer.

External Threats to the Investigation

On occasion we were required to walk on a virtual tightrope; if we fell off, the investigation could be exposed and D'Urso could be killed. For instance, in 2000 Aparo ordered D'Urso to kill Aparo's godson James Soldano, which I'll turn back to in a minute. But Soldano's brother Anthony had also been disrespectful to Aparo during a conversation, which D'Urso witnessed. Even though D'Urso was cooperating, he knew he had to stand up for Sammy and slap Soldano to avoid suspicion. When he went to do so, Soldano sat in a car with a guy named Radar. D'Urso had to back off because Soldano saw D'Urso approach and told Radar to grab his gun.

As for James Soldano, he was bipolar and violent. He beat up Anthony and threatened their own mother. He was very dangerous. Sammy also feared for his own life, because he went to see James, and James would not let Sammy leave the apartment for a while. So Sammy did what mobsters do. He went to the treachery playbook and asked D'Urso to kill his godson the next morning. D'Urso said he'd take care of it, asking Sammy just to let him know when James was asleep and to leave the apartment door open.

This of course presented a massive problem for me and D'Urso. As explained earlier, a cooperator cannot commit violent crimes, let alone a murder. On the other hand, if he didn't carry out this order this risked a perception that he was insubordinate—leading to D'Urso's potential death or, at the very least, a lethal suspicion that he was not who and what he appeared to be.

After D'Urso recorded this meeting between Aparo and Anthony, we agreed James had to be taken off the street asap. D'Urso also told me that Anthony had a gun in his car. I went to Anthony's car myself when I was not able to get help. As Anthony approached his vehicle, I displayed my badge and told him I could see the gun. Anthony replied. "It's not a real gun." So I said, "Then you have no problem with me taking it." It turned out to be a toy gun.

More urgently, we had to deal with Sammy's order that D'Urso kill James. I asked agents Tommy Krall and Craig Donlan to speak with James. They got him to agree to quietly enter drug rehab. However, James backed out at the last minute. Krall then went to Nassau County about getting an arrest warrant, but then James's mother called the police for him threatening her, and he was arrested.

Part of the resolution was for him to enter a facility to treat his bipolar condition. That defused the situation because this behind-the-scenes creative orchestration permitted D'Urso to tell Sammy that James was gone, D'Urso couldn't find him. Over time the issue faded away and off Sammy's radar; out of sight, out of mind, he cooled down, and Soldano was his godson after all. Through treatment James was able to get back on his medication for the bipolar condition, and he calmed down.

Internal Threats to the Investigation

Unfortunately, I also had to continue battle with internal FBI bureaucracy—specifically, threats to the operation's success presented by Kingsley (Not his true name), the ASAC to the New York Organized Crime Unit. As I show below, not only did he attempt to undermine my effort to disrupt a major financial corruption racket involving the Genovese acting boss, but he also almost single-handedly destroyed the entire case takedown.

First things first. One part of the financial corruption involved acting boss Bellomo and an initially mysterious figure, "the Tax Doctor." Taking D'Urso further into his confidence, in late 2000 Cafaro told D'Urso about a guy who concealed and managed Bellomo's money through offshore accounts in the Bahamas; tens of millions of dollars. "Nobody meets him," Cafaro advised, "he's Barney's guy." Other Genovese confirmed that this "Tax Doctor" was "Barney's guy," and that Bellomo kept this relationship closely guarded; he didn't want any other gangsters to meet the Tax Doctor.

Seeing a prime opportunity, I devised a plan relying on the mob's basic greed for it to have a chance to succeed. D'Urso claimed to have an acquaintance who worked as an insurance adjuster. The fictitious adjuster supposedly found a way to regularly steal money due to the lax internal controls at this business. He could steal $130,000. Now he needed someone to help him manage the ill-gotten money and keep it off the IRS and law enforcement radar.

On March 24, 2000, D'Urso recorded his conversation with Cafaro utilizing a similar scheme we addressed earlier in this investigation involving a corrupt check-cashing business. Cafaro stated, "I can do it with this kid Peter, but he wants to talk to Patty (Falcetti) first." Cafaro arranged a meeting between D'Urso and Peter on Sunday to discuss the stolen check scheme. Cafaro used his cellular telephone to make this call and asked for "Mr Tarangelo please . . . Peter Tarangelo gets on the telephone and Cafaro described how he has a friend who wants to open an account offshore. Cafaro arranged a meeting for Sunday at about 11:00 or 12:00, by a Starbucks Coffee Shop on Military Trail. He described how Tarangelo "always has two or three accounts open, so he doesn't have to always run over to the Bahamas when someone wants to do something with them."

I had D'Urso incentivize Falcetti, who became involved in the discussions, to let D'Urso into the Tax Doctor's offshore scheme by promising Falcetti a large piece of the money, around $70,000. Likewise—promised a fee— Cafaro offered to serve as a conduit for D'Urso. Eventually, Cafaro disclosed that the Tax Doctor was an accountant named Peter Tarangelo who lived in Florida and frequently traveled to the Bahamas and internationally to conceal Bellomo's money. The plan was for Cafaro and D'Urso to travel to the Bahamas, meet Tarangelo, and do the deal. This was an excellent opportunity—it permitted me to target Bellomo, Falcetti, Cafaro, Tarangelo, and others for money-laundering prosecution, expose and disrupt an otherwise effective scheme to hide mob money, possibly give us access to Bellomo's account, and simultaneously position D'Urso for even more Genovese prestige because it would help establish him in their eyes as a more sophisticated "earner."

On April 5, 2000, Patty Falcetti met with D'Urso and provided him with a piece of paper with the name of the company that the stolen check should be made payable to. The company name was "Gibson Rigby and Company."

In addition to providing the money, the FBI would have to create a plausible fictitious business from which D'Urso's "friend" was supposedly stealing. I had to wade through considerable bureaucratic incompetence to get this done, and I did. But then Kingsley tried to stop me from progressing. I needed a minimum of $130,000 to make this work, a relatively insignificant amount of money in light of the outstanding outcome available to us. It was also necessary to have at least that amount of money to entice the mobsters. But Kingsley pushed back, disingenuously saying how he would love to support the investigative strategy, but he claimed they were at the end of a fiscal year and did not have enough funds to do so. He said he would support a lower amount, but he knew this would not be sufficient to catch Falcetti and Cafaro's interest. It was clear that for some reason Kingsley did not want to support this effort.

So—incredibly—I had to figure out a way to circumvent my own ASAC just to do my job. I met with our squad's NYPD lieutenant, making the case for this operation and the importance of getting a line on Bellomo's offshore bank account. We struck a deal: the NYPD would front the second half of the money I needed to fund the operation, and it would share in the amount of money seized through offshore forfeiture. The lieutenant agreed.

I immediately walked the lieutenant and others into Kingsley's office exclaiming "great news." I knew Kingsley had no backbone and would never reject the NYPD. I said Kingsley previously agreed to fund a smaller amount due to budget issues. Now that the NYPD agreed to fund half, "We can do this transaction." Kingsley agreed to the funding but looked furious as we left his office. It was surreal, whatever personal issues Kingsley had that needlessly interfered with everything. Based on our recorded conversations, we were identifying possibly tens of millions of dollars of offshore funds, money laundered funds, enabling us to charge people like the Genovese acting boss. Yet here was the ASAC trying to actually stop us from doing so.

During this time period, I had to contend with further unthinkable sabotage by Kingsley, which I discuss below. But first I'll let you know how this all played out. With the money in hand, we cut a check to a fake business, just like an adjuster paying a claim. Cafaro and D'Urso (as always, equipped with recording devices) then flew on a private plane to Nassau, the Bahamas, and stayed at the British Colonial Hotel. There they met up with Tarangelo at the bar by the hotel pool, where they socialized and had a few drinks. As usual, I was there too, accompanied by NYPD Detective Bob Vosler, posing as tourists and taking photographs of the meeting. D'Urso, Cafaro, and Tarangelo eventually headed up to a hotel room where D'Urso handed over the check. I continued to pose as a hotel guest heading to my own room and photographed them walking together. Tarangelo then left the hotel and walked directly to a nearby bank to deposit the check, with me discreetly following his every step. Incidentally, by following the money trail we subsequently learned that Tarangelo was kiting[17] the money that he was supposed to be investing for the mob, a move extremely hazardous to his life.

Through this accumulated effort I knew, as expected, that I now had enough evidence to get Bellomo and others, for tax fraud and other crimes.

Not only did I have to juggle multiple balls to keep the investigation alive—maintain the perception that D'Urso was a rising and powerful gangster while in reality he was my stand-in FBI operative—I had additional difficulties navigating continued internal FBI efforts to sabotage the case. Toward the end of the year, a cross-designated detective told me out of the blue that Kingsley was at it again. This time, Kingsley planned to pull the plug altogether; take D'Urso off the street and close down our ongoing historic investigation—*in two weeks*. I quickly confirmed there was indeed no urgent or pressing valid law enforcement–related rationale or logic behind this move. Instead, Kingsley, a do-nothing bureaucrat, appeared to have self-serving motivation simply to reward an outgoing U.S. attorney with a huge press release and accompanying news accounts for this takedown conducted under her term as the U.S. attorney. I have no reason to believe that the U.S. attorney knew of or approved of Kingsley's loony plan. George Bush had been elected president and would soon replace U.S. attorneys with his own selection. Bush's inauguration would be on January 21, 2001.

---

17 Kiting involves intentionally moving funds from one account to another, misrepresenting account balances due to the theft of funds.

There was no reason to take the case down. The process of taking down a highly complex, now three-year investigation in just two weeks—when we had not yet even appeared before a grand jury—proved Kingsley's monumental incompetence. We had not yet appeared before a grand jury because doing so too early created the terrifying possibility of a leak—either purposeful or accidental—which would place D'Urso's life at continuing and unknowable risk. It was critically important to keep his identity a secret. Informing a room full of twenty strangers, the grand jurors, what was going on, when many members of law enforcement themselves had no idea, would escalate the risks, creating vast amounts of unnecessary danger.

I immediately went down to Kingsley's office with my supervisor to explain the complexity of the evidence we were still actively gathering and explained that the case had not yet gone to a grand jury. Yet Kingsley—being, in my opinion, as narcissistic as he was incompetent—replied, "The first indictment still has to take place in two weeks." This order was completely unexpected, idiotic, and baffling. I approached Dan Gill, our skilled Head of Forfeiture, since the end of the investigation would involve a huge amount for forfeiture. Yet Kingsley was equally uninterested in hearing from Dan; he was immovable.

Kingsley single-handedly jeopardized years of promising work. Perhaps I should not have been too surprised; to put it mildly, Kingsley did not have the best professional reputation. I and others on my team were unaware of Kingsley's conduct in his personal life. We subsequently learned months later how he was on thin ice, under an Office of Professional Responsibility investigation—part of the U.S. Department of Justice, and about to lose his job or be severely disciplined. To me, his act of sabotage against the ongoing investigation for personal political purposes belied a whole new low level of irresponsibility.

It was stupid for Kingsley to think that an active investigation involving three years of undercover work—and against the most significant criminal organizations in America—could be suddenly taken down in two weeks. Reams of evidence had to be carefully evaluated and analyzed: what charges could be filed, against whom, what evidence was admissible, what would be sufficient to convict? What properties and other assets could be identified and forfeited? Then the prosecutors would have to draft a massive prosecution memo and indictments—all of which was in turn subject to appropriate intense internal AUSA supervisory scrutiny and review. And so on. The anticipated wrap-up would require months. Two weeks was literally inconceivable.

My extreme frustration with the desire to (try to) take a case down— particularly one that promised to be of historic proportions—purely as a self-serving political "favor" forced me once again to problem-solve out of the box. In the week that followed, I rushed to gather more evidence. I flew to Florida and tasked D'Urso with raising specific topics related to subjects such as the Genovese control of the ILA, the plan to murder George Barone, the Tax Doctor in the Bahamas, and more. I made sure that D'Urso recorded statements from gangsters that would inspire prosecutors to delay taking down the operation so that we could gather more to ensure convictions.

Whereas to get around Kingsley to investigate the financial crimes I had to go to an NYPD lieutenant, this time I had to approach the U.S. Attorney's Office to gain their cooperation and beat Kingsley. I created a list of criminal topics that still needed to be addressed to fully secure the evidence we needed against the Genovese administration. I planned to recruit the interest and support of the prosecutors who would benefit from this résumé enhancement by being involved in such a big case. The case had two AUSAs assigned to it at the time, Paul Weinstein and Paul Schoeman—Mark Feldman was their immediate supervisor. I wanted to make Weinstein and Schoeman realize that very significant convictions would be possible based on the recordings currently underway with high-ranking gangsters.

I met with them and presented a list I prepared of all of the evidence gathered and the evidence we planned to collect. The list consisted of about ten to twelve investigative steps to secure evidence against the Genovese administration. I knew the prosecutors would salivate and wouldn't be able to help but imagine how it might help them win cases and bolster their own careers. I also quoted from recordings we'd already made, promising that more was on the way. Prosecutors always want the most detailed recordings possible because it makes their jobs that much easier to do.

Paul and Paul appreciated the point and provided me with their support, enabling me to delay the takedown for months—until it made *actual* sense—and thereby ensure the operation's success.

But the plan worked even better than I could have hoped, to actual comical effect. What happened was the prosecutors passed the topics on my own list—the verbatim list I prepared for them and handed to them—to Kingsley. Unbelievably, Kingsley then summoned me and my team into his office and had my supervisor hand me a memo containing *the exact same language* I had provided to the prosecutors about a half hour earlier. Kingsley then directed me to read out loud to everyone assembled in the room each of my own steps. After I finished reading the details, Kingsley asked what I thought of this strategy—my strategy. I replied, "I think it's brilliant."

This became extremely awkward for Kingsley. The team couldn't help but giggle at the absurdity of the exchange that had just taken place, and Kingsley could see and hear their reactions. He had no idea that he had just had me read to him the same language that I had provided to the prosecutors, and that they had provided in turn to Kingsley. As we left the office, Agent Tom Krall remarked it was unbelievable how quickly things had changed.

Though I'd managed to pivot this into a win, I knew the investigation could not go on indefinitely. I'd bought a few more weeks and would need to start preparing for the operation's eventual conclusion.

CHAPTER TEN

INMATE PANIC

"You're Campi?"
"Return the money—Campi will find it."

By the early 2000s, I knew we were developing something big. D'Urso had gained entry to the Genovese's upper echelons. Whenever yet another detailed recording captured overwhelming evidence of crimes, we would say to each other, "there goes another schmackdown."

Having previously convicted the entire active Genovese administration with the Ida case, it was clear to me that this investigation was going to only further devastate the Genovese, and all other New York organized crime families. As described earlier, in D'Urso's very first recording Sammy Aparo described how they might not survive another big indictment:

"We can't take another hit like that. If we have another takedown, this life is over."

Well, it was coming.

D'Urso had by now been undercover for years. Remarkably, while essentially acting as a day-to-day undercover operative for the FBI, the amount of respect and trust shown to D'Urso within the Genovese family *increased tenfold*—and he was repeatedly positioned to receive greater and greater status and assignments. All of the street-hardened, naturally

154

suspicious gangsters who surrounded him were completely fooled. These men lived and died by their wits, and many are constantly literally paranoid about any hint of law enforcement's presence.

Yet under my direction, and combined with his stellar performance under the harshest stresses, D'Urso was fooling them all. He was being introduced to more and more valued relationships, and he was recruited to commit important murders.

After three years of operating him and getting so much more than I ever conceived, however, it was time to begin to focus on the takedown. Every day risked a leak, internal pressure was mounting and at some point, you have to take the case down so you can make the arrests. As it was, we'd accumulated so much evidence that we could arrest literally dozens of highly placed mobsters from all five crime families.

One might think I was floating high in view of what we'd accomplished and in anticipation of a second massive Genovese takedown. I'd like to agree, but unfortunately it wasn't so. Certainly, there were moments such as when we'd made some of the most successful recordings when I'd felt deeply pleased by our ongoing success collecting a staggering amount of evidence against such a large number of very bad people. But there had always been corresponding setbacks, failures where more could have been accomplished, and there was the continuing daily depressing reality of having to deal with incompetent managers who at times tried to actively undermine my work and who excelled at leaving even the most successful agents feeling resented and/or underappreciated.

To give a sense of the types of criminal schemes we were uncovering, here are some: One involved Genovese associate and former NYPD Mike Norrito, who introduced Sammy and D'Urso to a man named Abe Weider. Abe owned multiple apartment buildings, with tons of tenants. Local 32BJ was the union that handled the buildings, their cleaning, etc. Abe was looking for a way to pay off mobsters who could rid him of an obligation to 32BJ and the high costs of dealing with their union.

We made recordings with D'Urso about how the Colombo gangster Mike Donofrio had already ripped off Abe, taking $400,000, yet providing Abe with no relief. Abe was now wary but willing to listen to other ideas. The Genovese brought in associate Glenn McCarthy, who was their union go-to guy. McCarthy is the son of Jack McCarthy, a historical associate of the Genovese family. Jack McCarthy, Glenn's father, had a relationship with the Genovese family going back to the 1950s. He was convicted multiple times on labor-related racketeering counts. Jack provided George Barone with $25,000 upon his release from prison. Glenn McCarthy reported to Genovese powerhouse "Quiet Dom" Cirillo, a conduit and street boss representing Chin's interests, and Cirillo guarded this relationship tightly. Yet D'Urso was brought within this tight inner circle. Alongside his father's involvement, between the two of them the McCarthy's long-standing ties to the Genovese went back decades. Nevertheless, McCarthy did not know it but the mob's treachery had almost resulted in his being killed years before, since he was suspected of being an informant alongside Pete Savino. Even decades later, when D'Urso asked Falcetti about McCarthy, Falcetti responded, "I don't trust him, if that's what you're asking."

McCarthy in turn introduced Frank (not his true name), who had a track record of creating his own unions, from which Weider could then oust 32BJ. As McCarthy put it in a recording made by D'Urso, "Frank, to understand who he is, was the finance manager of [a named high-profile New Jersey politician]. I normally get ten percent of whatever the billing is that he ends up with." McCarthy vouched that Frank worked wonders with union corruption: "The streets are still paved with gold through Frank. I got no complaints."

D'Urso recorded conversations from multiple highly secretive meetings that followed. At one, Frank outlined to Weider how it would work:

> Get three or four competitive bids. . . . You don't want these people on your payroll anymore. . . . You're going to negotiate with the union "in good faith" to an impasse. Assuming you can accomplish that, you're no longer able to achieve what is viewed as satisfactory. . . . You want to save 25 percent of your costs because it's too much money. You're making an economic decision not based on any animus towards the union, or towards any of the employees.

Weider responded, "that part I understand." Frank described how on the day Weider decided to make his move, "you tell these people here's your final check and here's a letter from the new contractor who will be happy to interview you tomorrow at nine o'clock."

The end result was an agreement granting the Genovese 25 percent of Abe's savings of $1,000,000 per year. Sammy, Vinny, D'Urso, and McCarthy were to split their take. However, in the end, Frank couldn't get down to Abe's numbers. D'Urso then took the situation to Falcetti, who had an Albanian guy, Izzy, who was a 32BJ delegate and would help solve their problems.

The takedown ended up happening before the scheme could come to fruition. Still, it was a conspiracy, and so there were a lot of arrests just from this one scheme. (A funny postscript to that: On the day of the arrests, capo Alan Longo told me he thought I had made a mistake because Weider, looking so out of place in his Hasidic clothing, was arrested alongside the mobsters. I responded, "You don't recognize your boss? That's Chin." All of us laughed.)

Another scheme concerned McCarthy again, in addition to Genovese associate Dominic Rabuffo. When I heard Rabuffo's name mentioned in a conversation, I instructed D'Urso to try to coordinate a meeting with him, as I knew Rabuffo was a potentially important figure. McCarthy made the introduction. The fact that he did so spoke volumes to D'Urso's continually rising stock.

I hoped D'Urso could capture Rabuffo discussing details of crimes he coordinated for the Genovese. Rabuffo was former partners with Irwin Schiff, who was brutally murdered by the mob in the 1980s while having dinner at a Manhattan restaurant. Rabuffo was involved in everything from skimming construction profits, to bank, mail, and tax fraud. He was also involved in a massive mortgage fraud scheme using shell companies to acquire residential developments and using straw borrowers to make purchases on those developments. Rabuffo would later be sentenced to nearly thirty years for his role in this scheme.

I soon learned from D'Urso's conversations with Aparo and McCarthy that McCarthy and Rabuffo were involved in further fraud through a guy named Jack Quinn. McCarthy described Quinn as the most skilled, sophisticated con man he'd ever met, which is saying quite a bit. They were all involved in real estate fraud involving major construction projects, like a Ritz Carlton hotel in Florida that McCarthy suggested D'Urso might manage. At one meeting, D'Urso observed that there was not a lot of money to be made, to which McCarthy responded:

> I don't think you quite got it. We're not here for the construction. We're here for all the perks afterwards. We're here to move the parking, retail space, the laundry, the cleaning and put a union in the joint. That makes long-term sense. Short-term is not what I'm talking about. I'll take short term money like everybody else. I like annuities, long-term. I like knowing every month something is coming.

All of this was being pushed through thanks to the help of a corrupt local mayor of a major city. Under the mayor's scheme, high-rise buildings were being built with his approval after receiving a bribe. The buildings often violated established rules, such as for housing density, but the mayor made "magic" happen for the mob-connected developers. So long as the cash flowed, he ensured the rules did not apply to them. D'Urso personally met with the mayor and made recordings of him discussing these extralegal changes.

Another scheme which helps to illustrate the everyday depravity of the mob concerned a plot to have capo Longo's son Danny, a plumber, block a building's sewer, causing massive flooding and damage. Through a corrupt contact who worked at the building, they would then hire Danny on an "emergency" basis to "fix" the problem he had just caused. Sammy Aparo described the scheme further:

> Like a super that's able to sign for the money. The manager or the super is capable of signing for the thing, so they're checking that out now. If he can do that, we go ahead. You got to have somebody that calls and is able to sign for the boss. [Danny Longo] gets 350 [$350,000] and the rest [out of an anticipated $900,000] is ours.

Paul Geraci also described how Longo tried to recruit his participation as well. Longo told him, "You don't understand, we can make six hundred thousand from one morning. Give the money to us on the street in a shopping bag the same day. No, well, they have to get paid, and they get a million dollars and give us six hundred thousand."

Massive and needless property damaged, insurance premiums raised, rents raised, or prices for goods possibly raised to spread the costs to the affected businesses and their customers, jobs possibly lost as employees are blamed for the flooding, the list goes on. Meanwhile, the mob pockets their profits. This is a sample of the type of damage they inflict on the rest of us while they laugh all the way to the bank.

Here's another example. Employment at the Jacob Javits Center in Manhattan has long been under Genovese control. Recorded conversations with Tommy Cafaro described how Fat Tony Salerno used to be in charge of it but that it caused him headaches because Chin "would ask for everything," meaning employment for his friends and family in addition to other benefits. Cafaro further described how Barney Bellomo later took over, but the Genovese abused their control because they treated it like their own candy store. The intended use was for mobsters, or "friends," as Cafaro said, who needed to show paper employment when they came home from prison. But this was extended to dozens of others, including, as Cafaro put it, Bellomo's whole family. "That was the ruination. He put his brother-in-law in there." Do you think any of these people actually worked? No, they simply take jobs from those willing to work, and they collect paychecks and benefits at great cost. The costs of these handouts simply get passed on in the form of needlessly inflated expenses for which those downstream must pay. This is known as the silent "mob tax"— paying for their criminally inflated standards of living for which all New Yorkers and those across the country must pay.

Likewise, Longo and Geraci described their involvement in stock fraud. This can take many forms but often involves inflating the price of worthless "penny" stocks, and then selling to hapless victims who may lose their life savings on the other end of the transaction, having no idea they are being conned out of their money. Longo advised that, "I got involved in the stock business several years ago. Made two million dollars." Geraci followed up in another conversation that in the past couple of years he made "about four, maybe three [million]. That's only a couple of months. I saved it, I spent it. I bought my house. I got a house in Florida. I got a house here. January of last year until now I got about seventy thousand. I did a little deal between this month and last month. I gave him [Longo] half the money. Like me and him are partners in the stock deals."

This is just two mobsters. Many more make similar amounts using associates to provide some insulation from law enforcement scrutiny. As an investigation occurs, it's the associates who may be killed due to the lack of trust by the gangster.

Incidentally, on the treachery theme, Cafaro had aided Longo and Geraci's stock fraud by making an introduction for them. But apparently, he had kept this from Bellomo because he informed D'Urso, "I never need that fucking guy to find out."

Before the takedown took place, in addition to routine criminal discussion, the early months of this year were explosive—filled with murder plots, D'Urso receiving murder assignments, and other hair-raising moments.

One scary moment took place when D'Urso showed up for a meeting with Falcetti in the Bronx. Falcetti arrived in a rented car, which was unusual, because he usually drove his own car. First big reg flag. Falcetti then told D'Urso to get in the car with him, which he did.

D'Urso asked where they were going, and Falcetti answered, "A funeral home." Second big red flag.

At this point D'Urso was unsure what to do. Had they learned he was cooperating? Were they going to take care of him and then cremate his body?

When Falcetti pulled the car into a mob-owned funeral parlor run by soldier Ralph Balsamo, the situation seemed even more dire. More screaming red flags. D'Urso planned out his violent response if this was a trap; hit Falcetti first, then take out Balsamo.

He texted his location to the agents who were following him. But one of them lost him, and the other could see that Falcetti was looking at his car, so he had to drive straight past. D'Urso was completely on his own.

Thankfully this was a false alarm. For whatever reason, Falcetti had simply decided to conduct this meeting at the funeral home.

"Guys Like That End Up Getting Clipped, Guys Like This Fucking Georgie."

In addition to Soldano, another murder assigned to D'Urso was legendary Genovese soldier George Barone.

Barone was an old-timer who played a historic role in the Genovese's control of the ILA. He had been a longshoreman decades before, and cofounded the street gang the Jets, memorialized in *West Side Story*. Various powerful Genovese such as Vito Genovese and Fat Tony Salerno saw Barone's criminal potential and took him under their wings. As Barone was to later testify, he killed so many in the service of the mob that he lost count: "I didn't keep a scorecard . . . Black, green, yellow, whatever." He explained, "I did whatever [Fat Tony] told me to. . . . He is my boss."

Over time, he became the president of an ILA local and, during the transition from loading ships manually to the process of containerization, solidified the mob's iron grip on the waterfront. New union locals formed with containerization, which presented the Genovese a chance to control a larger union membership. New Jersey had the land in Newark, Elizabeth, and Bayonne to store the containers, and the Genovese had previously agreed with the Gambinos that the Genovese would control New Jersey and Manhattan, while the Gambinos got Brooklyn and Staten Island.

As Barone described, this in turn gave the Genovese control over who would be elected ILA president. Barone also held meetings with shipping executives to obtain favorable ILA contracts. These contracts were always corrupt, and always slanted to benefit the mob.

Eventually, Barone got caught and went to federal prison. By the time he got out, he had been pushed aside by a new generation of gangsters and felt disrespected. As he was to later testify, he became "very bitter. I went to jail, and that was the end of everything." Having moved to Miami prior to going to prison, he formed an alliance with Cuban gangsters there to control Miami's waterfront.

Many years before, as a favor to Chin, Barone had placed Chin's son Andrew with associate Bert Guido in the shipping business. More recently, Barone received a message that Andrew needed his help getting a lucrative contract for Guido, but Barone first wanted to get paid on an old debt because Guido owed him about $90,000. On top of that, Barone felt contempt for Andrew Gigante, who he described as "a drunk, a junkie. . . . He'd go in the bathroom and come out flying like a kite, for chrissakes." Barone asked Falcetti and Ernie Muscarella to have Guido pay him.

Barone had been close with Chin going back to the 1950s, but according to Cafaro, Chin later detested Barone: "That guy I'm talking about, this guy," pointing to his chin, "hated him, hated him." Cafaro explained that once Barone was in Miami, he constantly concocted excuses not to help the Genovese: "The piers down here [in Florida]. We're finished. Where all the key jobs were given out. Hundred-and-fifty-thousand-dollar checker jobs were given out to all the Cubans. They're pieces of shit." D'Urso: "Who gave them out?" Cafaro: "This guy, George. He gave them out. They're gone. So say we want to put somebody there. You're dead. We could have put a guy there for 150 [thousand dollars], the guy gives you 25 [thousand dollars back]. . . . They're making big mistakes. I wish my friend [Bellomo] was home [back from prison]. Now they're going to put guys in to be president of certain things up there [New Jersey]. All these guys do is take money." D'Urso: "Who the fuck is controlling it?" Cafaro: "Patty is in charge of the one up there. We just have the companies. I take care of the companies. There's two companies I take care of. Whatever we get out of them, me and my Pal [Bellomo], you know, that's it. It's ours. I stayed out of the union. I went with the companies . . . [Barone] ain't stepping down. He's got all those Cubans. He will go to war if he has to. . . . Guys like that end up getting clipped, guys like this fucking Georgie."

Cafaro also discussed an idea to set the Cubans up for drug arrests:

It's easy to set them up. We get somebody down here that we know, that's got a fake badge, we throw something in the fucking car, make a fucking bullshit thing. Let it get into his [Barone's] ear. We say, "George how can you have guys who are in the fucking junk business, that are fucking around with junk. You got to get rid of this kid. Don't let him lose his job, but get him a job. He can't have this [high-level, high-pay] position no more. Give him a regular [job], put them out on the pier. He did something wrong." They're not going to know they were set up by us. And that's how we'll get rid of them. We'll put them down with the rank and file.

D'Urso also discussed this topic with Patty Falcetti, who said that Barone "was told to stay away from the International, don't communicate with the president, stay away from a couple of delegates, stay away from Jersey, okay, and stay away from another guy that he's close with [ILA President Harold Daggett]. . . . We're not going to lose Florida."

So the anger with and desire to kill Barone had been building, and Barone's condition that he would help Andrew Gigante only if the Genovese first collected payment from Guido struck Patty, Ernie, and Andrew as a direct insult to Chin. They gave Barone a few thousand dollars instead, and Barone responded by saying to tell Chin to stick it up his ass. He let them know he had an army of armed Cubans willing to stand alongside him. This sign of perceived disrespect, combined with Barone's aligning with the Florida Cubans more closely than with the Genovese, and his cold stubborn character, was the tipping point that led to a death sentence.

D'Urso was assigned to eventually carry out the hit. Falcetti had D'Urso to his home in the Bronx and asked D'Urso to follow him to an upstairs bedroom. There, Falcetti gave the lethal order. He pointed to his ear to indicate Barone, who was elderly and hard of hearing. Falcetti said, "We are having a problem with this guy getting out of hand with these Cubans. We have to do this." As Falcetti said "this," he made the shape of a gun with his hand. D'Urso was being ordered to kill a made man, Barone, orders that could have only come from the very top.

Playing his role to the hilt, D'Urso responded that he needed only to be told when and where. This moment also signified that D'Urso had earned the Genovese leadership's ultimate level of trust. This was no everyday murder like Soldano, but rather a prestige assignment in that world. He was tasked to take out Barone, a legend within the family, and a very powerful man. At the same meeting, in further confirmation of D'Urso's rising stature, Falcetti asked him how he would feel if he was moved out from under Sammy Meatballs, to report directly to capo Falcetti himself.[18]

---

18 This in itself was further testament to D'Urso's rising stock, as associates normally report to soldiers.

D'Urso replied that while he loved Sammy, he also knew Sammy would want him to do what's best for his mob career.

To implement the plan for Barone's demise, Falcetti arranged to meet him in Florida, where he handed Barone half the money owed. Falcetti brought D'Urso along with him so that he could observe Barone's appearance, and promised the remainder when Barone was next in New York. Barone had the support of dozens of loyal and heavily armed Cubans in Miami; the Genovese needed him, alone, in New York. I videotaped the payment during my surveillance, capturing Barone laughing as he counted the cash while sitting next to an armed Cuban friend.

Barone knew the lure of the second payment was to bring him back to a place where it would be easier to kill him. As confirmation, Jimmy Cashin, a former ILA Local 1804 secretary treasurer gave Barone the same, "If I call for you, don't come," speech that Sammy Meatballs provided to D'Urso years before.

"We're Not Dead Yet. We're Strong. Don't Let Anybody Tell You We're Dead."

In early 2001, capo Alan Longo summoned D'Urso to meet at Campagnola restaurant. In yet another sign of his increasing stature, Longo informed D'Urso that he had been handpicked to participate in another prestige assignment: a massacre.

The Albanian mob had a particularly vicious reputation and did not fear or respect Italian gangsters. On one recording we made, Falcetti said that when he met with them, he always brought a gun and that "if you have a beef with them, you have to kill them right away. There's no talking to them. They respect you if they know you, but if they don't know you, they do what they got to do and see who's coming out of the woodwork. But believe me, they ain't gonna be around forever. I hate these fucking Albanians. I hate them. If you have a beef with them, you have to kill them right away. There's no talking to them."

D'Urso's recordings with Longo described how the Albanians took disrespect to an entirely new level. A group of them walked into a Bronx social club controlled by a crime family and assaulted a Lucchese soldier and a Colombo capo and threw them out. The Albanians not only physically threw them out, but also changed the locks and took over the club. Even more unbelievably, when a pair of Lucchese and Columbo capos arranged a subsequent sit-down, the Albanians simply beat up the capos.

This meant war, as it challenged the very premise by which organized crime rules: owning the streets through raw fear and intimidation. Telling D'Urso he would be one of those to wreak vengeance, Longo said, "We're not dead yet. We're strong. Don't let anybody tell you we're dead."

Longo also stated that the mafia had lots of "capable guys"—which meant capable of murder. In a moment of precious irony, and of course with no clue that D'Urso was recording every word, Longo added, "We're going to pull together. You'll be one of them. We go to the guys we can trust. We ain't going to put guys on the line who are going to become rats one day." The Genovese have four hundred made men and thousands of associates. From this very large pool the Genovese powers viewed D'Urso—who had been working with me and for the FBI for around three years by then—as one of their most trusted and reliable killers.

As Longo explained, the plan was each of the mafia families would supply five handpicked shooters. They would enter five clubs known to belong to the Albanian mob, and simply murder everyone inside, armed with machine guns. They estimated the total body count to be fifty to one hundred people.

The massacre was to take place in about six months. Waiting so long would lull the Albanians into a false sense of security. Just when they would assume that hostilities had died down was precisely when the mob would strike and kill them all.

"This Was an Investigation of Historical Scope and Significance."

With the looming planned Albanian massacre, I finally made the decision to take the case down. We had copious evidence against high-ranking members of all five crime families involved in serious crimes. I could also tell that D'Urso was under growing stress, although some of the extraordinary stress I only found out about years later, which I discuss later in this book. As for what I knew, among other things, the premature effort to close the case was weighing on him, as was his concern about whether or not Aparo would himself decide to cooperate. It must have been rough for D'Urso to gather evidence every day against someone he regarded as a father, deceiving Aparo all the while. When he initially cooperated, D'Urso thought Aparo might join him as a cooperator because of Farby's abusive behavior. To my knowledge, he did not try to get Sammy to cooperate because had he approached Sammy to discuss this topic while still on the street it would have meant a death sentence for D'Urso.

With all of this, plus the constant concern of an eventual law enforcement leak, I decided to take the case down. The longer the investigation continued, the greater that risk became. We shared the numerous recordings D'Urso made with the other crime families with the squads investigating them. And we made numerous follow-up recordings to assist these squads with future indictments to decimate the mob.

With knowledge that the takedown was coming, D'Urso's family also prepared to enter witness protection, and in the recesses of his mind he knew he would still have to go before a federal judge to be sentenced himself.

The prosecutors began the grand jury work and drafting the voluminous memorandums and sealed indictments to support the arrests.

When we were about two weeks out, and everybody knew the takedown was imminent. D'Urso asked me to meet his father-in-law, a retired police officer, and now explain what he had secretly been doing. We met at a Brooklyn McDonald's, and they were already seated when I approached. His father-in-law had no idea who he was meeting until I arrived and identified myself as an FBI agent.

D'Urso asked me to explain that we'd been working together for the past three years, and also what changes the future would bring. D'Urso was thinking in particular that his wife would join him in the Witness Security Program. The father-in-law took it all in and said that he understood. He had grown up in the Chin's neighborhood. Though he was clearly in shock, he did not articulate his feelings too much.

"It is what it is," he pronounced. I asked whether he would be interested in entering the Program himself and he said he'd think about it.

A few days after this meeting, D'Urso asked me if I would also meet his own parents and his sister at a hotel near the Museum of Natural History off Central Park. D'Urso's wife, Vanessa, also joined, as did the prosecutors.

During this meeting, some of D'Urso's family became emotional, while some simply sat in stunned silence. I came away with the impression that D'Urso had done his utmost, faithfully silent during the past three years, and, with the exception of his wife, told not even his closest family members about the operation. I knew this must have placed a huge burden and increased stress for him. But it doubtlessly helped to ensure his safety and the safety of the entire operation. It was also critical that they learn of what had happened before he was taken off the streets. I also extended a witness protection offer to these family members.

There is a tail end to the Albanian story. After D'Urso was taken off the street, Albanian leaders met with Gambino member Arnold Squitieri. The sit-down took place at a gas station in a rest area near the New Jersey Turnpike. A large contingent of armed Gambinos accompanied Squitieri. For the Albanians, Alex Rudaj came with a half dozen crew members.

The conversation got heated and the Albanians and Gambinos pulled out their weapons. Outnumbered, the Albanians threatened to blow up the gas station with all of them in it. This ended the "discussion," and both groups pulled back. The Albanians were subsequently charged with various crimes, and I testified at their trial. On cross-examination, one of their defense lawyers asked, "You're telling this jury that these Albanians took on the Italian mafia and they're still alive?" My response, "That's exactly what I'm saying," and I cited the above recordings about the Albanians beating up the mobsters and the planned retaliatory massacre. I also described historically how numerous other ethnic crime groups such as Irish, Jewish, Cuban, and Russian gangs had conflicts with the Italian mafia. These also typically resulted in murders that led to negotiated resolutions.

The D'Urso takedown itself occurred in April 2001. Dozens upon dozens of mobsters from all five crime families were arrested when law enforcement swooped-in during early morning raids. It was one of the biggest hauls in history and sent shock waves through the ranks of organized crime. As EDNY United States Attorney Roslyn R. Mauskopf put it:

The investigation resulted in the arrests of dozens of members and associates of organized crime. *This included the top leadership of the Genovese family for the past twenty years* including acting bosses Liborio Bellomo, Frank Serpico, and Ernest Muscarella.[19] Six captains, numerous soldiers and dozens of Genovese associates involved in criminal schemes that ranged from money laundering, labor racketeering, and sophisticated frauds. The investigation also expanded their efforts to the other crime families, resulting in the arrests of the acting boss of the Colombo family, Jackie DeRoss, as well as two Gambino family capos, two Gambino family soldiers, two Bonanno family soldiers and a Lucchese soldier.

Clearly this was an investigation of historical scope and significance. It was accomplished by FBI agents Campi, Krall, and Donlon, and by NYPD Detective Vosler.[20] Because they had encyclopedic knowledge of their subjects, their tactical decisions during the investigation were superb, and their talent cultivating cooperating witnesses and operating them on the street was remarkable. Indeed, the organizational skill and sheer hard work that this investigation required was breathtaking.

As Mauskopf stated, we arrested the *entire administration of the Genovese crime family.* The second time in less than a decade they had taken such a hit as a result of my investigations. Additionally, various acting bosses, capos, soldiers, and associates from the Genovese, Gambino, Lucchese, Bonanno, and Colombo families went down. As summarized by the official FBI statement on the matter, this was perhaps:

> "*The most significant and successful undercover operation in law enforcement history.*"

---

19 In follow-up indictments, the Chin and multiple capos and others were charged.
20 Jane Doe, who remains anonymous, was also recognized for her attachment to the team.

The eventual historic list included:[21]

Genovese Family

Vincent "Chin" Gigante—boss; Ernie Muscarella—acting boss; Barney Bellomo—acting boss; Frank "Farby" Serpico—acting boss; "Quiet Dom" Cirillo—administration; Andrew Gigante—Chin's son, and direct spokesman for his father; Patty Falcetti—capo—powerful, with a direct line to Barney Bellomo; "Little Larry" Dentico—capo and member of acting administration—powerful, with direct line to Chin; Anthony Antico—capo; "Johnny Sausage" Barbato—member of Chin's crew; Charles "Chuckie" Tuzzo—capo; Patty Deluca—capo; "Fritzie" Giovanelli—capo; Sammy "Meatballs" Aparo—capo; "Petey Red" DiChiara—capo and later acting boss; Ross Gangi—capo; Alan Longo—capo and part of the ruling administration; Joe Zito—soldier, high-ranking and with more clout than some captains; Vinny Aparo—soldier; Frank DeMeo—soldier; Sally DeMeo—soldier; Mickey Ragusa—soldier (later reputedly street boss); Bobby DeBello—soldier; Paul Geraci—soldier; George Barone—soldier; Tommy Cafaro—associate—respected as a power and conduit to Bellomo in prison; Abe Weider—associate/victim; Glenn McCarthy—associate; Mike Norrito—associate, retired NYPD; Peter Tarangelo—associate (a.k.a. "the Tax Doctor" and "Barney Bellomo's money man"); Carmine Polito—associate (now an acting capo); John Cerasulo—Polito cousin and wannabe; John "Gingale" Imbrieco—Polito cousin and wannabe; Mario Fortunato—associate; Izzy Kukic—Albanian associate; Frankie Schwamborn—associate; David Grossman—associate and former New York State Trooper and attorney; Bobbie Santoro—associate and major money launderer to the mob; Ralph Balsamo—associate; later a soldier and capo; Anthony Bruno—neighborhood guy and wannabe; Andrew Albin—associate; Tommy Barrett—associate; Jerry Brancato—associate; Phil DeSena—associate; Alan Green—associate; Patty Marmo—associate; Louie Monaco—associate; Scott Mulligan—associate; Joe

---

21 There were multiple indictments and superseding indictments, so it is quite possible that this list is not exhaustive.

Savarese Sr. and Joe Savarese Jr.—associates; Louie Colonna—associate; Daniel Longo—associate; Frank Pizzolato—associate; Michael Squillante—associate; Harold Daggett—associate and ILA President.

Bonanno Family
"Johnny Green" Faraci—capo; John "Boobie" Cerasani—soldier

Colombo Family
"Allie Boy" Persico—acting boss; Jackie DeRoss—acting boss; "Wild Bill" Cutolo—underboss, murdered before arrest; Frank Campanella—associate

Gambino Family
"Big Lou" Valario—capo; "Skinny Dom" Pizzonia—capo; Gerry Brancato—capo; "Johnny Beano" Setaro—soldier; Joe O'Kane—associate, directly under John Gotti Jr.

Lucchese Family
Ray Argentina—capo; Johnny Sorrentino—soldier

Despite the historic magnitude of this takedown, I never experienced the kind of excitement or high that came with a "win," like back when I was playing sports and my team beat another team. But good feelings? Sure. I thought about the great agents I worked with on C-5, like Tom Krall and Craig Donlon, who were quality agents who dealt with D'Urso on the street and continued to work with him and others in later trials and hearings. I would hire them in a second as corporate security executives. I thought about NYPD Detective Bob Vosler, who was also a member of the team on this investigation. We received the FBI's annual National Director's Award for Significant Investigations.

I felt good for everyone who helped: the prosecutors, Jenny Ng—the squad's most valuable clerical employee who maintained the case files for our squad—and for all the remarkable people who helped make such a good thing happen. Even so, to be perfectly honest, in the moment I had only feelings of emptiness. I think a big part of it comes from how much of our support came from the U.S. Attorney's Office—and *not* from FBI management.

I also found it hard to celebrate because the investigations and subsequent court cases had so many moving parts. Convictions would always be appealed, and surprises could always happen (chapters 14 and 17 contain particularly jarring examples). Things always seemed to be in transition. And there was always a hefty to-do list collecting on my desk, full of loose ends that required additional work for future organized crime indictments.

Oh—I also had an ASAC, Kingsley, who hated me and who was determined to reward my dedication by preventing me from putting in for a desk as my squad's supervisor. My interest wasn't to leave the squad but to groom the new agents on the most efficient method to investigate organized crime.

Arrests

The majority of the arrests took place in New York, but we also arrested several mobsters in Florida and conducted a search warrant on the Tax Doctor's office. I traveled to Florida for these arrests and court appearances. The arrested were shell-shocked when the haze parted and the sheer scale of the takedown emerged. They also simply could not believe or accept that the reason was D'Urso, the devoted, through-and-through hardcore, loyal gangster they had been positioning to obtain power in the inner circle. That he had been working undercover all those years—recording their private conversations and handing those tapes over directly to me—shook them to their core. And it was a monumental humiliation for the Genovese, who prided themselves as standing apart from their fellow crime families with their sophistication and fortitude.

The Florida arrests were quite eventful. When we arrested the Tax Doctor, Peter Tarangelo, in the early morning hours, he greeted me with:

"*You're* Campi?"

How on earth did the Tax Doctor know my name? Tarangelo explained: Tommy Cafaro had told Bellomo that D'Urso wanted to deposit funds with Tarangelo. Bellomo immediately instructed Cafaro to return the money to D'Urso:

"Campi will find it."

And I had. In fact, *I* was the one who sent D'Urso to them with the money in the first place.

Apparently, my reputation preceded me. It was kind of remarkable to hear how the Genovese acting boss was so acutely concerned about me.

As for Tarangelo himself, it was clear from the outset he was terrified and a strong bet to cooperate. His terror was well placed because, as noted above, he had been stealing some of the money that he was supposed to have invested for Bellomo. Once that became known, he was as good as dead. Within days of his arrest, sure enough, Tarangelo did sign on to become a witness against the Genovese. That is the way these types of cases unfold. Arrest scores of bad guys, some of whom agree to become witnesses, and you strengthen your case even more and possibly arrest more bad guys.

A final, surreal moment regarding Tarangelo occurred when I eventually flew home. In a hallway in the West Palm Beach airport, I saw a ten-by-twenty-foot print advertisement for Tarangelo's wealth management services. The header? "The Tax Doctor." The nickname, it turned out, had been his own invention.

By the way, Tarangelo is now deceased, so it presents no risk to let you know that he refused witness protection and spent his remaining years working as a maître d' in an Italian restaurant.

Back in New York, Tommy Krall arrested Falcetti. When Krall told Falcetti that his arrest was due to D'Urso's cooperation, Falcetti didn't believe a single word. He considered it literally impossible, just could not happen. He suspected Krall was lying to prompt him into making a statement that could be used against him. When Falcetti eventually grasped that Krall had told him the truth, he sought some consolation, telling Krall the FBI made a grave mistake because we took down the operation prematurely; this statement confirmed how D'Urso was being groomed to become a major power.

Falcetti may not have realized at that time the sheer scope of evidence that we had already accumulated. He also probably could not yet conceive of how long D'Urso had been on the street working for us. Likewise, little did Falcetti know that I may not have permitted D'Urso to go through an induction ceremony or kill Barone; I already had such good content from D'Urso that at this point it would present a possible unnecessary risk. If we knew we could go through with it safely, we would have authorized D'Urso's induction. It would likely have included recordings instructing D'Urso and others to get undressed.

As mentioned above, one person who D'Urso always hoped would eventually flip was his mentor and father figure, Sammy "Meatballs" Aparo. Aparo always resented Farby's abusive management style and his hair-trigger willingness to put a hit on D'Urso until Aparo and other emissaries calmed Farby down. D'Urso also knew that Sammy believed Chin did not care for him due to the incident involving Aparo's former capo, Salvatore Palmieri, also known as "Sally Young."

However, Aparo had no interest in cooperating. He had been in the life for so long, his son Vinny was in the life, and Sammy had health concerns suggesting he could die any day (he actually made it until 2017). I visited him in prison after it was all over to, among other things, let Sammy know that D'Urso was sincere in loving him like a father and meant nothing personal by his cooperation. Sammy told me to pass on his best to D'Urso and that he understood why D'Urso cooperated.

D'Urso and his family were placed in a secure location, a safe house under FBI protection. Sometime after this relocation I brought my own father to meet D'Urso. I had been planning to go over and pay a visit, and my father showed up at my home right as I was about to leave. I decided to take him along with me to see if meeting D'Urso might make him open up about our own family's encounters with the mafia. He had no idea where we were going as I drove. All I mentioned was that I was going to introduce him to a friend whose parents are from Italy and speak Italian. As we headed to the safe house, I was mindful that my own uncle had been shot by someone, similar to D'Urso's shooting. This uncle was tough, boxed, and didn't take any shit.

When we got to the safe house, D'Urso and his family chatted for a while with my dad in Italian, but they did not reveal the reason for their living situation, or how D'Urso and I knew each other.

Afterward, as I drove back home with my father, he asked how I had met such nice people. I tried to distract him with conversation to avoid discussing any specifics. But he asked me about the scar along the side of D'Urso's face and neck. Then I told him the whole story, and I hoped this would prompt him to share details about my uncle's shooting. But it didn't happen. My dad didn't react or share his story.

This reminded me of something he'd told me several times as a child.

"What's a secret?" he would ask.

"When you and a buddy know something that nobody else does," I would respond.

"No," he would reply. "A secret is when you know something nobody else does. Once you tell someone, it's no longer a secret." I imagine he made these statements to me at about the same time his brother was shot. He would always say to me as a child, "Don't let anyone hurt your brothers." I never feared a confrontation.

It turned out that D'Urso, too, had been harboring a horrible secret for many years. But he didn't tell me until years later. Instead, once installed in the safe house he called me and launched into a bizarre tirade. I was in Florida at the time meeting with Barone, who had decided to cooperate after his arrest.

D'Urso railed against Jane, one of the several FBI agents who had been working with him on our team for the past several years and who I previously discussed. "I hate working with this woman, Mike. I can't stand it. Some people, you just can't stand? Well, I can't stand her. We don't get along. She just makes my skin crawl. Mike, I'd rather go to jail than keep working with her. *I hate her even more than Polito.*" Carmine Polito is the man who orchestrated D'Urso's cousin's assassination and the attempted murder of D'Urso. For D'Urso to say this against Jane was just remarkable. He didn't provide any specifics, and I concluded that this had to do with Jane's recent withholding funds for living expenses from D'Urso and his family, which she had responsibility for distributing. This coupled with the accumulated overall and overbearing stress D'Urso and many others were under, including D'Urso trying to prepare his family and in-laws for witness protection.

Then another striking event took place. One night I was called to a hospital emergency room by D'Urso's wife because he thought he was having a heart attack. I came to the hospital and met with them. It turned out he was having a panic attack, not a heart attack. I understood how this could happen from all the stress that D'Urso was under. When D'Urso reiterated that he did not want to spend any further time with Jane, I thought his request still came from the stress D'Urso was feeling trying to adjust himself and his family to a new life.

Believe it or not, my supervisor at the time was Jane's husband. I told him to reassign Tom Krall to D'Urso (I was handling George Barone debriefings and another matter related to the case in Florida), and to keep Jane completely away from D'Urso. He asked me why with an incredulous tone: "Because D'Urso told me he hates her more than he hates Carmine Polito. That's why. Now remove her from all contact."

CHAPTER ELEVEN

FLIPPING GEORGE BARONE—THE FIRST GENOVESE MADE GUY SINCE VALACHI

"There's no way George Barone is cooperating."
"The mafia is not the paternal, wonderful organization that it
proposes to be. The esprit de corps does not exist. Greed, violence,
betrayal: that is what exists."

As part of the sweeping arrests made in the D'Urso case, after Barone's Florida arrest, we arranged to meet with him and his lawyer. This in and of itself was a miracle. When mobsters are arrested, and as Martin Light—a former prosecutor who became a defense attorney representing mobsters—testified in front of the President's Commission on Organized Crime, mafia families assign their trusted attorneys to represent the gangsters. These mob lawyers have several tasks. In order of importance, they first ensure that the mafia family and its higher-ups are protected; second and closely related is preventing the arrested mob member from any form of cooperation. If and only if these two primary conditions are satisfied, then the third goal is to actually represent their assigned client's best interests.

Conversely, for the gangster, his best move is often cooperating because this almost completely eradicates the risk of a lengthy jail term. But because that would violate the lawyer's first two priorities, it cannot happen so long as the assigned attorney represents them. Simply put, the lawyers would *never* bring their gangster clients in to meet with prosecutors. To cooperate, the gangster must figure out a way to reach out to law enforcement without their own lawyer finding out they did so. For instance, they might walk into the FBI offices, à la Al D'Arco, or they secretly employ "shadow counsel" to help them, à la Sammy Gravano, or they approach the FBI with a handpicked lawyer prior to being arrested, as did D'Urso.

It always amazed me that the system was permitted to function in this manner and a blind eye was directed toward this topic.

When the D'Urso case arrests took place, however, it happened so suddenly, at such a massive scale, and was so unexpected that the Genovese did not have the chance to coordinate the Florida arrested men with trusted mafia legal representation. In New York alone they had to quickly arrange for dozens upon dozens of lawyers to handle those arrests. Each arrested administration member and capo had to arrange for *their own* lawyers to help them out. It was just mass shell shock. Of course, an additional important factor for Barone was that he suspected the Genovese planned to kill him, and so he may have defied their instructions as to which criminal defense lawyer to hire in the first place. That in itself however would have signaled that he may be considering cooperating and could have led to his swift ending.

Genovese old-timers were absolutely confident that Barone could not possibly cooperate. So when mobsters cooperate it's because they first make the decision to do so independently, and then they figure out how to approach law enforcement. Here the situation was very different, as Barone expressed no interest in cooperating. I had to persuade him to do so. Barone was a tough gangster legend and he had spent many decades deeply embedded in the life, murdering and scheming throughout. For example, Al "Chinkie" Facciano, a powerful Genovese in his nineties who had been partners with Meyer Lansky back in the day, and was still living at that time, was cited at a Florida diner assuredly asserting, *"There's no way George Barone is cooperating.*" But they had been equally wrong about D'Urso.

In any event, Barone secured a very capable local defense lawyer who had no connection whatsoever to the Genovese or other mafiosi. He was on the board of directors of Legal Services of Greater Miami, Inc. and the director of pro bono services at a local law school. This well-credentialed lawyer did what any lawyer not obligated to the criminal organization would do—he sought the best outcome for his client. After all, as an attorney he was ethically obligated to do so. We asked to meet with Barone, a practice that is custom with most arrested criminals, and the lawyer advised his client to give it a shot. Among the whirling frenzy of surrounding events, our meeting quietly took place in Florida on the same day of his April 6, 2001, arrest.

Barone was a hardened hardcore gangster through and through. He was in his late seventies by that time, and over the course of decades he had killed countless numbers of men. He had been a loyal and committed mobster his entire life. Made men from his crime group, the Genovese, simply did not cooperate. Period.

Moreover, despite his own hard feelings toward the Genovese, law enforcement was always the undisputed enemy, never to be trusted, and Barone had spent many years in prison and kept his mouth shut. Distrust of law enforcement had been embedded in his DNA for decades. On top of that, we were the people responsible for his arrest earlier that same day. So even though his lawyer told him he should meet with us, every fiber in his body rebelled at the concept, which was apparent in the way he regarded us with a literal side eye. Barone was legally deaf, so we could hear as he and his lawyer bantered, with Barone angrily expressing, "Are you crazy? Why would I talk to *them*?" while his attorney worked to settle him with comments like, "Let's hear what they have to say. How can it hurt?"

Although the task was daunting, now that we had one foot in the literal door, we shared an optimistic outlook at our chances. I didn't plan to let this prime opportunity pass, to let Barone walk out the door without an agreement. We had no agreed-upon game plan to achieve this goal, instead relying on our respective honed instincts.

With his attorney's active assistance, we made friendly small talk with both of them, attempting to thaw Barone's inherent mistrust that had been built up over decades. Ironically, we needed to demonstrate to a career mafioso that we might actually be good guys and trustworthy. Not surprisingly, he remained on guard. One thing we had going for us off the bat was we did not seek his detention after arresting him, We agreed to a bail package while in court earlier in the day to permit Barone to remain at liberty pending his trial or plea. That seemed to carry some weight with him.

Another extremely helpful piece was that I was able to bond with Barone around small but significant things. I have always found that the best approach was to be genuine and to say what you mean. That gives a street guy, who lives by his ability to read people, the accurate sense that you're being authentic. For instance, Barone also happened to be a half-breed like me, as Barone was half Italian, and Hungarian with some Irish. I brought up the topic, and Barone mentioned he didn't even know he was part Italian until he was eight because his dad had abandoned the family. He grew up in an Irish community in the Chelsea section of Manhattan.

I laughed when Barone said eight and told him how I had moved towns, and that I had a similar experience when my own son was eight. As I picked my son up from his first practice with his in-town basketball team, I asked him about the team. He responded, "My coach can't read. He calls our team the Gunning Guineas." I asked what the team name was, and he held up the team shirt for the "Chicago Bulls." They were almost all Italian kids. My son didn't know he was Italian either because his grandfather proudly spoke about how he was American, and if America went to war against Italy, he was fighting for America. My father always teased how the Irish, such as my son's Nana, always talked about Ireland. With the Irish Americans, Ireland came first. Barone laughed hard and replied, "I want to see you again"—we just hit it off.

We joked a lot about our shared heritage. I said that George wasn't Italian, just a stubborn Irishman who could hold a grudge. Barone shook his head, agreeing as he laughed.

Anything to create a bond of conversation, of trust, was invaluable toward bridging the gap between our two worlds. This banter certainly played a critical role in Barone's ultimate decision to cross the void and become our witness.

But there was a long way to go before we reached that target. Moving past the small talk was almost like driving with the brakes on. Barone looked at us warily when we asked him to begin to transition to discussing criminal activity, as though we might have been setting a trap for him all along. He couldn't understand how that would possibly benefit him and was concerned we might be trying to trick him after all. On our side, it was simply not possible to evaluate our interest in working with him unless we could establish that he was at least willing to talk about his criminal past and to be truthful and forthright. I would never make an agreement with a liar because their information is worthless, and the last thing you ever want to do is put a liar on the witness stand. What was further explained was if we came to a cooperation agreement, and he testified, his criminal history would be presented by his direct testimony for the government at trial. It was important that we have these details rather than learn about them in a cross examination.

Barone's lawyer assisted our efforts, urging Barone to be open with us. The way meetings like this work, called proffer sessions, is that we couldn't use his statements to make further arrests or charges against him or others unless he ultimately signed up as a witness. That protects people in his shoes because they can be completely truthful without having to fear that law enforcement will double-cross them. This is a somewhat challenging intellectual concept, and it took a bit of time for Barone to get comfortable with the idea.

As we circled around with him, one of the questions Barone asked was, "Why should I trust you?"

I knew a lot about Barone's past, and I was confident that Barone had a long trail of dead bodies. Beyond explaining how a proffer session worked in response to Barone's question, Barone was asked to describe a murder he had committed, "How about the first one, who was it?"

"I'd have to be crazy to tell you that," was his initial response.

It was explained to Barone how a cooperating witness is required to provide information about his role in all criminal activity—and that this is how it works. The government cannot learn about crimes in a cross-examination. To Barone this was sheer insanity. Turning to his law-yer in a kind of "Can you believe these guys?" type of gesture, the attor-ney nodded his head and suggested that Barone just answer our question. Barone, who had a great sense of humor, looked at his lawyer and said, "I thought you represent *me*." We all laughed.

We briefly left the room to permit Barone and his lawyer to talk it over further before he decided whether to answer. When we reentered, Barone seemed to better appreciate the need to play by our rules if we were going to move forward. Hesitantly, he described in very broad strokes a murder in which he had participated decades before.

The floodgates of trust didn't open wide in that single instant, but it served to loosen Barone up a bit. He seemed amused and began taking small steps. We ended up meeting for a few days, largely consisting of Barone and me discussing details of his criminal past. The details included numerous murders and ILA corruption. At the conclusion, we all had an excellent rapport and Barone agreed to become a cooperating witness.

This was momentous. Other mafia families had numerous cooperators in positions of power, but the Genovese stood completely apart. Barone became the first made Genovese to fully cooperate since Joe Valachi in the early 1960s.[22] There was now a big crack in their wall. As Barone testified at trial years later: "I wanted to get even. I wanted to survive. I didn't want to get killed by them. I decided that the Mafia is not the paternal, wonderful organization that it proposes to be. The esprit de corps does not exist. *Greed, violence, betrayal: that is what exists.*"

In the end, in all likelihood, the most compelling factor for Barone's decision was just as he put it on the witness stand—the betrayal, ingrati-tude, and treachery of his own crime family. This, all originating from a modest amount of money owed by a multimillionaire associate to a made member of the Genovese family. A clear example of how the crime family *did not* come before the blood family.

---

22 As noted above, Vincent "Fish" Cafaro became a cooperating witness but was not usable in many critically important cases (such as against Ida and against the Chin) because his claimed inability to recall certain events and people left a lot to be desired, to put it very mildly.

Barone elected not to enter witness protection because he was confident in the quality of protection his Cuban friends could provide. At one trial this topic came up and he testified that the mob had "been trying to kill me for years now. They haven't made it yet and they're not going to."

Just as D'Urso's cooperation opened the door to others' cooperation, such as Barone, Tarangelo, and a former attorney and New York State Trooper, David Grossman, so did Barone's cooperation lead to additional arrests, convictions, and cooperation. Other Genovese made men now had a model to consider the question, "Why shouldn't I do the same? George Barone, a historic, loyal, and old-time Genovese soldier did." Barone's cooperation, in combination with the collective stunned reaction to D'Urso's multi-year infiltration, really broke the impenetrable Genovese dam. A precedent had finally been set, making the inconceivable suddenly possible. Later on, two Genovese capos cooperated—the first Genovese ever to cooperate at such a high ranking.

Not only was Barone's cooperation historic for the above reasons, but it also led to more convictions and provided an invaluable store of knowledge about this highly secretive criminal gang.

Barone's lawyer allegedly committed suicide in 2007. This death happened three months after I retired from the FBI. I and many others highly suspect that his death was not by suicide, believing that he may have instead been killed because of the pivotal role he played in Barone's cooperation. It reminded me of a recording D'Urso made with Tommy Cafaro and Patty Falcetti about a historic New Jersey gangster, Long Zwillman. Longy was a powerful Genovese associate similar to Meyer Lansky. Zwillman was believed to have committed suicide in his West Orange home. Falcetti cited how, "We killed him" ("we" meaning the Genovese family). Cafaro replied that Longy committed suicide because he was depressed. Falcetti's hilarious response, "Let me tell you something. If I'M depressed, I am going to kill a whole bunch of people before I kill myself." If Barone's lawyer was in fact killed, it was because he did his job ethically, the way society expects, and as he was supposed to do.

Other Fallout

mafiosi from all five crime families had been arrested, and the entire organized crime ecosystem was deeply shaken. The fact that as trusted a gangster as D'Urso had flipped, fooled, and recorded the secretive Genovese and all other crime families for years shattered their foundation, sent shock waves down their spines, and created huge mental stress. They knew about all of the criminal conversations and schemes they had with D'Urso, including their violations of omertà. They also knew the multitude of secrets they shared with him, often instructing him not to tell anyone because it may jeopardize their life. Exploring potential cooperation is a common process during FBI organized crime arrests. As you've read throughout this book, those who do not want to be exposed as cooperating witnesses willing to testify frequently provide information as informants.

CHAPTER TWELVE

DOG EAT DOG? . . . "DOG KILL DOG."

"I'm here to tell the story of the ungratefulness of all the bums that I put in jobs that turned against me."
—George Barone

My relationship with George Barone involved his understanding of how critically important it was for him to be truthful. I knew George wanted revenge on the gangsters who mistreated him. After our first meeting, I described how it is never too late to change one's life and do some good. George, who was a crusty blunt person cited how, "We both know where I'm going Mike once I die." As he said this, he smiled and gestured down to hell.

He confirmed being baptized as a Catholic, whereby I cited the penitent also known as the "good thief." There were two men crucified at the same time with Jesus. I reminded him how this thief was rewarded by Jesus. He was familiar with this Bible story and raised his eyes, smiled and said, "You know, you may be right. Maybe there is some time left to do some good." He was a fearless gangster who provided an abundance of information about the murders he committed and the historic corruption of the International Longshoremen's Association (ILA) by the LCN.

George was born in Brooklyn on December 16, 1923. Shortly there-after, he and his family moved to the west side of Manhattan known as the Chelsea section. He spent two years in high school before he decided to discontinued this and began to work. He joined the Navy and served approximately four years during World War II. During that time, he par-ticpated in five invasions that included Iwo Jima, Saipan, and Guam, where he received medals for his role.

After the Navy, George returned to New York and subsequently became involved in working at the ports on the west side with the ILA. During this period around 1953–1954, he became friends with Johnny Earle who was described as the toughest man he ever met. Earle was frequently in and out of prison and known as the youngest criminal in New York state to be charged as an adult.

Redmond Cribbens, a.k.a. "Ninny," was killed by George and Johnny Earle in approximately 1955. Ninny was Irish and a member of a gang that robbed approximately $650,000 from a bank. Earle learned the details of the robbery and where Ninny was hiding. Ninny wasn't home when he and Earle broke in and located the $650,000 in a large suitcase at this location. Both George and Earle waited until Ninny arrived home to kill him. Ninny arrived and stepped into the room. George pushed him into a chair, where he was shot numerous times. They placed Ninny's body into the trunk of a car and drove it to a parking lot of a supermarket located in the area. Earle had arranged for another individual to pick up the car and take it to another location. The purpose was to give Ninny's other gang members the impression he took the money for himself and ran off with it. The $650,000 that they took from Ninny was used to start his West Side gang known as the Jets.

During this same time frame, George Scalise, another member of the Genovese family who was previously in prison with Earle, told Earle that Vito Genovese wanted to meet George and Earle to ask for a favor.

They were directed to meet Genovese at an export packing com-pany located on Thompson Street in the Greenwich Village section of Manhattan. George accompanied Earle to the meeting that happened in the doorway of this business. Also present for this meeting was Tommy Eboli, a.k.a. Tommy Ryan, and Vincent Gigante, a.k.a. Chin. Upon arriving for this meeting, Earle was greeted with a big hug from Gigante. Earle and Gigante were previously inmates in prison together and became friends.

Vito Genovese explained how Scalise spoke very favorably about them and how Earle could help Genovese's company with the ILA unions at the piers. Genovese wanted a union contract for his company but also wanted to hire his own people as employees. Earle agreed to help Genovese with this request and allowed him to use his own people that included non-union workers.

Genovese developed a strong friendship with both Earle and George, and they were introduced to numerous members of the Genovese family to include all of the capos.

George subsequently became an ILA official and very involved as a union organizer for Captain William Bradley, the president of the ILA. Earle was a friend of Bradley's and introduced George to him. During this same time frame, the McLoughlin brothers came down from Boston and met with Earle. These brothers wanted Earle's gang to take over the gambling in Boston. The McLaughlins were friends with Henry "Buster" Bell and descibed the potential money that could be made with this operation. Earle had the gang go up to Massachusetts and grab numerous bookmakers persuading them to become partners with Earle's gang. This persuasion came through threats, intimidation, and violence. One of the bookmakers was Jerry Anguilo. According to Barone, at that time, Anguilo was an associate of the Genovese family under Jimmy "Blue Eyes" Alo. Jimmy Blue Eyes was a historic member of the Genovese family and wanted Earle to leave Anguilo's gambling operation alone. This dispute was ultimately resolved by Vito Genovese. Genovese refused this request and sided with Earle. This operation went on for about fourteen months before Earle's gang decided to discontinue it.

Shortly after this, there was turmoil in New York involving Vito Genovese, Frank Costello, and Albert Anastasia. Anastasia and Costello were conspiring to kill Vito Genovese. One of the primary circumstances that prompted this murder conspiracy was the gambling money generated in Las Vegas. George described how Anastasia, Costello, and Genovese were feuding over this money. In addition, Vito did not care for the relationship between Frank Costello and Albert Anastasia that developed while Vito was a fugitive hiding in Italy. During this period of time, Costello was the acting boss.

Anastasia and Costello met with Michael Miranda, the consigliere of the Genovese family, to obtain his consent to kill Vito and replace him as boss with Costello. Miranda had a close relationship with Anastasia and gave him the impression that he would consider this and circle back to them in the next few days. Miranda was also close with Vito Genovese and warned him about this plan to murder him. Genovese told Earle and Barone about Costello and Anastasia's plan to murder him. As part of the effort to corroborate Miranda's meeting with Costello and Anastasia, which happened at a Brooklyn restaurant, Miranda identified John "Sonny" Franzese as someone present who observed this meeting. Franzese corroborated the meeting and Vito directed Chin Gigante to kill Costello.

As discussed earlier in this book and historically, Chin shot Costello as he returned home late at night on May 2, 1957. Costello survived this shooting. Costello confirmed Miranda's meeting and his intent to coordinate Genovese's murder with Anastasia. He would deceive Anastasia that his shooting was not related to their conspiracy to kill Vito. Anastasia was subsequently killed on October 2, 1957. A couple weeks later, November 14, 1957, the infamous Apalachin meeting occurs to formally address Anastasia's murder based on his violation of the commission rules. In addition to this topic, Carlo Gambino becomes the official boss of this Cosa Nostra family now known as the Gambino family.

Earle was shot on June 18, 1958, while in a cafeteria located at 57th Street and 8th Avenue in Manhattan. His murder was planned by the members of his gang with the exception of Eddie Crowe, Mickey Ross, and George. After Earle is killed, Vito Genovese sends word that he doesn't want to be involved with the gang anymore. Genovese was very fond of Earle.

When Earle was killed, George was working for the ILA and at the piers servicing a complaint.

George anticipated someone else from the LCN trying to control him and the union in the future. He already knew and liked Fat Tony Salerno and wanted to align himself with someone he liked. Salerno and George subsequently became good friends. During this period, Benny Squint Lombardo was the capo of the Harlem crew. Salerno was part of this crew and subsequently became the capo when Benny Squint was promoted to Genovese boss. In the capacity as an associate of Fat Tony Salerno, George committed a number of murders.

On March 17, 1967, George killed an infamous Genovese gangster Johnny "Futto" Biello, in Miami, Florida. Biello was a historic gangster with the Genovese family going back decades in New York to Lucky Luciano days. George stated "Futto had a dance club on 79th Street in Miami . . . named Candystripe or something like that." He described the infamous club and its popularity with the famous dance known as the twist. Futto and Fat Tony didn't get along and they had a recent dispute. George knows Futto's routine to frequent "a jewelry store at 79th Street and the causeway every day." Futto parked in the back. George wore a black T-shirt and wool ski cap for this murder. He also placed cotton in his mouth to alter his appearance as he sat under a tree. As Futto walked out and approached his car, he walked up to him and shot him multiple times. This gun had a silencer. He then walked around the corner and was picked up by Louie Rotunda.

Another Barone murder involved a black male in Covington, Kentucky who was interfering with a Genovese gambling operation. This was on or about 1975/1976. A Genovese associate, nicknamed Screw, originally from New York, operated the Genovese-controlled illegal numbers business in Covington, Kentucky. George flew out and stayed at Screw's residence for this murder. He was introduced to the black male under the guise that he was there to fix horse races that they could make money betting. George subsequently left with the black male in a vehicle to discuss this scheme. George asked the man to pull over to discuss the race-fixing scheme. He shot the black male in the chest to stun him and then shot him multiple times in the head leaving him in the vehicle parked on a curb. After killing this individual, he met with Screw to drive him to the airport. This murder preceded George's induction. Fat Tony appreciated George's role in conducting murders. It was his role in the murders and friendship with Salerno that justified Fat Tony poposing him for induction. George cited how he really didn't care about whether he was inducted or not inducted.

George's induction happened in about 1969, during the period when Benny Squint was the official boss of the Genovese family and Frank "Funzi" Tieri was the "decoy" boss. Eli Zeccardi conducted the induction ceremony because Funzi couldn't remember the process. This induction happened in an apartment located in the vicinity of 116th Street in the East Harlem section of New York.

George described how only one other person was inducted into the LCN at that time who wasn't a full-blooded Italian. This individual was identified as Joe Massi, who was based in Detroit. Each induction was done individually. Funzi identified himself as the decoy boss at this ceremony explaining how Benny Squint is the "real boss." Funzi started the induction with the question, "Do you know why you're here?" George responded, "No." There was a gun and dagger on the table with Funzi forgetting to mention them. Eli Zeccardi reminded Funzi to prick his finger, which did not occur. There was also no burning of the saint.

After the inductions, they attended a breakfast with about fifty to sixty others from the Genovese family who were all part of the Harlem crew.

At first appearance, if you interacted with George in public, you would consider him a nice old pleasant man with a sense of humor. I once picked him up from a train station in Trenton, New Jersey and watched as he politely allowed a woman access to a concession stand before him. She obviously viewed him as a kind old man. However, knowing the details of his treacherous life, the total opposite is the reality. A classic response by George during one of his depositions in describing his life and the violence on the west side involved the question posed, "Was it as dog eat dog?" with George's cold response "Dog kill dog." George once described how he left the West Side and joined the Navy to get away from the neighborhood's violence. This was during World War II.

George Barone played a critical role in the Genovese family's control of the ILA as it transitioned from the manual loading of ships to the containerization process. The Genovese family was able to facilitate control of the ILA executive board through rigged elections. Below is a portion of George Barone's details of his historic role in this criminal process:

In the early 1950s, the ILA, Local 1804 was based in New York City. The members of this local worked in the capacity as maintenance for the ships. Henry "Buster" Bell was the president of Local 1804, and Harry Cashin was the secretary-treasurer. In approximately 1957, Barone became an international organizer for the ILA. Harry Cashin died and his son, Jimmy Cashin, replaced Harry as the secretary-treasurer. Jimmy Cashin was like a younger brother to Barone. Patrick Connelly, also known as "Packy," was a very close friend of Barone's family. Packy was also the international executive vice president for the ILA. Packy was the brightest individual Barone ever met in the ILA and a mentor to Baronem teaching him about the unions.

Packy predicted how the shipping industry was going to dramatically change as a result of containerization. This change would require thousands of mechanics. Containerization was the new process to load products into containers on land and then hoist the containers onto ships. This would significantly reduce man-hours and be a much more cost-effective method for the shipping industry. Packy knew mechanics would be needed to make repairs to the containers and equipment utilized in this process. Packy also knew there would be a significant reduction in the need for longshoremen when containerization was fully implemented by the shipping industry.

Local 1804 previously consisted of members who would clean, paint, and do other maintenance related work. Local 1804–1 became the local for the mechanics who worked in the shipping industry. As a result of this new role, the ILA requested local 1804 issue another charter for Local 1804–1. It was Barone who went to the International to request the paperwork for this new charter. Packy told Barone to stay with Local 1804–1 because Local 1804 would play a diminished role with the ILA.

Barone became the vice president for Local 1804–1 with Henry "Buster" Bell the president. Jimmy Cashin was the secretary-treasurer and the charter for this local was obtained from Captain William Bradley. Sealand was the first company that implemented containerization. Local 1804–1 became one of the most important locals in the ILA.

Barone succeeded Bell as the international vice president for the ILA. He maintained a close favorable relationship with Anthony "Fat Tony" Salerno, a future member of the Genovese family's administration.

The Metropolitan Marine Maintenance Contractors Association, referred to as METRO by George Barrone, was an employers' association that consisted of the companies that handled the maintenance of the ships. METRO entered into a labor relations agreement with Local 1804–1 and Local 1277. Local 1277 was represented by Joe Colazzo and Anthony Anastasio, who were with the Gambino family. Prior to containerization, the METRO association consisted of maintenance men. It now transitioned to an association that predominantly dealt with mechanics.

Having the mechanics companies join the METRO association was very important because Barone controlled METRO. Barone was responsible for placing numerous people at METRO. D'Urso made numerous recordings with Tommy Cafaro and Patty Falcetti about Barone's historic power in the ILA and providing them roles in this corrupt operation.

METRO was jointly controlled by both the Genovese and Gambino families. Barone represented the Genovese family interests while Anthony Scotto represented the Gambino family and Brooklyn-based interests. Anthony Scotto was a capo in the Gambino family and the son-in-law of Anthony Anastasio, Albert Anastasia's brother.

Barone was involved in organizing every major container leasing company's contract with the ILA. The piers in New Jersey grew over the years as a result of the abundant land that they had to store containers. These piers were located in Port Newark, Elizabeth, Bayonne/Jersey City. The Gambino family Brooklyn piers union membership diminished in size. Barone noted that 90 percent of the work in the New York metroplitan area is handled at the New Jersey piers.

Barone became extremely active with the ILA organizing various locals all over the country. He traveled to Houston, Miami, North Carolina, and numerous other locations to organize locals to address containerization. It became evident that Local 1804–1 was a very important local. Vincent "Chin" Gigante and Bobby Manna (future Genovese boss and consigliere) began to pay close attention to this local. Gigante was a capo at the time, with Manna, his acting capo. Philip Lombardo, a.k.a. "Benny Squint," was the boss of the Genovese family with Eli Zeccardi the underboss and Thomas "Tommy Ryan" Eboli the consigliere. Benny Squint, prior to becoming a Genovese boss, was the capo of the powerful Harlem crew for the Genovese family.

One of the meetings cited by Barone involved Vincent "Chin" Gigante asking Barone to stop leaning so hard on Umberto Guido, a.k.a. Bert Guido. Bert Guido was a cousin of Albert "Kid Blast" Gallo, who was in Chin's crew. Kid Blast was Crazy Joe Gallo's brother. He was released by the Colombo family to the Genovese family after Joe Gallo's murder. Guido became extremely wealthy as a result of ILA business facilitated by Barone and the Genovese family. Chin expressed his love for Barone and wanted Barone to make it appear as though Chin's son Andrew Gigante, looked good to Guido. Chin would greatly appreciate any assistance Barone could provide to strengthen the relationship between Guido and Andrew. Barone agreed to comply with Chin's request.

This was during the same time frame that Chin was not getting along with Fat Tony Salerno. Benny "Squint" Lombardo was the boss and attempted to have Salerno step down as underboss after having a stroke. Benny Squint supported Chin in the dispute with Fat Tony, instructing Fat Tony to stay at his upstate farm. Benny Squint subsequently died and Chin became boss while Fat Tony became the decoy boss.

Barone subsequently went to prison, and when he was released years later, in 1990, he had no idea what his role was with the Genovese family. Barone had facilitated the ILA influence at the Florida piers with significant support from the Cuban membership.

Tommy Cafaro eventually contacted him to arrange a meeting with Barney Bellomo, the current acting boss for the Genovese family. Bellomo took an active interest in the ILA business at the piers. Bellomo would travel to Florida every few weeks to discuss Bellomo's plan concerning the piers and ILA. One of the first requests Bellomo made was to provide Anthony Schettino, a.k.a. "Rocky," with a position at the piers. Barone provided Schettino with a position as a planning clerk at the Sealand Shipping Company in Florida. Schettino received approximately $160,000 salary in this position the prior year. This reminded me of the recording D'Urso made with Tommy Cafro who cited how Barone was not helping them any more with providing jobs at the Florida piers. Cafaro described how they would receive about $25,000 a year from the guys they placed in employment at $150,000 a year.

Bellomo went to prison on my Ida investigation in 1996. While Bellomo was in prison, Cafaro always told Barone how he would regularly travel to New York to meet with Chuckie Tuzzo, Ernie Muscarella, Patty Faletti, and Andrew Gigante.

There came a point in time when Andrew Gigante and Bert Guido wanted to obtain a contract with Maersk involving the container repair work in Florida. Andrew began to travel to Florida to meet with Barone and reacquant himself in order to secure this contract. Andrew attempted to ensure they won't have any labor problems with the local union. During a meeting, Barone asked Andrew to assist him with collecting a modest debt of approximately $70,000 owed to Barone by Guido. The debt was owed prior to when Barone went to prison. Guido was a multimillionaire who had benefited greatly due to Barone's assistance at the piers.

Gigante learned that Tommy Cafaro, Joe Perez, and Salvatore Catucci were also bidding on this Maersk contract. Tommy Cafaro was Andrew's best man at his wedding. Andrew Gigante was livid with Cafaro after learning this. Barone agreed to help Andrew secure this contract under the condition Andrew obtains the money owed to him by Guido. Barone cited how both groups, Gigante and Cafaro, paid bribes to the individual at Maersk making the decision.

Guido and Gigante's company began work in Florida for Maersk. This company made about $400,000 during less than a year, and Barone still had not received any money from Gigante concerning Guido's debt. Barone requested Gigante come and meet with him in Florida. Two months passed without Gigante responding to the request. Barone decided to cause problems for their company with this Maersk contract. Subsequent to causing these labor problems, Guido scheduled a meeting with Barone in Florida. While in the restaurant bathroom, Guido attempted to provide Barone with $3,000 and cited how Gigante wanted him to have this money. This was supposed to be a Christmas gift for assisting with the labor peace. Barone became angry and told Guido to take the money back and tell Andrew Gigante to stick it up his ass.

The labor problems continued with Gigante and Guido's company. A few months later, Andrew Gigante traveled to Florida and met with Barone. This involved another heated argument because Gigante refused to assist Barone with getting his money owed to him from Guido. Andrew refused because Guido was an associate under his control. He believed he didn't have to pay this debt because Chin Gigante was his father and the boss of the Genovese family. Additional hypocrisy knowing how Barone placed Andrew with Guido as a favor to Chin. Chin was not the boss at that time. Barone was a member of the Genovese family while Andrew Gigante was not a made member but the son of the boss. It appears with the Gigante family, blood family came before the crime family.

Shortly thereafter, Ernie Muscarella and Patty Falcetti traveled to Florida and met with Barone. Muscarella questioned Barone's behavior with Andrew Gigante and why have such an abusive argument. Muscarella also explained to Barone that he was shelved and not to have anything to do with the ILA. He was prohibited from seeing Harold Daggett, Jimmy Cashin, or John Bowers, and he wasn't to have any contact with Local 1804–1.

Barone explained to Muscarella how Andrew Gigante agreed to help obtain the money owed to him by Guido if Barone assisted with labor peace with the Maersk contract. Barone reminded Muscarella that he asked him on three separate occasions to help Barone obtain this money from Guido. Muscarella was embarrassed by having to reprimand Barone. He knew Barone was friends with his father. Barone also noted that Muscarella, as his superior, his capo, should have represented Barone in this dispute. Barone also questioned Falcetti's loyalty. Barone was the person who provided Falcetti with his first job at the piers, and all of them were members from the same Harlem crew.

Barone told them he was prepared to go to war with the Genovese family and had 2,000 Cubans who would support him in this war. After hearing this, Muscarella asked who the four individuals were who accompanied Barone to the meeting. Barone explained the Cubans were there for his protection. They were strategically placed in close proximity to Barone for his safety. This dispute was not resolved, and Barone continued to cause labor issues.

Falcetti returned to Florida after a few months to request Barone's help. This assistance was in getting Harold Daggett the position as general organizer for the ILA. The plan was to get Daggett on the executive board and replace John Bowers with Daggett, who was controlled by Falcetti and the

Genovese family. Barone explained how John Bowers's father was Micky Bowers, a Westside ganglord over a very powerful gang. Micky and his gang had a very close relationship with Jerry Catena. Catena was the boss of the Genovese family who succeeded Vito Genovese.

Once Daggett was on the executive board, Barone would be asked to have Bowers retire. Bowers would retire in a non-convention year. During a convention year, the election would be open to the full membership of the ILA. The Genovese family may not be able to control this large an election. In an off year, when a president can't complete his term, his replacement must be a member of the executive board. Only the members of an executive board can vote for the next president. Barone further cited the executive board was already controlled by the LCN, primarily the Genovese family. Barone helped Falcetti with this process. A few months later, Falcetti traveled to Florida and met with Barone to provide him with $45,000 in cash. Falcetti told Barone he would be back in March with the remainder of the money owed by Guido.

D'Urso was recording his conversations with Falcetti and Cafaro during this meeting and the months that precede this payment. D'Urso was actually sitting as a passenger in Falcetti's vehicle as Falcetti left the vehicle to walk over and pay Barone this money. I was taking photos of the transaction as it occured. D'Urso was able to see Barone. Barone was sitting in another vehicle with a Cuban associate for security protection. These recorded conversations by D'Urso describe the turmoil Barone was causing for Andrew Gigante and how they ultimately decided Barone had to be killed. Falcetti actually met with D'Urso to have him kill Barone. Barone knew he was to be killed if he came to New York.

George was such a unique, bright, and blunt cooperating witness who was authentic in his testimony. He was a loyal member of the Genovese family until they violated their oath of allegiance, screwing him out of a modest amount of money owed to him. His testimony included statements related to why he was cooperating. Barone cited: "My mission is to tell the corrupt story of all those years I did their bidding, all those years I was a very faithful mafia soldier. . . . I want everyone to know what went on in the ILA. . . . I'm here to tell the story of the ungratefulness of all the bums that I put in jobs that turned against me."

CHAPTER THIRTEEN

CONCLUSIVELY ENDING THE CHIN'S ACT / SEPTEMBER 11

"A plane went through the Pentagon . . . and two planes in the Trade Center."

The year after I had convicted Ida, Bellomo, and Generoso in my first Genovese takedown in 1996, the Chin had been finally brought to justice and convicted in a separate case. Gigante faced sentencing of twenty-five years but was able to whittle that down to twelve and a half years based on the testimony of well-credentialed psychiatrists who swore in court that although Gigante may have faked or exaggerated mental illness in the past, by the time he faced sentencing his mental capacities ironically actually had deteriorated in fact. They supported this testimony with a battery of tests and medical brain scans purportedly proving their point. Because he had been sentenced to twelve and a half years, Chin would be out in ten based on how federal sentences are calculated.

Yet while D'Urso was taping the mobsters in later years, he had made many incriminating tapes that established this beyond a doubt that Chin was still running the Genovese and firmly in control. The evidence included statements by highly placed figures who certainly were in a position to know: Chin remained the foundation of power for the Genovese. For example, capo Falcetti told D'Urso, while touching his own chin, "Whatever the kid says [Chin's son Andrew, who visited Chin in prison], it comes from him [Chin]. Who's going to challenge that?" Likewise, D'Urso recorded capo Longo saying, "Vito (Genovese) ain't here no more. Vincent is." And soldier Geraci was recorded saying that although Farby Serpico was "still there, he ain't the guy." Pointing to his own chin, Geraci concluded, "This guy is the guy. Don't say nothing."

Acting capo Aparo further explained that Gigante "still sends messages [from prison] . . . how he gets them and how he sends them, I don't know." This was a critical point, because when it came to violence, "You're always doing it for the boss. No matter who you are killing, it's from the boss." Also, confirming our long-held conviction that some of Gigante's doctors were corrupt, Aparo stated that Dr. Wechsler—who often visited Gigante in prison—might be the one passing messages. "He's a good guy, the doctor. So I don't know if he gives a message. He's got this doctor for years and years and years. So actually, he can trust him."

I came up with the idea of obtaining Chin's recorded prison conversations along with videos of his prison visits. When he was a free man, Gigante studiously avoided using phones, and had been recorded basically mumbling and whistling on the rare occasions that he did. But now that he had been locked up for years, I considered whether Gigante perhaps finally let his guard down, figuring the feds would have no interest in him since he was simply serving out his sentence. Maybe Chin used the phones to contact family and others? Maybe we would find some nugget? Maybe he risked issuing some orders over the phone?

I obtained six months of tapes from Chin's Texas prison calls, which was the maximum period of time such tapes were retained by the prison system. I asked Tommy Krall to travel to Texas, recover this evidence and see where it led us. Tommy enjoyed the trip and there witnessed, firsthand, the boss conduct himself as a completely normal person. The one thing he learned that Chin still held on to indicate he was "crazy," though, was to end his conversations with anyone within listening distance, "Pray I don't hear those voices tonight as I sleep." Tommy, me and others joked that another word for this is "dreaming."

What we found was a virtual and stunning gold mine. Chin had indeed, for the first time ever, completely let down his guard. The prison tapes contained half a year of recordings that captured him speaking like a regular person—perfectly coherently and normally. Moreover, this raised the question: How was Gigante even making these calls? Remember, he was supposed to have the intellect of a damaged caterpillar, incapable of understanding what a phone even was and liable to smash it into the wall. Every prisoner is allocated a certain number of outside calls. Just to even make those calls, a prisoner had to memorize a series of numbers to gain access to an outside line, and then had to dial the number he wanted to reach. The act of doing this alone would be way beyond the capacity of someone with such purported limited capacities as Chin, according to all of the credentialed psychiatric "experts."

In addition, we obtained video recordings of Chin's prison visits. Forget the feeble man from his trial five years before, needing both a wheelchair and a cane and mumbling to himself incoherently. Now Gigante assumed a commanding presence, walking around in dominant fashion with pointed instructions to his captive visitors.

All of this was the breakthrough news. But there was sobering news as well. He was canny enough to still maintain his guard to some degree. In none of the taped recordings did Chin discuss anything remotely of a criminal nature. Those conversations were reserved for his prison visits, as Falcetti and Aparo made clear. So in essence, Gigante dumped his crazy act while on the phone but maintained his ingrained mobster's cautious and wily ways.

We now had fantastic evidence to definitively establish that Gigante was perfectly sane. We could prove by commonsense inference that he had always been this way, that he didn't magically have a full recovery, and that his multi-decade act was a farce. But was there a criminal legal theory to fit this evidence, a crime to charge? Or was this merely a moral victory—confirmation that, as we knew, law enforcement had been right all along? Chin was eligible to be released from prison as early as 2007. Could we use this new evidence to extend his sentence and delay or prevent his reentry?

We decided to charge him with obstruction of justice. The idea being that by *faking* insanity, Gigante had—for decades—avoided and therefore obstructed the effort to bring him to justice. Obstruction of justice *is* a federal crime.

The tape recordings with Chin speaking in his own voice were priceless evidence. For the very first and only time he had no way around his own words, and no way to refute it. His lawyers couldn't argue that the speaker was a lying sociopath who would say anything to reduce his sentence, because it was Gigante himself who was speaking. So why did he take this risk? Probably a combination of two considerations had led him to speak so freely. First, ironically—*to preserve his sanity*—Chin needed to speak with those who were dear to him. He was in Texas and he was locked up for a long time. He still had two families, a wife in New Jersey and a paramour in New York City, with multiple children between them. These were the people who mattered to him and who he needed to speak with, and on the phone was the only way to do so with any regularity.[23]

Second, Chin likely figured the feds were done with him and had moved on. On this point, he was absolutely correct, all subsequent speculating news accounts and reporting to the contrary. Until I suggested it, nobody ever bothered to obtain the tapes of his prison phone calls—or even thought of it. And Chin would have remained absolutely correct, had D'Urso's tapes not kept pointing back to Gigante as still being in active charge. It was only for this reason that we determined to refocus efforts on Chin. It may also have been that Gigante didn't consider that speaking on the phone about normal everyday topics might constitute evidence of the crime of obstruction of justice.

September 11

One of Chin's most remarkable calls of all followed the horror of the September 11 attack on America. But before revealing for the first time what he said on that tragic day, let me tell you about what happened with me on that day.

---

23 It may be that with our limited six-month sample we didn't know the full extent of who he reached out to, but all of the calls we listened to were placed to his New York City family, not to the one based in New Jersey.

I was in a hotel in Miami waiting to meet with Barone since he had secretly begun to cooperate, and watched the news as the second plane flew into the towers. Jimmy Cashin with the ILA was supposed to fly to Florida to meet with Barone, but I realized he would not make that flight. In fact, his plane was ordered down. I sent Barone back and thought of how many of my friends working in downtown New York City may have died, learning later that many of them had. I immediately called my wife, who worked at a pharmaceutical company located near Newark International Airport and some sensitive buildings. At the time, we did not know if there were other terrorists controlling other planes. All planes had been ordered to land. I told my wife to leave work and pick up our children from school. She said her company hadn't made any announcement. I explained how at risk she was due to the location of her business and told her, "You don't need to wait for someone to authorize this evacuation. Leave *now* and get our children home."

On television, I also saw FBI agent Gary Pontecorvo, a good agent who investigated the Colombo family, running as the Trade Center fell. He clearly had moved directly into the line of fire and was there to assist with the evacuation process. Thank goodness Gary was not killed. This was a very difficult time for me.

In Florida, I previously had a horrendous encounter with the clueless FBI head of their Miami Organized Crime squad, who had ordered me to pack my bags and leave Florida. That, combined with the terrorist attacks, made me so furious that I thought about leaving to work terrorism.

I also called my supervisor, who told me, Kingsley, our ASAC, didn't want me to return. My supervisor suggested I go to San Juan and enjoy. "You're lucky you're there." He didn't have a clue. I couldn't help but think how messed up this all was—I wasn't going to use the terror attack on our country as an excuse to take a beach vacation. I ended up driving my rental car with NYPD Detective Bobby Vossler straight to the New York City command post on the West Side Highway.

I learned shortly thereafter how Agent Lenny Hatton, with the Bank Robbery Squad, responded to the Towers to assist with the evacuation. Lenny was a former Marine, bomb technician, and a volunteer firefighter. He was clearly a man of great courage who that day demonstrated his compassion and bravery with his remarkable response. He perished after evacuating some and reentering the towers to assist with additional evacuations of others. The FBI street agents and NYPD detectives who knew Lenny were so proud of his bravery on that day, and we will never forget him.

Gigante: Chin had his own reaction to the attacks. Imprisoned and isolated in Texas at the time, he nevertheless quickly learned what had occurred. His New York City–based family, though, living just a few miles from where the Twin Towers burned, were clueless. Less than an hour after the attacks, Gigante had them on the phone. He called them, and not his New Jersey–based family, because that's where the planes had crashed. They were the ones he needed to make sure were safe.

I believe that the exchange which follows has never before been publicly revealed.

Chin: What's happening over there?
Vince Esposito (one of his sons): Nothing, Dad, what's a matter?
Chin: Everybody says there, there's plane crashes over there.
VE: Plane crashes?
Chin: In New York.
VE: I don't know.
Chin: The Trade Center, Washington D.C., all over they say.
VE: Plane crashed?
Chin: They, the, the terrorists they said.
VE: I don't know, Dad. I don't know nothing.
Olympia Esposito (Chin's paramour): We didn't hear anything yet, hun.
Chin: What?
OE: I didn't hear anything.
Chin: You alright?
OE: Yeah, sure.
Chin: That's what I'm worried about. They just come and tell me that it crashed in the penta, in, in, I don't know, Washington D.C. They went, a plane went through the Pentagon.

VE: I don't know.

OE: Really?

Chin: And, and two planes in, in, in downtown, what is that, the Trade Center.

VE: Yeah, I don't know.

Chin: Put the news on. See what's going on.

Standing entirely by itself—*this call, alone*—proved the criminal obstruction charge against Gigante.

More specifically, it exposed Chin's act as a fraud that was perpetrated over many decades. To make the call, Chin needed to, among other things: (1) know the complex series of numbers to dial an outside line; (2) know to call his New York family as opposed to his New Jersey family—or a complete and random stranger; (3) be able to speak beyond a mumble; (4) string together a series of logical and coherent sentences; (5) accurately remember what he had been told; (6) accurately convey it; (7) understand what a plane was and what it meant to crash; (8) know that New York and Washington DC had been hit; (9) know about the World Trade Center; (10) know about the Pentagon; (11) know two planes crashed at the Trade Center; (12) know that this was cause for real concern; (13) warn his family about possible danger; (14) alert them to turn on the television; (15) know that they should watch something called "the news" to get more information; (16) appreciate and understand the import of the topic; and (17) his family members talked to him as someone who was completely lucid. And Chin knew all about this *immediately* after the attacks—all the way from *Texas*—before his New York City–based family even knew anything had happened. This call also likely illustrated that Chin's blood family was more important to him than his criminal family. He didn't call any of them (although he never called them from prison). That was one positive takeaway from this hypocritical life.

Obviously, this call took place on September 11, 2001. However, psychiatrists swore—as far back as *thirty years before*—Chin was already *insane, psychotic, and schizophrenic, a candidate for electroshock and with an IQ of 55.* Two years later, they swore he had somehow seriously *deteriorated* from that condition. In the 1980s, intercepted calls from his Upper

East Side mansion recorded him whistling and grunting on the phone, apparently unable to speak even a single sentence (Chin assumed the FBI was listening, as they were). In 1989, assuming it was even possible to do so, his doctors swore that he had *deteriorated even further*. Was he then a complete vegetable? Then, to avoid trial, in 1996 they represented that he had *continued to go steadily downhill in the intervening period of time*. It is not even possible for the human mind to conjure the wreckage of the shell of a human being that would remain.

In sum, over the years he was diagnosed as insane, psychotic, retarded, schizophrenic, suffering from organic brain disease, demented, practically mute, an electroshock candidate, infantile and delusional. All of these diseases were degenerative and irreversible. Yet here Chin was, miraculously crisply and clearly alert, immediately warning his family about the devastating September 11 attacks. [24]

But there were *six months* of daily calls like this. Chin conversed about every day, mundane, boring, regular topics that everyone talks about, albeit he did so from the perspective of an inmate:

Chin: They didn't give me turkey legs. In fact, they gave me a sliced ham. I gave it away. Somebody wanted me to eat the turkey leg. I tasted the turkey leg. It was salty . . . I gave it away. I had the rice and, and, ah, and Jello.
OE: That's all?
Chin: And a little salad. And tonight, I ate again. I had a little tuna, a little tuna fish salad and egg salad. And ah, what else. Oh, I had a watermelon.
OE: Oh, yeah.
Chin: Yeah. They gave us a watermelon. It was nice. The watermelon was good.

---

24 Gigante's daughter has referenced this call as the one that did him in: "9/11 happened. And he picked up the phone and he thought God forbid something happened to one of us. And he called and he spoke like, normal. Like nothing. *And that's all they needed.*" Mike and Tommy had obtained half a year of continuous and perfectly lucid conversation. So although this phone call is fascinating, in fact it was not needed to prosecute Gigante for obstruction of justice

And he talked about other regular everyday topics like the weather, such as in this December 2001 conversation:

Chin: Yeah, we got bad weather here.
CE (a daughter): Rain, Dad?
Chin: Ice. Skipping on, sliding on the floor, everything.
CE: Mmm.
Chin: Very bad weather. It's down in the twenties.
CE: Yeah.
Chin: It's raining and it's turning to ice.

In most of his conversations, though, as do many aging regular people in full possession of their mental faculties, he talked about his health. For example, two days after the September 11 attacks, Chin called his New York family again to have this discussion:

Chin: I went to the dentist.
VE: Okay.
Chin: And uh, he, he says he, he put me on antibiotics.
VE: Why?
Chin: What?
VE: Why?
Chin: He says because I have some work to be done. But he can't do it this week, he's gonna do it next week. So he gave me forty antibiotics I gotta take. Erythromycin.
VE: Okay.
Chin: So he put me on, he gave me some moxycill, amoxycillin something like that. I said I can't take penicillin.
VE: Right.
Chin: So I had to make two trips to go back to change it.
VE: Hm.
Chin: And, an, an' I got the erythromycin—I'm taking erythromycin now. Four of those a day.
VE: How many milligrams, do you know?
Chin: Yeah, 250 milligrams.

Plenty of people have parents or other relatives of perfectly sound mind with no clue as to the names of their medications and dosages—and yet here somehow was an insane, psychotic mute with an IQ of 55 who had easy recollection and access to this information and could remember and pronounce the complex names of his medications.

Some other examples among multitudes worth sharing:

Chin: Then he told me about the heart doctor . . . is a fine doctor, I said, I didn't say he ain't. He says, you know, your ejection, w-we done the echocardiogram there, your ejection fraction is down to 35. Normal is 60.

OE: So?

Chin: So I says what do you want me to do? He says well I'm just telling you. I say then I'm in trouble. Oh no, he says, don't worry, he says, you'll be alright. You're doing fine. I said thank you. I said but the pains in the chest don't mean nothing, doc? Oh I take the nitro. I said I do, but it gives me headaches. Oh. Things like that, hon.

And . . .

Chin: (relating a conversation) He says, uh, I don't know. I don't know if you know, I don't think you got a, a rupture. I said okay. Still got the pain, is all I can tell you hon.

OE: Well if it's not a rupture, what did he say it is?

Chin: He says it could be a torn ligament. What do I know it is, huh? He's a D.O. [Doctor of Osteopathy], he ain't a doctor."

And . . .

Chin: I got up at 7 o'clock.

VE: Right.

Chin: I had to wait, and then they did the count.

VE: Right.

Chin: They had us over till about 10 o'clock. I went over. And uh, they took the cardiogram. They took the cardiogram.

VE: Right.

Chin: Come back at uh, one o'clock. [Ever alert] What's that noise?

VE: That's the phone, Dad. I don't know.

Chin: Okay. And then I went back at one o'clock. I stood there 'til 2 o'clock. I, he, he examined me. He examined me in like, forget about it, through my shirt he examines. You want me to take off my shirt? No. No, I can hear. Take deep breaths. That's no examination. They do what they want. That's the best care they put in the, in the paper about me, right?

VE: Hmmm.

Chin: What a laugh.

And on, and on, and on. For six solid months. And we could have obtained another six months to find more of the same. But there was no need.

Chin even commented when his criminal colleagues were arrested in the big sweep of arrests that April. He told his paramour, "They say I'm indicted on something." She responded, "They said you were with a family, and you were running it [in prison] from Texas." Gigante added, "I'm running it? I'm running around the park."

Remarkably—for *decades*—this man persuaded esteemed psychiatric "experts" that he *could not be faking mental illness*, along with the courts who relied on their testimony—and that he was a complete mental vegetable. After his 1997 conviction, additional psychiatrists persuaded yet another judge that his mental faculties had deteriorated sufficiently to warrant a reduction in his sentence by slightly more than half.

Like no other mobster in history, Gigante manipulated, abused, and made a mockery of the American system of justice. With these and countless similar recordings in hand we had enough to finally bring the fraud to a conclusive and irrefutable finale.

In fitting irony, the crazy act—which had forever shielded Chin—would now become our sword to convict.

As an initial matter, though, none of this evidence appeared to deter Chin. When he was brought into court to answer for these new charges, he reverted to the old playbook. He slumped in his chair and appeared not to understand any of the proceedings. One of his lawyers, Gary

Greenwald, told the court that his client could not respond to these new charges against him because of mental incapacitation.

But the recordings had changed everything.

CHAPTER FOURTEEN

TRIALS AND CONVICTIONS

"You knowingly and intentionally misled doctors evaluating
your mental competency?"
"Yes, your honor."

It was time to bring it all home. Paul Weinstein and Paul Schoeman very capably obtained guilty pleas from the vast majority of the arrested mobsters—dozens and dozens of them. Faced with the overwhelming evidence that D'Urso and I compiled, the powerful mafiosi took the only realistic avenue available—pleading guilty. Bellomo, Falcetti, Muscarella, Cirillo, Aparo, DiChiara . . . the list goes on and on and on.

That left just a remaining handful, against whom the evidence was much more questionable, usually because they had not been captured on any of the recordings discussing their criminal activity. These men pushed toward trial.

Other recordings D'Urso made with DeRoss, Colombo associate Campanella, and Aparo also were used as evidence in a later trial of DeRoss and acting boss Alphonse Persico regarding Colombo underboss Billy Cutolo's murder—resulting in their life sentences. The prosecutors also worked hard to build a case against the five who murdered Tino Lombardi and who put a bullet in D'Urso's head. Eventually they were all convicted. Two of them, Anthony Bruno[25] and Angelo Cerasulo, were convicted via their guilty pleas to murder and they agreed to cooperate and testify against the others. That was the key to breaking the case open, and I played a major role in getting their cooperation by visiting each of them in advance and informing them of what was coming and that they were best served by becoming witnesses and not letting it all fall on their heads. When Polito attempted to silence them each by offering to provide them with lawyers (who would never let them become cooperating witnesses), I had prepared them in advance with enough information that they knew to turn down this offer and to instead retain their own counsel. Their guilty pleas in turn persuaded a third murderer, Gingale Imbrieco, to plead guilty prior to trial. Gingale agreed to a multi-decade jail sentence. Gingale and Cerasulo were Polito's cousins. And the remaining two, Polito and Fortunato, were later convicted at trial. They received life sentences.

Bobby Santoro's money-laundering operation made him the largest check-cashing company in New Jersey—City Check Cashing, located in Jersey City. The Genovese used him to convert large check payments for their crimes into cash. D'Urso recorded numerous conversations about this check-cashing operation. On October 2, 1999, D'Urso recorded Aparo telling him that he is involved in a five-million-dollar check fraud scheme with Alan Longo, Paul Gerace and a number of other people. Aparo's share of the proceeds from this crime could amount to $400,000.

Aparo stated, "we got it all worked out pretty good . . . opened up accounts already, deposit this check and then go up to the check-cashing guy that we got and let the bank wire it to them. . . . Once they wire it the guy will give us the money. . . . Even if they (the bank) find it's no good, they got to give it to him. Then they'll look for the guy that cashed it. . . . He goes in the wind. . . . The name's a phony, everything is all phony already, it looks good. . . . It looks like it will work." Aparo further

---

25 Bruno was the one who shot D'Urso in the head, which D'Urso knew since Bruno was standing directly behind him when he was shot. So we arrested Bruno first in the hope that he would cooperate against the others to avoid the full brunt of the case falling entirely on him. Once his cooperation was in hand, we arrested the others.

described how they were going to conduct this scheme that should occur soon. Aparo stated "We got an account with the guy, a phony account that he had for years, so it isn't you just opened it. . . . Now when he gets the check, he'll notify the bank. . . . Listen I just sold a business, I'm expecting a large amounted check, so they're prepared for it. When it comes, forward it to my account and the bank wires to the check-cashing place the money. Once the check-cashing place gets the okay from the bank it gives you the money, his money, and he gets paid. Then he gets five percent."

On October 4, 1999, Aparo again discussed with D'Urso the five-million-dollar check scheme that Longo, Geraci, Frankie Schwamborn (a.k.a. Frankie the German), Aparo, and others are involved with. One of the coconspirators in this fraud is employed at the check-cashing facility in New Jersey and has a five-year contract with this facility. A new company bought this check-cashing facility and gave this individual a $600,000/year contract to stay because he knows this business very well. This check-cashing facility in New Jersey is open until ten or eleven at night. Aparo described how this individual cashed checks in the amount of two million dollars for Frankie Schwamborn. The check will concern a company that was supposed to have been sold.

This was when we decided to get involved by providing our own check under the guise it was stolen. We facilitated additional meetings to address Santoro's role. On November 16th, 1999, D'Urso met with Frankie "the German" Schwamborn and discussed the stolen check scheme. Schwanborn's contact at the check-cashing facility already has accounts set up to negotiate these stolen check schemes. He told D'Urso to have his stolen check made out to New York Energy Service. He did not want D'Urso to meet his contact because he wanted to protect D'Urso and others from law enforcement in the event this individual was to cooperate. He also told D'Urso that if they wanted to do a multimillion-dollar theft in the future they would have to do it with multiple checks. The maximum amount of each check would be $250,000. Schwamborn asked D'Urso how many people were involved in this scheme. D'Urso cited just Aparo, him, the insider (FBI) and Schwamborn. The insider required $40,000 from the $125,000 check. Schwamborn was anxious to do this scam and cited how there would be no problems at the check-cashing facility. He asked D'Urso when can he get the check?

The numerous recordings made by D'Urso with Schwamborn and other participants discussed specific details that charged and convicted Schwamborn, Bobby Santoro, and David Grossman (a former New York State Trooper/attorney). Grossman subsequently cooperated with me and the FBI. These recordings provided the specific details of who to make the check payable, mailing address etc. Below is one sample of a discussion just before we provided the check:

Frank Schwamborn, Vinny Aparo, Sammy Aparo and D'Urso were recorded and photographed on surveillance as they exited Florio's restaurant on Grand Street in Little Italy to discuss this stolen check scheme. Schwamborn instructs D'Urso to mail the check. If law enforcement comes around, he will tell them "I got a check in the mail, I thought I won something. What am I going to do. I spent the money. . . . Now if I didn't get it by mail, then somebody made an error, somebody gave it to me. . . . One way is an insurance company fuck up and the other way, even for him it's a fuck up. I mailed it to the wrong guy." Schwanborn described how they will do the "Little one first" (the check in the amount of $125,000). When they do the large theft involving millions, he will need time to set up offshore accounts in the Channel Islands. Schwamborn described how they need to be cautious because if they get caught "The money-laundering statute, they'll give us twenty years (in jail)."

Schwamborn also described how the insider at the check-cashing facility (Bobby Santoro) wants to do the multimillion-dollar schemes. He stated, "He wants to do that, what we do is we can all set up our own account, each one of us, get the check then wire it, what do you think, a hundred thousand apiece."

In another related conversation: Aparo described the details of how Bobby (Santoro) protected Alan Longo's son who was arrested at Bobby's check-cashing facility. When the son was arrested, Longo asked him to help. Aparo sent Frankie Schwamborn to Bobby and said, "Whatever you have to do, do and get these kids off that pinch and he did." Bobby told the police that Longo's son was not responsible.

Santoro took the stand in his own defense at trial. In desperation, he presented a fake document which he claimed contained financial information proving his innocence. I located an expert witness who testified to details of the document based on how the lettering was not aligned properly. This indicated to the jury the document had been forged, and I watched the jurors as they realized Santoro lied, all immediately turning their heads with disgust toward him.

Santoro was convicted. One interesting anecdote is that Santoro wore a toupee. When I arrested him, we chatted, and Santoro revealed that his wife had never seen him without the toupee. I replied, "If she visits you in prison, she'll see a bald Bobby Santoro."

Finally, Finally: Chin Fesses Up

In the face of the overwhelming evidence out of his own mouth, Chin ultimately elected to plead guilty—and finally, finally fess up. He would swear under oath that his entire decades-long act that had fooled so many mental health professionals and judges was a complete and continuing farce, a fraud, a prolonged scheme to simply avoid being brought to justice or serving an appropriate sentence.

The plea would be taken by the Honorable Leo Glasser, a bright, respected, and very no-nonsense judge. The courtroom was jam-packed with family members, along with press and onlookers who wanted to see the true Vincent Gigante, his act finally shed.

Waiting in court for what might prove to be the strangest court appearance in history, I wondered whether Chin's ego would permit him to carry through with it. He had staked nearly his entire criminal career on persuading others that he was a mental vegetable. Could he finally let go, raise his hand, and swear under oath it was all a lie? By doing so, among other things, he would necessarily reveal that all of his family members who advocated publicly for him through the years, such as his brother Louis—the priest—had lied all along.

When Gigante wandered into court, he shuffled in under his own power, a sharp contrast to his trial five years prior in which he claimed to need a wheelchair. But he also tried to look confused and arrived in ill-fitting clothes while clutching a prescription bottle of heart medication.

When instructed to raise his right hand to swear to tell the truth, he initially raised the wrong hand and then quickly corrected it, and when asked to sign a document merely jotted an "X."

That said, when asked to confirm that he had been malingering all along, Chin gave complete answers in the affirmative.

The Court: Do you understand why you're here?
Chin: Yes.

And,

The Court: You knowingly and intentionally misled doctors evaluating your mental competency? Is that true?
Chin: Yes, your honor.

Judge Glasser pronounced that Chin was: "both mentally and physically fit to proceed," and accepted the guilty plea. Before he left court, his lawyer asked whether Gigante could meet briefly with his son, Andrew. Andrew Gigante was also set to plead guilty right after his father. The judge allowed it, and they briefly and quietly conferred. I appreciated the judge's decision to allow Andrew the opportunity to meet with his father. This was most likely the last time they got together and an opportunity for them to express a love a father and son shared. This reminds me of Barney Bellomo's daughter representing him at the sentencing at his guilty plea in this D'Urso investigation. She described how he missed many of her important life events while he served a prison sentence. The events = included her graduations, proms, etc. You could see the genuine love a father and daughter shared. Barney is now out of prison, and as I understand, the current official boss of the Genovese family.

On a secretly taped conversation, Genovese capo Alan Longo once related how John Gotti told Chin he had inducted his son, with Gigante responding disapprovingly. Gotti said, "Now I'm doing my son too. [Chin] says I'm sorry to hear that. Sorry to hear that." Although Gigante did not have his sons inducted, he brought them deeply enough into the criminal life for Andrew to likewise become a convicted felon. Another son,

Vincent Esposito (from Chin's paramour), would likewise later become a convicted felon in the SDNY for union extortion. In 2017, Vincent's conviction was obtained in part on cooperation provided by one of his own cousins, Chin's nephew, Vincent Fyfe.

As reported by the Department of Justice upon the guilty plea of Vincent Esposito, "At the time of Esposito's arrest, the FBI executed a search warrant on his home and seized more than $3.8 million in U.S. currency hidden throughout the residence, along with an unregistered handgun, ammunition, brass knuckles, and lists of made members of the Genovese Crime Family. As part of today's guilty plea, Esposito agreed to forfeit the more than $3.8 million seized by the FBI as criminal proceeds resulting from the offense. I view this as a bit more of LCN hypocrisy."

How does a relative of Chin's, who is not a made member, have a list of made members' names? This is clearly another violation of LCN secrecy.

It could not have been easy for Gigante to plead guilty, to publicly confess that his enemy, the United States government, was right all along. As his daughter has stated publicly, "I'm sure that devastated him because I'm sure he didn't want to give them [law enforcement] that." The extended farce of his manufactured mental illness was finally and fully exposed for what it was and for all to see. Moreover, the dangerous potential of Chin returning to freedom one day had been further delayed. Incarcerated, this gummed up the works for the Genovese to the benefit of the law-abiding American public. And it served as a reminder to the mob that the government was ever ready to pursue them, even if they were already convicted and serving out a sentence.

As summarized by the United States Attorney: "Gigante's legendary charade has finally and conclusively been put to rest and exposed for the fraud that it is. There is no further debate about his mental competence."

In a *New York Times* article, Clyde Haberman added "It was the end of Gigante as capo di tutti frutti. . . . The clownish affair was finally over. . . . This was all a serious business, of course. The mafia is an enemy of the American people, the scourge of American business, *a source of embarrassment and pain for Italian Americans weary of seeing these bozos glamorized in film and on television.* Presumably America is safer—if less entertained—with Mr. Gigante behind bars for a good long while."[26]

The judge added an agreed-upon three additional years to Chin's sentence, and Gigante would eventually die in jail in December 2005.

Years later, even the priest, Father Lou, finally acknowledged Chin's status and his own long-standing fraud to an enterprising journalist: *"Was my brother the boss of the Genovese family? Yes. He rose to that, picked purposely by Vito Genovese."* One of Gigante's own children recently added her own confirmation: Chin was "the boss of the Genovese crime family" and "he was also the head of the commission."

Father Lou was sued in 2021 for allegedly sexually assaulting a nine-year-old boy and a nine- or ten-year-old girl decades before. He died in 2022—his will and testament revealing for the first time that the priest fathered and raised a son of his own, to whom he left many millions as an inheritance.

A statue of the priest stands outside a church in Brooklyn.

As I noted above, Chin was able to remain at liberty for so many decades based in part on the testimony of psychiatrists and other mental health professionals who claimed that he was a mental vegetable. The only mental health professional who previously swore Gigante was nuts and who then had the decency, integrity, and courage to step forward and offer to testify was Dr. Wilfred Van Gorp. After Chin died, Dr. Van Gorp offered public commentary: "I wonder how the guy did it? Is he just a great actor? I don't think we will know.[27] It's all so compelling, and it was all such a fraud."

As the article recounted: "While behind bars, the Chin had normal conversations with his family—all of which were recorded. Those chats became the basis of his final conviction. . . . Van Gorp remembered listening

---

26 Clyde Haberman, "NYC; No Madness as a Method for Mob Boss," *New York Times*, April 8, 2003, https://www.nytimes.com/2003/04/08/nyregion/nyc-no-madness-as-a-method-for-mob-boss.html.

27 Gigante's own daughter has definitively answered this question: "Quite honestly, he could have won an Academy Award he did it so well."

to an hour and a half of those tapes and being stunned. *'It's phenomenal. The guy is as normal as you and me. The guy is completely normal.'"*[28]

And so my work with D'Urso had resulted not only in the conviction of dozens of powerful mobsters, but now included the Genovese boss. However even this victory was limited. For instance, though Gigante was forced to confess to his "crazy act," we were not able to disrupt his creation of intergenerational wealth for his family. Sammy Aparo was recorded saying that Chin's wealth exceeded $100,000,000. Additionally, many of his descendants including children and grandchildren now hold or can look forward to lucrative sinecures in a variety of mob-controlled industries. As one example, Chin's nephew Ralph Gigante (deceased) testified that his waterfront job paid him as though he were working twenty-seven hours a day, seven days a week—the extra three hours coming from paid meals. And New Jersey's governor recently endorsed a position in favor of eliminating the Waterfront Commission—the bistate police agency created to attempt to insulate the waterfront from mob influence.[29] In my experienced eyes, this is likely a huge mistake that will only benefit the mobsters.

The work with D'Urso was finally concluded, a resounding success, and I could put it all behind me. At least that's what I thought. But over the course of years, I learned that in fact it was not all over. Some shocking, explosive, and devastating aftermaths were yet to come.

28 Greg B. Smith, "Crazy Act Fooled Shrinks," *Daily News*, December 20, 2005.
29 New Jersey plans to have their state police assume the roles that the Waterfront Commission served.

CHAPTER FIFTEEN

FIRST SHOCK TO THE SYSTEM

The first shock took place in 2004, when the Second Circuit Court of Appeals threw out Polito and Fortunato's murder convictions. This just blew me away and made no sense. We had convicted them based on D'Urso's testimony, based on Bruno's testimony, and based on Cerasulo's testimony. Cerasulo was Polito's cousin and described his role in this murder along with Bruno and Polito's participation. And we had offered other corroborating evidence into the case. Clearly, Polito had organized the hit because he wanted to erase a debt and because he wanted to switch to Malangone's crew so that he could commit bank robberies to help pay his gambling debts. That is what the evidence showed. This was also corroborated by the numerous recordings D'Urso made with Sammy Meatballs, Alan Longo, Tommy Cafaro, and others.

But the court completely rejected D'Urso's testimony, which had explained Polito's motivations. They essentially called him a liar and ruled that his testimony was not to be believed. The court basically concluded that since they rejected D'Urso's testimony, the murder was a private matter and not a mob hit, and that therefore there was no federal jurisdiction. The murderers were set free.

Needless to say, myself and my fellow agents were crushed by this ruling. All of our dedication and hard work to accomplish justice was vitiated in an instant, just evaporated into thin air. There was a second trial involving Tino Lombardi's murder conducted in state court by the Brooklyn District Attorney's office. Chris Blank was the prosecutor and did an excellent job securing convictions for both Fortunato and Polito. This also was overturned after it was appealed.

As of this writing, Polito is an active capo in the Genovese family and has been observed meeting with Barney Bellomo, the current Genovese boss. Polito was recently arrested for operating an illegal gambling operation for the past decade.

It also, of course, had a severe impact on D'Urso, who devoted himself to three years of dangerous undercover work in part for the hope that justice might one day be his. The way he had wanted to make things right—to punish his cousin's killers and his own would-be killers—would never happen.

CHAPTER SIXTEEN

LOYALTY VERSUS HYPOCRISY

"The entire top leadership of the Genovese family, the largest and most powerful mafia family, including its boss, Vincent Gigante, and every acting or 'street' boss in power for almost the past twenty years."

I left law enforcement in 2007 based on the anticipated costs of my children's college tuitions. Prior to leaving the FBI, I was a supervisor of a Public Corruption squad for a while after Kingsley blocked me from becoming an Organized Crime supervisor. One of my most memorable cases there involved arresting a corrupt judge/auction referee, Edward S. Reich. Reich had been a vice president of the New York State Bar Association. He had frequently been appointed by Brooklyn state judges to serve as the referee in the sale of foreclosed property, and took bribes so people could rig it to win these auctions.

On the morning of his arrest, Reich thought he was flying out for a vacation. I told him, "You're not going to the Bahamas. Your wife can go, but you're coming with us." The look on his wife's face toward her husband was akin to "do something because you're usually in charge," and Reich adopted a completely arrogant tone of voice: "I've got a flight to catch." My response was, "Not today. Today, you have an arraignment to make."

Two other significant investigations were charged while I was the supervisor. One involved Brian McLaughlin, a corrupt Queens assemblyman who was being considered as a candidate running for New York City mayor. He was also head of the NYC Central Labor Council and historically attached to Local 3 IBEW of the electricians' union. He was helping to further bid rigging schemes on New York City street lighting contracts. This investigation also helped lead to a new organized crime investigation involving Santo Petrocelli Sr., who pleaded guilty to making illegal payments to McLaughlin. Petrocelli was a Genovese associate who maintained annual calendar logs of his meetings with Quiet Dom and other Genovese powers. These logs were similar in size to old-fashioned encyclopedias. They were seized in a search warrant at his office.

Ultimately, the ASAC who replaced Kingsley asked me to return to the OC Unit as the coordinator, overseeing all the organized crime squads. Among other things, in this capacity I testified as an expert witness on organized crime.

The same year I retired from the FBI, his cooperation now completed, Mike D'Urso was sentenced in 2007. Coming full circle, the Honorable Sterling Johnson, who ran the District Attorney's Office that prosecuted D'Urso when he was a teenager, and who also took D'Urso's secret guilty plea in 1998, now was D'Urso's sentencing judge. Likewise, the assistant district attorney who originally prosecuted D'Urso now represented him at his sentencing.

In recognition of the work D'Urso accomplished under my daily direction, the accolades poured in. Law enforcement officially recognized the extraordinary and singular contributions. Excerpts from the sentencing letter provided by the U.S. Attorney's Office included the following:

> D'Urso devastated "*the entire top leadership of the Genovese family,* the largest and most powerful mafia family at the time, *including its boss, Vincent Gigante, and every acting or "street" boss in power for almost the past 20 years.*"
>
> "D'Urso's cooperation was historic in its scope and impact."
>
> "Michael D'Urso was responsible for the arrest, conviction and imprisonment of a *substantial portion of the most powerful gangsters in the mafia.*"

"Michael D'Urso has provided the government with cooperation that is fairly described as *among the most successful and far ranging in the history of the prosecution of American organized crime.* By
any measure—be it by the number of defendants arrested, the number of defendants convicted, the significance of defendants convicted, the intelligence on organized crime gathered, the personal
danger faced, the length of undercover operations, or the amount
of testimony provided—Michael D'Urso's cooperation is virtually
unprecedented."

"He met on a continuous basis with some of the most dangerous
and violent members of organized crime, while wearing a recording
device. He exhibited remarkable courage in doing so."

"By the time his cooperation on the street was over, D'Urso was
a trusted confidant of one of the most powerful Genovese family
crews."

"The significance, therefore, of Michael D'Urso's cooperation is
singular."

Taking this into full account, Judge Johnson recognized D'Urso's truly
historic contributions and ordered that he remain at liberty. This both
served as a just reward for his assistance to the American public, and also
encouraged others to attempt the same.

Long ago, I had trusted D'Urso and I had taken a risk on him. It had
paid off better than I could have ever hoped or expected. Due to our work
together, I had for a second time taken down the leadership of the most
powerful, secretive, and feared gang in America.

Other Cases

As you've seen, cases and cooperation often springboard to other cases
and cooperation. And occasionally ongoing investigations overlap. For
example, younger agents Bill Inzirillo and Jon Jennings had a cooperating
witness who was problematic and would never make a credible witness.
After meeting with the witness, I directed the agents to have him introduce an undercover detective, who then could accompany the cooperating
witness and make recordings and testify. I instructed the detective how

to maximize his effectiveness with the gangsters by minimizing speaking, which they would interpret as his demonstrating sophisticated criminal caution. Let the wiseguys speak about crimes while you sit back and record them.

The UCA in turn once showed up to capo "Petey Red" DeChiara's social club while D'Urso was also there. We were conducting surveillance and observed our fellow squad agents in the same area. We found out the UCA was also in the club, recording conversations with Ross Gangi and others. I immediately called D'Urso to provide an alert and minimize any potential reaction on his part.

The efforts with the detective proved fruitful as well. This separate but concurrent investigation lasted for over two years and concluded at the end of 2001 with large-scale arrests in the SDNY of dozens of Genovese, including capos Patsy Parello (from the Robert De Niro *A Bronx Tale* party described in chapter 5), and Ross Gangi, who took a hit in both investigations. And after that, another C-5 investigation, resulting in the conviction of powerful capo Louie Moscatiello, came down. Genovese associate mob lawyer Pete Peluso was arrested in this investigation as well, and Agents Inzerillo and Jennings quietly obtained his cooperation. As a cooperating witness, among other things Peluso recorded his conversations with a historic old-time capo John "Buster" Ardito, resulting in Ardito's arrest, along with Bellomo and others.

In 2005, Peluso pled guilty to participating in numerous crimes committed with the Genovese, including murder, extortion, and obstruction of justice. One of the ways that Peluso assisted the Genovese was by exploiting his status as an attorney to deliver important messages to and from the gangsters, some of whom were incarcerated. Because he was a lawyer, his communications were presumptively shielded from law enforcement scrutiny as "attorney-client" protected and privileged. It is exponentially easier to obtain a court's permission to listen to conversation between two gangsters than it is to legally "protected" conversations between a gangster and his lawyer. Mobsters are fully aware of this loophole, which they have always exploited to their full advantage.

As one example of how they use lawyers, Peluso pled guilty to participating in Genovese member Ralph Coppola's murder. Specifically, Peluso admitted carrying the imprisoned Bellomo's message to other Genovese leaders that sanctioned the hit. D'Urso had also gathered evidence related to Coppola's murder. For example, we recorded Aparo stating that Coppola should never have been straightened out nor made a capo. And we recorded Tommy Cafaro citing how Bellomo assigned Coppola to the Jacob Javits Center and that Coppola "screwed up there." When D'Urso asked whether Bellomo had any input into Coppola's disappearance, Cafaro responded, "Nobody goes against him (Bellomo)."

Cafaro also described how Coppola had been disrespectful to Bellomo: "I knew where you fucking came from. In the fucking street. You were ready to be killed if it wasn't for us. . . . Barney told him, I put my neck out for you. You fuck up, you deal with me." Cafaro's cited Bellomo's previous statement to Coppola about preventing his murder years ago related to a dispute with the Lucchese family. Al D'arco's prior cooperation with the FBI cited how Coppola was originally with the Lucchese family. The Lucchese family released Coppola to Bellomo and the Genovese family. Bellomo cited at the sit-down with D'arco and others how he saved Coppola's life with his release.

Soldier Paul Geraci also made clear that Bellomo specialized in murder: "He was all about it. Don't worry about that. That whole Harlem regime was doing all the work [mafia-speak for murders]. He was doing all of it. How old do you think Barney was when he got straightened out? Nineteen."

Bellomo was obviously impressed with John "Sonny" Franzese, a powerful, former underboss of the Colombo family. He knew Chin was close to and respected Sonny Franzese. This was most likely due to his status with the Colombo family back in the time frame when Costello was shot and Albert Anastasia was killed. As previously noted, Franzese corroborated the meeting between Anastasia, Costello, and Michael Miranda to kill Vito Genovese. Joe Gallo was supposedly one of the shooters who killed Anastasia. I imagine Sonny also could have participated in this murder.

The Colombo and Genovese families were aligned due to this historic murder. Years later, after Joe Gallo was killed, the Colombo family released Joe Gallo's brother, Albert "Kid Blast" Gallo, and Frank "Punchy" Illiano to the Genovese family and Vincent "Chin" Gigante's crew. Joe Gallo was killed in a Little Italy restaurant operated by a future Genovese acting boss, Matty "the Horse" Ianiello. As I understand from a reliable source, while in prison, Bellomo told Franzese how Chin loves him because of the role he played in Frank Decicco's murder. Chin promoted Bellomo to acting boss of the Genovese family after this murder. These details were shared by Sonny with other members affiliated with the Colombo organized crime family.

Frank Decicco was murdered in April 1986, and Hickey DiLorenzo was killed in November 1988. Bellomo was the acting boss when Dilorenzo was killed. He met with Al D'Arco, acting boss of the Luchese family, to address Hickey's murder. D'Arco subsequently cooperated with the FBI and testified at Ida's trial about his meeting with Bellomo, Ida, and Generoso about this murder. This eight-month window of time from Decicco's murder coupled with Hickey's murder is very interesting evidence from a timeline perspective. It was in 1987 that Bobby Manna, Genovese family consigliere, was recorded discussing the murder of John Gotti for the unsanctioned killing of Paul Castellano.

If I was a current FBI agent, I would be reviewing the telephone records and photographs in the Manna investigation to address the Decicco homicide. There is a possibility of an unknown male, Bellomo, meeting with Manna. I did this type of review when I was addressing the indictment of Bellomo, Ida, and Generoso. Back in the early 1980s, Bellomo was identified as an unknown male as he was photographed entering the Palma Boys Social Club controlled by Fat Tony Salerno, the acting boss. Timeline evidence is very important in complex organized crime investigations.

In addition, the role of Paulie Geraci, Gaspipe Casso's son-in-law in Bellomo's crew, is very similar to Jimmy Ida having Hickey Dilorenzo's brother in his crew. I also recall Ida losing a dispute with the Luchese family regarding the release of George Zappola to the Lucchese family. George's father, also named George, was a member of the Genovese family, and was killed in 1982. His father's hand and head had washed up on a beach in Long Island. According to D'Arco, Ida had George Zappola, the son, under him as an associate and did not want him released to another crime family. The primary concern was to minimize his activity. To prevent any future cooperation with law enforcement in retaliation for his father's murder. Benny "Eggs" Mangano, underboss for the Genovese family, authorized this release. According to D'Arcao, Ida and Chuckie Tuzzo played a role in Zappola's father's murder and wanted to maintain control of his son to prevent cooperation with law enforcement.

So, it should be clear that investigations need not live and then die. They can bear further fruit through creative approaches and hard work. My hope is that current FBI agents make use of the many years' worth of recordings and insights that the D'Urso investigation produced, and that is fully within their grasp—all they need to do is review the files and recordings. Under the right circumstances the tapes can still bear additional fruit, including serving as evidence in support of current investigations or charges in addition to further investigations and prosecutions.

And just so there is no misimpression, plenty of powerful gangsters in addition to the ones we've described here have become cooperating witnesses, many of them disgusted with the mob's hypocrisy that we've chronicled throughout this book. That is not to even mention the exponentially higher numbers of informants who secretly provide information about their fellow mobsters to the FBI on an ongoing basis.

Below is just a partial list of these cooperating witnesses. For the sake of brevity, the list is not close to exhaustive. For obvious reason, the numerous informants are not included on this list.

Bonannos
Boss Joe Massino
Underboss Salvatore Vitale
Capo Frank Coppa
Capo James Tartaglione
Capo Frankie "Curly" Lino
Capo Dominic Cicale
Capo Peter Lovaglio
Acting capo Nick Pisciotti
Acting capo Jimmy "the General" Barbieri
Soldier Joe D'Amico
Soldier Michael "Sonny" Maggio

Soldier Peter Rosa

Luccheses
Acting boss Al D'Arco
Acting boss Joe DeFede
Underboss Anthony "Gaspipe" Casso (agreement violated due to his
    deception and violence after he cooperated)
Capo Peter "Fat Pete" Chiodo
Capo Anthony "Tumac" Accetturo
Soldier Thomas Ricciardi
Soldier Frank Gioia Jr.
Soldier Frank Gioia Sr.
Soldier Vinny Salanardi
Soldier Frank Lagano
Soldier John Pennisi
Associate Henry Hill: *Goodfellas* movie was based on his story and the
    Lufthansa heist at JFK Airport

Colombos
Consigliere Carmine Sessa
Capo Salvatore "Big Sal" Miciotta
Capo John Pate
Capo Greg Scarpa (longtime FBI source)
Soldier Larry Mazza
Soldier Reynold Maragni
Associate John Franzese: son of power Sonny Franzese and brother
    of capo Michael Franzese. Testified against his father, who was
    convicted

Gambinos
Underboss Sammy "the Bull" Gravano
Capo Mikey Scars DiLeonardo: denied permission to avenge the mur-
    der of his brother, who was killed in a dispute with another mob
    family

Soldier Craig DePalma: son of capo Greg DePalma, who proposed undercover FBI agent "Big Jack" Garcia for induction into the Gambinos. Craig's mother always resented Greg influencing his son to enter the mob.
Soldier Dominic "Fat Dom" Borghese
Soldier Frankie Fappiano
Associate John Alite

Genovese
Capo Renaldi Ruggiero, South Florida: post-Barone/D'Urso cooperation after they set the precedent.
Capo Felix Tranghese, Springfield, Mass: post-Barone/D'Urso cooperation after they set the precedent.
Capo Vincent "Fish" Cafaro: not a fully usable cooperator
Soldier Anthony "Bingy" Arilotta: former capo, and post-Barone/D'Urso cooperation after they set the precedent
Soldier George Barone
Soldier Joe Valachi
Associate Mike "Cookie" D'Urso: proposed for induction multiple times
Associate John Bologna: Springfield, Massachusetts crew
Genovese attorney: Pete Peluso

Decavalcante (New Jersey)
Acting boss Vinny "Oceans" Palermo
Capo Anthony Rotundo
Soldier Anthony Capo
Soldier Frankie "the Beast" Scarbino

Other Crime Families
The Philadelphia crime family has had multiple high-level defectors, including a former boss and underboss. Chicago, Cleveland, and other gangs were similarly devastated by former members, disgusted with the life, who realized the only way out was to turn on their treacherous former colleagues.

So even if for some reason you're not yet convinced and *still* want to enter the mob, you're forewarned that anybody you deal with, no matter what they say about how much they hate cooperators, and even if they try to kill cooperators—might be the guy to turn you in one day. Gaspipe Casso used to despise cooperators so much that he killed guys just because he thought they *might* cooperate—and then he spilled all the beans and tried to become a cooperator himself.

No loyalty, no brotherhood, no honor. Most of these gangsters are out for themselves no matter what they say. You're totally on your own if you believe the false hype and join them. The risks versus rewards can devastate a blood family, even one that obtains great wealth.

CHAPTER SEVENTEEN

CLEAR VIOLATIONS
OF OMERTÀ

This chapter will address in a timeline manner recordings made by D'Urso that demonstrates the trust and respect high-ranking members of the Genovese and other LCN families had for him. From the very beginning of his cooperation in June 1998 through March 2001, there were numerous recordings made about how he was going to be inducted into the Genovese family. The recordings also will provide instances of regular violations of omertà and show how/that the secrecy of this criminal organization is ridiculous. The gangsters in this life have egos and personality disorders that prevent most of them from maintaining secrets. The purpose of citing these details is not to insult made members but to have them discourage young, blood family members from getting involved in this type of life. If a gangster has the money, he can create a legitimate business opportunity for a son to succeed in life by raising his family with love rather than jail.

The recordings will also cite some of the incredible schemes and crimes involving numerous members and associates from the various LCN families:

9/4/98: Mike Norrito, former NYPD detective, told the source he has someone that is looking to launder approximately $5 billion. Adding that it was being stored in an airplane hangar. A friend of his saw this money. (Norrito had so many criminal schemes that D'Urso recorded.)

9/11/98: Sammy Aparo was recorded telling D'Urso about Joe Zito's meeting with Frank Serpico, Genovese acting boss, that occurred the previous week. During this meeting, Serpico authorized D'Urso to collect the money owed to him by Johnny Zero. Serpico also approved the source for induction into the Genovese family.

Aparo told D'Urso that originally when Serpico decided not to have him killed, he refused to approve D'Urso as a candidate for induction. A clear example of the criminal hypocrisy of this criminal life. The recordings made with Zero, in Florida, cited how Zero already provided Serpico with this money. He took out two separate mortgages to pay him. Serpico learned about D'Urso's meeting with Zero in Florida and cited how D'Urso could only collect this debt from Zero in New York. He again stalled D'Urso's induction.

9/29/98: During the meeting, John Cerella, a.k.a. Johnny Sideburns, a Genovese associate at that time, currently an acting capo in the Lucchese family, told D'Urso that Danny Pagano is unhappy with how Anthony Palumbo, a.k.a. "Tony D," wants to plead guilty on their case. Pagano doesn't want this. Sideburns also told D'Urso that Pagano doesn't want Jimmy Tanaglia, a.k.a. "Jimmy T," to be "made" in the Genovese family. Palumbo sponsored Jimmy T, who is part of Dom Cirillo's crew.

10/12/98: A second instance where weapons were provided to D'Urso. At this meeting, Aparo provided the source with a brown briefcase containing several weapons and silencers. Aparo opened the briefcase briefly to show him the weapons and told him to keep these weapons for him. He did this by providing them to me and the FBI as evidence.

11/9/98: Jimmy T (Tenaglia) discussed with D'Urso how the LCN life is so treacherous. He cited how Mikey "Bats" (Michael Cardello), a former capo with the Bonanno family, was released from prison and moved to Texas. Mikey Bats did this because he no longer wanted to be involved with his LCN family. Jimmy T cited this as an example of how the LCN life is no longer a popular life.

11/10/98: Johnny Sideburns complained about Alan Longo requesting him to return to New York from Florida. The complaint was based on Sideburns additional expense to live in New York without Longo providing him with an opportunity to earn. Sideburns and other crew members went with Longo to Scores strip club. He didn't like that Longo gave strippers a thousand dollars while he had difficulty earning money.

11/17/98: Sammy Aparo told D'Urso that he currently is involved in discussions regarding Carmine Polito. The discussions concern Dom Truscello, who is trying to save Polito from being killed by D'Urso. Dom knows Polito from prison and met with Petey Red DiChiara. Petey Red brought up the benefits of allowing Polito to be released to Truscello. He qualified this as a favor that could be repaid. Truscello could be elevated to a higher rank in the Luchese family and the Genovese family could benefit. Clear hypocrisy to D'Urso and provided comfort with his decision to cooperate with the FBI. The decision by Joe Zito, Aparo, and others was to support D'Urso and not release Polito.

Aparo described how he has had about five different capos and three to four different acting capos during his life. Vito Genovese came from the "West Side" and Lucky Luciano organized the Cosa Nostra in the United States and put the commission together. During this portion of their conversation Aparo also described the shooting of Frank Costello. He explained how Albert Anastasia and Costello conspired to take control of everything. Costello did not want to give up the position to Vito (Genovese) who was in hiding in Italy because of a pending murder investigation. (These details were voluntarily corroborated by George Barone's debriefing after his cooperation in 2001. As I discussed earlier in this book, Barone was an associate of Vito Genovese at the time of Costello's shooting and Anastasia's murder. Vito also shared these details with Johnny Earle and Barone. Aparo also described animosity that Gene Gotti had toward his brother John Gotti. The animosity stems from how John's family has been cared for financially by the Gambino LCN family while he has been imprisoned. However, Gene's family does not receive the same type of financial support. A bit of hypocrisy on crime family coming before a blood family. Here is an example of both a crime family member and blood family member who feels mistreated.

3/25/99: Aparo described how Gigante was arrested in the same case with Vito Genovese whereby Vito subsequently died in prison. Their arrests concerned "junk" (heroin). The rule to prohibit the LCN from dealing in narcotics occurred in 1957 while Vito and Chin were arrested in 1959 during a period when it was prohibited. Aparo also described Chin's participation in the shooting of Costello and Aparo the Genovese historic administration to include how Fat Tony Salerno was never the boss of the Genovese family. He was "our consigliere." In describing the circumstances concerning the commission case, Aparo described how they made Fat Tony a decoy boss because "The boss was the guy walking around in a bathrobe at that time."

6/4/99: Aparo told D'Urso that John Gotti did not like Carmine Persico. Gotti was always on Vinnie Aloi's side in the Colombo war dispute. Now that Gotti's in prison, he does not want anyone to remove him as boss. This is another example of egos coupled with hypocrisy in this life. Aparo further described how nobody in the Gambino family wants to be boss, noting that Joe "Butch" Corrao does not want it. (Note: Corrao was a powerful Gambino capo frequently observed with Gotti.)

7/22/99: Aparo described how Jimmy Ida calls him from prison and sends messages through Louie Casalini, a.k.a. Louie Black, Genovese soldier. D'Urso observed how odd it was that Jerry Dilorenzo would be around an individual who was responsible for the murder of his brother. Aparo explained how this is part of the LCN life and cited as an example the murder of John DiGilio. They killed his father and straightened him (John Gilio the son) out. Aparo went on to describe how Ida could have probably obtained a plea that would have had him do twelve years in prison if the three of them (Ida, Generoso, and Bellomo) would have stuck together. Aparo's tone was one indicating a lack of loyalty to one another.

7/28/99: Aparo describes Joe Bonanno, former boss of the Bonanno family, as a "terrible guy." This concerned the biography on Joe Bonanno who is about ninety-two years old and became a rat indirectly. Bonanno gave up that there was a commission and that the orders must come from there. (Note: This discussion relates to the 1999-produced biographical film called *Bonanno: A Godfather's Story.* The film chronicles the rise and fall of organized crime in the United States. Bonanno was portrayed by Martin Landau.)

9/7/99: Vinny told D'Urso about his induction into the Genovese family last night. He also described how to conduct himself as a made member. The rules that he had to comply with. Aparo stated, "You can't raise your hands to another friend. You can't fuck around with counterfeit money. No drugs. You can't go off with another friend's wife." Aparo also told the source how, "You break any one of these rules we'll kill you and if we can't get you, we'll go after your family." They had to undress for the induction. Ernie (Muscarella) told him, you are not to tell anyone you're made, and Larry (Dentico) responded unless there's a situation that requires an introduction to resolve a matter. This recording by D'Urso happened hours after the inductions. Clearly a violation of the rules. I imagine this happens all of the time.

A few minutes later, Petey Red Dichiara and Frank Demea arrived at Florio's. D'Urso recorded the Aparos explaining how Dichiara came to officially introduce Sammy to his son Vinny as made so that they can conduct LCN business. This is comical having a father and son officially introduced as though they are following protocols.

10/4/99: During this same meeting, D'Urso recorded Sammy Aparo how he is going to lie at the next day's meeting with Jackie DeRoss.

This concerned a prior dispute involving Billy Cutulo, Colombo acting boss. Aparo is going to tell them that the $37,000 that John's Gourmet Salads (JGS) business owes to Aparo. How this was agreed to by Billy Cutolo. The only reason Cutolo did not pay Aparo this money was because of the dispute between the Colombo and Genovese families. This dispute required a pause in payments. Aparo told D'Urso they can't go out and ask Cutolo if this is true, he's dead. Aparo stated, "You can't ask nobody; you have to take my fucking word for it."

Another conversation on this same day involved Aparo describing his induction. Aparo explained how he was inducted on a Sunday morning. He overslept and almost missed the induction. There were about fifty guys there and Sally Young (Palmieri) and Aparo had to knock on the window to get into the induction. At that time the person who sponsored you to be made, brought you to the induction. Sally Young pricked Aparo's finger at this induction. Aparo was in Tommy "Ryan" Eboli's crew and described Eboli as an extremely powerful figure who had a hundred guys in his crew. When they broke this crew up, the Genovese family made ten captains and gave each crew ten guys. Eboli became an acting boss for the Genovese family and may have been killed as a result of his speaking in a disrespectful manner about Jerry Catena, a future boss.

10/12/99: Aparo described Petey Red as being very naive in that he believes that made guys don't lie to each other. Petey Red was further described as someone who pays money out of his own pocket for others around him to avoid confrontations. Aparo cited how Petey Red was not very bright and similar to Nicky "the Blond" (Frustaci). These discussions were in relation to the role Petey Red was to play in resolving a dispute involving Joe Cammarano, a.k.a. Joe Saunders, and D'Urso.

11/8/99: D'Urso recorded Aparo discussing the beating Benji Castellazzo received from the Albanians in the Bronx. (Note: Castelazzo, a.k.a. "the Claw," became the Underboss of the Colombo family). Aparo heard the Albanians broke Benji's legs. This group of

Albanians were around Torre Locasio's son. (Torre Locasio is the former consigliere under John Gotti)

Aparo also cited how he was at the Gulfstream racetrack with Jimmy Clemenza and discussed the Colombo LCN family dispute. Aparo shared with Clemenza how Alan Longo cited how the Genovese family was supporting the Persico faction. Clemenza told Aparo that he personally met with Joe Massino, boss of the Bonanno family, who supports their side in this dispute. Massino was to meet with representatives from the other LCN families to resolve this dispute in their favor. Clemenza also explained that he knows someone who was close to Ernie Muscarella who also supported Clemenza's faction. This contrast between the way the powers of multiple organized crime families communicate their position can facilitate a comfort zone for future murders of the participants.

12/17/99: D'Urso, Patty Falcetti, Ralph Balsamo, Sammy and Vinny Aparo attend Joe Zito's Christmas party at Dinino's restaurant on 2nd Ave in Manhattan. Numerous discussions include inductions, check cashing scheme, Carmine Polito, FBI bug in meter outside Florio's Restaurant, etc. The recordings demonstrated a trust in D'Urso coupled with his future induction.

12/23/99: D'Urso placed me on a three-way call with a woman who was employed at a tow truck business in Brooklyn. This business was affiliated with the Genovese family through a relationship with D'Urso. There was another competitive business affiliated with the Bonanno family, specifically Joe Cammarano, a.k.a. Joe Saunders (future acting boss). While D'Urso was on the telephone with me we could hear the woman crying as she explained how the people affiliated with the Bonanno family came to seize a car towed by the Genovese-affiliated business. To prevent this tow, an employee named Danny pulled a car in front of the vehicle. The Bonanno associate backed up over Danny's vehicle to tow this car. Danny was not seriously injured. As the tow truck pulled out of the station with the car attached, he hit additional vehicles. This was another dispute between two LCN families, that I recorded with D'Urso. When we learned nobody was seriously injured, we had a laugh at the stupidity of this dispute. As I understood, a vehicle broke down on the Belt Parkway and was towed. The tow truck business affiliated with the Bonanno family cited that as their tow. Can you imagine being the owner of this vehicle watching it get towed and damaged as it was taken to another business.

12/28/99 through 1/5/00: D'Urso made numerous recordings with Aparo and others regarding the check-cashing scheme. Aparo gave "the Fat Guy" (Petey Red) half of his share from these proceeds. The remainder of the money Aparo provided to Vinny Aparo. The only portion Aparo kept was the $10,000 he skimmed from the top when he lied to Frankie Schwamborn about the amount of money the insider (FBI) was to get. He told him $50,000 when the actual amount was $40,000.

Aparo then provides $60,000 in cash in a sealed envelope later opened by me and another agent. This money was the share for D'Urso's contact who provided the stolen check. That would be me and the FBI. Our share of the $125,000 check that was laundered through City Check Cashing (CCC). D'Urso recorded his conversations to include asking how the attorney, David Grossman, would respond if law enforcement comes around investigating. Aparo cited how Grossman has forty to fifty clients and was only following his client's instructions. Grossman cooperated with the FBI after his arrest. Robert Santoro, who operated this corrupt business, was convicted at trial.

Vinny Aparo was recorded telling D'Urso how Petey Red was all smiles when Sammy gave him his share of the money. D'Urso reminds Aparo to tell Petey Red who put the plan together. D'Urso also provided me with a receipt from CCC for $2,249.60. This amount was the processing fee for cashing the check.

1/5/00: Falcetti wants D'Urso to meet with Tommy Cafaro in Florida. He was supposed to be at Joe Zito's Christmas party in New York City but could not attend. After meeting with Falcetti, Joe Zito calls D'Urso and described how Patty Falcetti loves D'Urso and how he put him with the best kid (Falcetti) that you could ever have as a contact.

Falcetti was an extremely powerful, respected member in the Genovese LCN family who was close to Ernie Muscarella. Zito adds that D'Urso can do whatever you want with Falcetti without having to contact Zito. (This period of the investigation was an eye opener. We were now with Barney Bellomo's faction and making recordings that could be utilized in current investigations since Bellomo, Falcetti, Muscarella, and others from the uptown faction are currently the power base for the Genovese family.

2/24/00: While D'Urso was at Gulfstream racetrack today with Sammy Aparo and Jimmy "Brown" Clemenza, he learned that Richard Fusco, a.k.a. Richie "Nerves" Fusco, is the new boss of the Colombo family. Clemenza met with Fusco who wanted Clemenza to join the Persico faction. Fusco told Clemenza they only want "the other guy" meaning Vinny Aloi. This statement was concerning the Persico faction's interest in killing Vinny Aloi. Clemenza cited how half of Aloi's faction already left Aloi for the Persico faction. Clemenza is looking to go to another LCN family rather than join Persico. He knows that he will be killed if he agrees to rejoin the Persico.

D'Urso left Gulfstream and met with Cafaro. One of the topics discussed involved Tino Lombardi's murder. Barney Bellomo, Patty, and Tommy Cafaro all knew and liked Tino. Cafaro told D'Urso how he advised Bellomo to take his guilty plea in my Ida case. If Jimmy Ida accepted the jail sentence that was offered to him by the prosecutors, Bellomo would have received a lower sentence.

Cafaro described how his father loved Jimmy Ida and helped Ida win his trial in New Jersey. Vincent Cafaro would argue with the prosecutor in this trial. D'Urso cited how he heard Tommy's father never really hurt anyone in the Genovese family with his cooperation. Cafaro cited one instance concerning Bobby Manna, former consigliere.

2/29/00: Tommy Cafaro told D'Urso how Patty Falcetti has had a job with the International Longshoremen's Association for eighteen years. The job provides Falcetti with union benefits. Falcetti is under Ernie Muscarella while Cafaro is under Chuckie Tuzzo. Cafaro travels to

New York to meet Chuck once a month. Barney has Cafaro doing all Bellomo's business while he is in prison. Cafaro has not complied with Bellomo's instructions. Bellomo placed Michael Coppola as the acting boss prior to Farby. A few months later, Coppola became a fugitive regarding a prior murder, and Bellomo placed Farby as the acting boss.

3/2/00: D'Urso records his conversation with numerous LCN figures on this day beginning with Vinny Aparo. Vinny is recorded describing Andrew Albin's arrest in Arizona. Albin was ripped off by drug dealers when he went to Arizona to purchase marijuana. He was robbed of $100,000. Albin was involved in a gun battle with these drug dealers while driving through the streets and was arrested under the fictitious name of Angelo Bello. Albin was released because his previous arrest record didn't come up because of the fictitious name used. He is trying to get his money back from the drug dealers by giving them the impression he will cooperate with law enforcement if they don't return his money. Aparo and D'Urso believe the circumstances concerning this arrest are strange.

D'Urso and Vinny Aparo meet with Joe "Black" Gargone, Colombo soldier. Gargone cites the LCN life and how they don't need "tough guys" anymore, they need lawyers. Gargone cited how when you have a hundred made guys, only ten of them are tough. Years ago, Gargone claimed that there were eighty to ninety tough guys out of a hundred.

D'Urso then met with Falcetti at Divino's restaurant where Falcetti provided details of his conversation about D'Urso's induction. Muscarella told him D'Urso should be patient because Farby will not be in this position forever. Muscarella was the one who removed D'Urso's name from the induction list. Falcetti told Muscarella he wanted to use D'Urso to earn money and described him as a smart guy in construction and legitimate-type deals. They can earn money with D'Urso, and he could also be used for murders.

Ralph Balsamo is also with Falcetti at this restaurant and is recorded discussing the numerous crew members from Harlem who are inmates at Ottisville Federal prison. Balsalmo's father-in-law "Sal Larca" is at this prison. Larca received a twenty-four-year sentence, and has two and a half years left. (NOTE: Larca was subsequently indicted by my old squad. This was a forty-two-count indictment)

Falcetti instructed D'Urso to stay close to Tommy (Cafaro) and described how there are different types of people made in the LCN life. The types include, "Politicians . . . union guys . . . business guys." D'Urso need not worry about his induction. He stated, "This thing (the LCN life) is not what it was years ago, believe me . . . believe me . . . You're cut out for it. You got the brains and the balls . . . Let's make some fucking money."

3/14/00: D'Urso recorded Cafaro describing numerous details about his life and current problems. He was recorded describing "Scop" (Pasquale Deluca) and Farby (Frank Serpico) are "No fucking good." Scop and Artie (Nigro) claimed Cafaro insulted them at a wake a few months ago. This insult happened because Scop claimed Cafaro did not go over and greet them at the wake. Scop and Nigro went to Serpico to complain. Cafaro would be dead if it wasn't for his relationship with Barney Bellomo and Ernie Muscarella. He also described how nobody wanted to be the acting boss when Barney went to prison. They did not want to be the focus of law enforcement.

3/20/00: D'Urso recorded Cafaro explaining why Bellomo put him under Chuckie Tuzzo. Tuzzo was a powerful capo who turned down the acting boss position. Cafaro was already doing ILA ports business with Tuzzo. He explained how the ports in New York and Florida are controlled by the Genovese family, and that's how he makes his money. He stated that George Barone has run the ILA for forty years for the Genovese family and provided Cafaro with his first job at the ILA. Cafaro used to be Barone's driver. Andrew Gigante was Cafaro's best man. (Another example of treachery and hypocrisy. As a member of a team or family, you would think they could have provided Barone with the modest amount of money owed to him)

Cafaro described how Chin's kids did not get along with George Barone. Andrew Gigante abuses people because of his power and blood relationship to his father.

Cafaro provided details of a dispute involving Rao's Restaurant in East Harlem. This concerned the control of tables and how the LCN family who controls a table makes money off of it by controlling access. Bellomo is aware of the situation but is not aware of all the facts, and he will not make a decision on this one table until he receives all of the facts. The table concerns a Salerno and a DiNapoli. Cafaro explained how Peter Peluso, attorney, relays messages to Bellomo every few weeks. D'Urso stated in this recorded conversation how, "If agents (FBI) were listening to these conversations, they would laugh at what's going on now. The agents have locked up all the brains of the family and the idiots are out on the street." D'Urso knew I would laugh as I reviewed this recording.

3/22/00: Cafaro described how Bellomo paid the attorney fees for all of the attorneys on the case Bellomo went to prison. Cafaro also is recorded telling D'Urso that he is partners with Bellomo with the trucking business. D'Urso questioned Cafaro if Bellomo had any say in Ralph Coppola's murder with Cafaro responding, "Nobody goes against him [Bellomo]."

D'Urso made numerous recordings with Glenn McCarthy, a Genovese associate actively involved in numerous crimes. McCarthy recordings included so many schemes. One involved a corrupt mayor of Miami and the construction of a hotel. McCarthy introduced D'Urso to Dominic Rabuffo, a Genovese associate and former partner of Irwin "the Fat Man" Schiff. Schiff was killed on August 8, 1987, while sitting in a Manhattan restaurant. He was shot in the back of the head while others sat for dinner. This was an infamous murder featured all over the news. Bobby Manna, the Genovese consigliere, was convicted at trial for his role in the Schiff homicide. McCarthy was recorded explaining Rabuffo's role generating millions for the Genovese family. D'Urso recorded his meetings with Rabuffo, McCarthy and a corrupt mayor regarding a hotel development in Florida.

Rabuffo was previously arrested in March 1988 by the Manhattan DA's office investigating the Schiff homicide. He was partners with Schiff involved in bank fraud and cooperated testifying in federal court. The recorded D'Urso conversations with McCarthy indicated Rabuffo testified for the government in the homicide of Schiff. Rabuffo did not provide any evidence against organized crime. His testimony convicted some corrupt bankers. Rabuffo was partners with Schiff and the vice president of the Luis Electrical Contracting Corporation. The recordings made by D'Urso described Rabuffo's sophisticated skills to defraud people and banks based on large-scale transactions.

CHAPTER EIGHTEEN

SECOND SHOCK TO THE SYSTEM

D'Urso called me in 2011, four years after he was sentenced in 2007. What he told me shocked me to my very core. For years—literally within weeks of having first cooperated a decade before—D'Urso harbored a dark secret. He was too cautious and concerned to tell me about it until now, after he had finally been sentenced. Because he thought it could somehow destroy his sentence.

FBI agent Jane ███████████████ for years.[30]

That was what he said. He had been too afraid to bring it up to me. His fears had been many—the entire investigation would be blown up and fall apart by this revelation; his cooperation agreement might get torn to shreds and he'd receive his full life sentence; Jane would of course brand him a liar; on and on. He had eventually told his wife, though, who wanted to kill Jane herself. And cited how he had long ago told his attorney and the private investigator who his lawyer worked with. He had also confidentially shared this information with some in the news media whom he trusted. One was Jerry Capeci, who provides weekly news articles related to organized crime stories. He also told Kati Cornell Smith back in 2003. During that period of time, he wanted her to write a book about his story.

---

30 Jane was discussed first in chapter 7 and then again at the end of chapter 10.

Kati was a *New York Post* reporter covering trials in the Eastern District of New York court. Kati met with his wife and maintained this secret for years. His message: if I get killed, it's this crazy FBI agent, not necessarily organized crime. I corroborated these details by speaking with both Kati and Jerry who confirmed D'Urso statements.

After holding this secret in for more than a decade, D'Urso cited how he finally had to get it off his chest and tell me. This is what he said about how it all began: One evening, very soon after they met and only a couple of weeks after he began cooperating, Jane called D'Urso on his cell phone to meet at a hotel near Newark airport. When he arrived, D'Urso was surprised to find that only Jane was there. They had a meal and then a few drinks. Jane shared that she had been one of the agents keeping an eye on him before his decision to cooperate. She'd been looking at an alleged stock fraud scheme that she believed he and Aparo had been running. She had heard D'Urso speaking to Sammy Aparo on a T-III wire. My squad was addressing an investigation of Aparo and others.

The conversation took a shocking and unexpected turn when Jane confided that she listened to recordings of D'Urso and Aparo speaking, ██ ██.Seemingly out of the blue, Jane then said: ███████████████ ████.

D'Urso was stunned. Not only was this completely out of left field, but his relationship with the FBI was literally a matter of life and death. He wondered if what she was doing was some kind of test. Then he wondered if his response would impact his status as a cooperator. Jane of course knew the power she held over him as an FBI agent. Was she implying that if he did not follow her lead, she might try to destroy his cooperation agreement, even ensure that he faced the death penalty? She could easily claim that he ████████████████████████████████, or lied to her, which might well achieve these results. Or would she leak his cooperation to the mob so that they would kill him? Did he need to do whatever she wanted to keep her as an ally to literally survive?

In fact, and in hindsight, had D'Urso informed me of this, his cooperation agreement would not have been torn up nor would the investigation have been greatly disturbed. D'Urso did nothing wrong, and Jane's

████████ him would not affect cases against mobsters because it bore no relationship to the evidence of their guilt. But, in the middle of the fire and in the face of his guilty plea to murder, he was in no position to conduct a calm legal analysis and figure this out himself.

D'Urso was of course a street guy, and as a street guy he concluded his best option was to go along with her demand as the least risky choice. Later he could discuss it with his attorney if he wanted to go that route. I think it's also possible it crossed his mind that ████████████ may give him leverage over the FBI, because the organization would be publicly embarrassed if he leaked this information.

████████████████████████████████████

████████████████

████████████████████████████████████

████████████████████████████████████

████████████████████████████████████

████████████████████████████████████

████████████████████████████████████

████████████████████████████████████

Soon it became almost too much for D'Urso to bear. He couldn't just run away. Running would turn him into a fugitive and negate all his work, violate his cooperation agreement and expose him to a death sentence. ████████████████████████████ Nonetheless, this was ████████████ pure and simple. In the end, D'Urso concluded he had no safe alternative, ████████████████████

████████████████████████████████████

████████████████████████████████████ This continued for years, throughout the duration of his cooperation. ████████████ ████████████████████ He saw no way out, so he went along, all the way through the takedown three years later when he and his family were placed in the safe house.

At that point, he had called me on his cell phone to, as I described earlier, tell me that he hated her more than he hated Polito. He didn't say anything about ████████████████████████ because he was afraid I would arrest her, causing (in his mind) the case to blow up. For the same reason, even after he was hospitalized from stress, thinking he had a heart attack, D'Urso did not inform me about Jane. Instead, he demanded to have no further contact with her ever again.

As mentioned above, D'Urso did finally tell his wife and he let her know that if he was killed, it most likely ██████ not organized crime. ████████ ██ ██ Once his wife knew, she forbade him from ever spending time alone with Jane again, and Jane retaliated by diminishing disbursements for living expenses to D'Urso. To reduce the monthly money D'Urso received would not raise a red flag as though some inappropriate conduct happened. The FBI was paying subsistence for D'Urso and his family. D'Urso described this reduction of funds in a manner to ensure he continued with Jane's requests.

Sometime after Jane was pulled off any contact with D'Urso because I made her husband do this after D'Urso told me he'd rather go to jail than work with her, Jane met with D'Urso in a hallway at the courthouse months later when he was meeting with prosecutors. He said she told him she thought she might be ██████ after she had been directed to keep away from him. She likely believed a similar investigation as with Detective Simone was happening at the FBI. But this did not happen, because D'Urso hadn't told me what she had done to him.

Now, finally, hearing all of this from D'Urso, I was just floored. I was immediately reminded of former ████████████████████████ ██ This was in the late 1980s and a few years ago they made a movie about it.

In a flood, everything D'Urso related to me registered, crystallized, and came together. All of those bizarre, head-scratching pieces through the years—D'Urso constantly asking me who was in charge, me or Jane; Jane rushing to meet D'Urso while wearing sundresses; his hospitalization for stress and responding with a demand to have no further contact with her; D'Urso saying that he hated her more than Polito (who organized his assassination attempt). D'Urso also used to call me to let me know he was on the way to a meeting and needed to be wired up, which I would let the team know. Jane would usually immediately grab her purse and sprint out of the squad area. Mike Sharkey would look over at me and at the time we'd laugh at her behavior, never having a clue as to why she was in such a rush to set up for surveillance. We figured maybe she was hurrying because her bureau car was parked a distance from the office, and she had to get a head start to arrive in a timely manner. She would typically get there first and be seated next to D'Urso in the vehicle when we arrived to initiate our recording. Her presence wasn't needed or required. All of the recordings made by D'Urso would have been provided by me to those conducting related investigations.

All of these puzzling statements and behaviors through the years—now for the first time they fit together. And remember how I described that my supervisor tried to remove me from the D'Urso investigation just a couple of weeks after we began? And how he wanted to replace me with Jane, and Jane was sitting right next to him when he pulled this stunt? ████████████ ██ But who in their right mind—until D'Urso actually told me—would have suspected that Jane was so loony and criminal as to ████████████ our own witness?! I never viewed any FBI agent to be so stupid ██████████ with a cooperating witness in clear violation of federal criminal laws. This was, in my view, criminal extortion. The implicit threats included that Jane might: (1) reveal D'Urso's cooperation to the mob; (2) allege that he ████ ████████████████████████ so get his cooperation agreement torn up; and (3) deny D'Urso monthly expenses if he refused her ████████████ I reflected too that she may have found D'Urso an ██████████████████ ██████████████████████████

Almost immediately after D'Urso's call, I attempted to identify someone in power to address this allegation. I reached out to a friend of the chief inspector at FBI HQ in charge of the Inspections Division, who I knew from their prior assignment in the New York Division. The Inspections Division conducts sensitive inspections of each FBI Division and an assessment of FBI operations and performance, so it was the correct place to go. However, to my surprise and disappointment, instead of coordinating a meeting or a phone call to obtain details, the inspector communicated with others who instructed me to write up the allegation and mail it in. This made absolutely no sense. Given the extreme sensitivity of the claim, I was concerned that clerical staff opening and reading this type of communication might leak it, and it would undoubtedly spread like wildfire and compromise an investigation.

This direction to me appeared to indicate a lack of interest in addressing the matter. It would have been easy and appropriate to interview me in person (or even on the phone) and prepare a discreet internal FBI-302, just like we successfully did throughout the entire D'Urso investigation. My immediate thoughts were about the embarrassment this may cause to the FBI. If that was the case, that decision just allows more pathetic conduct to occur.

Years later, in October 2017, I tried a different approach. I shared D'Urso's details with a supervisor I trusted who was still on the job. The supervisor had also previously carried out a successful investigation with the Inspector General's office. Soon after, I met with an Office of Inspector General (OIG) supervisor and another agent and provided them with details. I also gave them investigative suggestions on how to corroborate these details through existing FBI records. D'Urso and I also believed a thorough investigation may uncover Jane engaging in similar ▓▓▓▓▓▓ with other cooperating witnesses.

A few weeks later, I learned that Jane was suspended while an internal investigation was being conducted. As I understand it, she was subsequently permitted to retire with her full pension. I wondered if FBIHQ addressed the ▓▓▓▓▓▓ or just the interference with another FBI division's access to evidence from a New York investigation. This was related to the Philadelphia LCN family ▓▓▓▓▓▓▓▓▓▓ This was also during a period of turmoil at the FBI with James Comey fired as director and Andy McCabe placed in position as the acting director at FBIHQ.

As I previously described, I was initially reluctant to participate in this story as an author. However, after certain conduct by D'Urso that I didn't approve of, I could not step away from completing this project. I also believe D'Urso may have made recordings of his meetings and/or calls with Jane. He also authorized Jerry Capeci to tell details of his story in his weekly column. When D'Urso originally provided Capeci with the details of Jane's behavior it was with the understanding he could not publish this story until D'Urso gave him the green light to go forward or was killed. In addition to Capeci, he provided these details of Jane's behavior to Kati Cornell years earlier.

I want to set the record and make it clear that I was unaware of this conduct by Jane until D'Urso shared it with me years later. I immediately attempted to escalate this matter and have it discreetly addressed in 2011. During the process of drafting this book, D'Urso attempted to have me support a topic that was not true. This provided me an opportunity to initially cease my participation. However, with all that is happening at the FBI, I cannot rely on others to share details as to what happened to D'Urso and exclude my multiple efforts to address it.

CHAPTER NINETEEN

COMING FULL CIRCLE

I eventually left the corporate world. For various reasons, I was not inspired or impressed by what I encountered—it just was not a good fit. Due to internal politics, both the corporate world and government have people who are weak and unable to do what is right versus wrong. In the corporate world, it typically relates to money. I eventually became a free agent of a sort, working on projects that presented themselves. I traveled to New Orleans as a contractor to review the paid claims to victims of the *Deepwater Horizon* oil spill. Louis Freeh was named the special master. This was a thoroughly enjoyable time working in a squad-like environment citing "red flags" of possible fraud. A couple of these matters involved trying to assist crime victims in their efforts to obtain justice. As part of one matter, I attended a wedding complete with bomb-sniffing dogs and armed security patrolling the area due to potential concerns about safety. Another matter I briefly worked on involved a land developer who was the victim of a local mayor's shakedown.

Then in December 2019, D'Urso asked me to assist him with a personal matter. We met in New York City and hit it off again as though almost twenty years had not passed. Joking around just like old times.

D'Urso soon learned that mobsters were meeting and talking about him at the T Bar Steakhouse on the Upper East Side. As is his wont, D'Urso forcefully took matters into his own hands. His open letter to the mafia was published in Jerry Capeci's authoritative weekly mafia internet newsletter called *Ganglandnews*, which is read by mobsters, law enforcement, and mob aficionados alike. The next day, the *New York Post* published a two-page spread covering the same topic and quoting from his letter:

> "Rest assured I WILL NEVER GET CAUGHT SLEEPING AGAIN. I am ready, able and willing to defend my family and myself. . . . If I feel my life is threatened, I WILL BE ON OFFENSE, NOT DEFENSE. I FEAR NO ONE AND NEVER WILL. . . . I still come in and out of the neighborhood every so often. If you see me, do yourself a favor and don't confront me."

CHAPTER TWENTY

A KID FROM JERSEY

Now that I've told you my story, I thought you might be interested to learn how I was raised and what influenced my formative years.

I was born in Newark, New Jersey. Like a lot of guys in my neighborhood, I'm part Italian, as my father was first-generation Italian. My mother was born in Ireland and sent to the United States against her will. My dad's parents were both born in Italy and spoke primarily Italian in their home. Theirs had been an old-world arranged marriage. Their parents arranged their marriage without my grandparents ever having met. I'd later joke with my grandmother how I'd run away before allowing my parents to pick my future wife. She laughed and pointed to all the grandchildren to make the case that it had actually worked out well.

I had uncles—Italians and Irish alike—who were boxers, some of them professional. Large noses and distorted features were not uncommon in the family photos. As an adult, I'd learn about historic violence on both sides.

I grew up in South Orange, where my parents opened a hair salon. We lived on a street with just sixteen houses, but this included thirty-five reckless children between the households. The families were primarily Italian, Irish, and Jewish. Many of the Italian families came from the same village in Italy and were literally interrelated. There were always friends to play sports with right outside my house.

As the new kid on the street, I was sometimes drawn into fights. One was hysterical. A friend asked me why I always wore "Guinea" T-shirts. I said because my mother bought me sleeveless shirts to wear during the hot summer, having no idea what the word "Guinea" meant. All the other boys had regular white T-shirts with short sleeves. At dinner I asked my mother why she bought Guinea T-shirts. My father froze, put his fork down, and asked, "What did you just say?" I repeated the question and my father explained that "Guinea" was an insult to Italians: "Anyone calls you a Guinea, you have my permission to punch them in the face."

I could not wait for dinner to end. Once back outside, I approached my friend, placed my finger under the strap to the shirt, and asked what he called it. He responded, "a Guinea T-shirt." That was when the fight started. We duked it out on a neighbor's front lawn, and soon the neighbor, Mr. Regan, came outside to break it up. I told him we were fighting about the T-shirt and because he called me a Guinea. This friend was so confused.

Mr. Regan laughed and explained that everyone in this kid's family was Italian (while I was only half-Italian). This was just kids using words they had heard their parents use, without understanding what they meant.

I have always loved joking around and making others laugh and learned along the way how easily humor could segue into teasing and fighting—I did my share of both.

In grammar school, I certainly liked joking more than studying, and would do practically anything on a dare. I became a class clown, frequently disciplined by the nuns, who were Sisters of Charity. On occasion, I would upset a nun to the point of physical contact. I've never responded well to authority figures I perceive as bullies and would typically be punished for challenging them. In one memorable instance, a nun slammed my head into a blackboard so hard I heard the board crack.

Yet the nuns who were most capable of dealing with me were kind and patient. One nun asked me to join her in the parking lot to deliver turkeys and food for Thanksgiving to less fortunate families based in Newark. I could sense the sadness while I passed food to someone my age. I could feel the boy's discomfort and embarrassment and never forgot the experience.

I think I always had a soft spot for people who were less fortunate. Some of the nicer clothes I had were hand-me-downs that came from wealthy Jewish clients of my parents' beauty business. In about 1964, my mother provided me with a relatively new bathing suit like what the other boys were wearing at that time. Rather than it being a loose boxer type bathing suit, it was a tight fitting, rarely used hand-me-down. As I swam that opening day at the community pool, I noticed another boy my age who had a hole the size of a quarter in the back of his swimming suit. The kid would crisscross his hands behind his back to cover the hole, and then dive back into the pool quickly. He would also not come back up the ladder unless he was the last one, to minimize the chances of anyone else seeing the hole.

I recognized him as a local who lived in a multifamily residence just four blocks from my own house. I felt bad for him, so after swimming, as we dressed in the lockers before biking home, I intentionally left my bathing suit on the floor.

I said something like, "Hey there, I think you forgot your bathing suit."

"Huh?" said the kid.

I just left the changing room.

The next day, I saw the same kid wearing the swimsuit that I left at the pool. He looked extremely happy. When my mother asked me about the bathing suit, I told her it must have fallen out of my towel when I rode my bike home.

There was nothing in the young me that seemed to forecast a future in law enforcement. If anything, to be perfectly honest, there were lots of indicators to the contrary.

For instance, my friends and I would sometimes tease police officers, or try to get chased on purpose. My local public high school, Columbia H.S., had a football team that was terrible. While in grammar school, my friends and I liked to sneak into the Columbia football games so that we could play football on the adjacent baseball fields during game day. I enjoyed getting chased by a local police officer whenever we hopped the fence to get access. I began to hop the fence in full view of the officer just so that he would chase me. I'd sprint for the bleachers. The officer would come after me, but his efforts were always to no avail. Once under the bleachers, I'd climb up into the stands and watch from above as the confused officer searched. Eventually, I'd climb back down and return to an adjacent field to play football while he continued looking for me in the spectator stands.

He never caught me. Years later, as a high school senior, I went to a movie in town and that same officer was standing outside the theater. Luckily, he had no idea who I was.

We also caused other neighborhood mischief. We enjoyed "pool hopping" in backyards in the Jewish section of South Orange where it was a little wealthy and the homes were new and fancy. My friends and I would hop fences and jump into pools—even when the residents were clearly home. The more brazen the adventure, the better. In one memorable instance, a group of men were playing cards inside a house beside a sliding glass window. I explained to my friends how difficult it was to see from inside a well-lit room out into a dark yard—so we could count on being more or less invisible to the residents. To drive home my point, I approached the window while explaining that I couldn't be seen. I leaned against the glass window, and all the men inside jumped into a panic. We all ran to our bicycles and sped off, as responding police drew closer in the distance.

* * *

In 1977, a friend, nicknamed "Dopsey" Iantosca, asked if I might be interested in parking cars at the Orange Lawn Tennis Club in South Orange. Each year this club sponsored a professional tennis tournament, and all the top tennis professionals attended. I wasn't really into tennis but agreed to do it because Dopsey was a friend who played on my summer softball team. Dopsey's father, nicknamed "Loaf," managed the parking for this tournament. Loaf—because he resembled a loaf of Italian bread—was one of the nicest men in South Orange.

On the opening day of the tournament there was a doubles exhibition match: New Jersey Governor Brendan Byrne and *Paris Review* editor George Plimpton versus two young tennis professionals, John McEnroe and Peter Fleming.

McEnroe arrived at the tennis club the day of the match and Loaf greeted him. As was his lighthearted manner, Loaf joked, "Mr. McEnroe, don't beat our governor too badly or he'll raise our taxes." In full view of everyone, McEnroe, in a rude and vulgar manner, told Loaf, "I don't give a shit," and to fuck off. I thought this was not called for and felt bad for Loaf and Dopsey.

The next day, the pro players had to arrive at 10:00 a.m. to be assured a parking spot in the immediate vicinity of the club. I told Dopsey that if McEnroe arrived after 10:00 a.m., I'd park him at the bottom of the hill where all other attendees parked.

Dopsey asked, "You would do that?"

"Absolutely," I replied.

McEnroe arrived well after 10:00 a.m. driving a sky-blue Mustang convertible with a pretty blonde in the front passenger seat. There was a 400-yard driveway leading up to the club, adjacent to the grass hill where I directed the public to park. This allowed me to gap the cars in such a manner as to ensure McEnroe a lousy spot at the bottom of the hill, as I had promised.

I waved McEnroe down the hill to his parking spot at the bottom. McEnroe shook his head "no" and eventually drove over to me.

"I'm John McEnroe, a tennis pro," he said.

"I'm Mike Campi, your parking attendant," I said in a serious tone. "This is your spot. Park the car." I explained that tennis pros forfeited their special parking if they arrived after ten.

"I'll have your job," McEnroe said.

"You can have my job," I said. "Maybe I'll go hit those fuzzy little tennis balls instead."

The back-and-forth continued. McEnroe threatened simply to drive to the top of the hill and park. I explained that his car would be towed if he did that, and it would take days for him to get it back.

In the end, McEnroe parked his car at the bottom of the hill. The girl had to assist McEnroe and carried a bunch of his tennis rackets.

Eventually, Loaf came running out to the field with McEnroe's keys asking where the car was parked. He later explained that he appreciated what I was trying to do, but he wanted to keep his parking job.

As with the nuns, I had stayed true to my impulse to stand up to bullies, no matter what kind of cars they drove or how famous they were. I was also a bit of a smart-ass.

* * *

As in many Italian families, Sunday dinner was an institution at the Campi household.

There were four topics that dominated the conversations my father would initiate: the Catholic Church, corrupt politicians, organized crime, and nutrition. I learned early on that whatever was being discussed—sports, the weather, and so on—my father could be counted on to bring it back to these four topics.

At that time, I was not very interested in these topics—even organized crime. Nonetheless, the names discussed at the dinner table made their way into my neighborhood lexicon: Jerry Catena, Longy Zwillman, Tommy "Ryan" Eboli, Richie "the Boot" Boiardo, the Campisi family, and others. If my grandparents, uncles, and aunts were present at dinner, these figures would be discussed at length. Conversations might range from how Jerry Catena was essentially a good man despite his association with crime families, to the treachery of "the Boot," to the various merits and drawbacks of the Campisi family.

In any event, I was simply bored and did not care about these dinner topics. Not about any of it. My goal for these Sunday dinners was that they should be over quickly, maybe have some laughs, and then get back outside to play ball with my friends. An Irish priest named Pat was a somewhat regular guest. He had a fantastic sense of humor and knew I didn't want to hear conversations about these topics. To provoke, when I was a bit older, he would always begin a conversation by stating something like, "Tony, what do you think about your son Michael, who doesn't think Hoover was corrupt?" This would send my father on a lengthy rant, with Pat smiling behind him as he walked to get another drink.

I would eventually learn that my parents withheld the juiciest and most personal detail of the local mob from their Sunday discussions.

My uncle Frankie was one of my father's younger brothers. As I understood, he was physically strong, boxed, and had a tough stubborn attitude. I originally was led to believe Frankie was injured in a war because when we visited him, he was in a veterans' hospital in Lyons, New Jersey. The truth of his incapacitation, which I discovered only years later, was that a friend of his, a Campisi, had shot him in retaliation for Frankie beating him up. The dispute originally stemmed over money and a woman.

According to my mother, Frankie looked like Paul Newman and had always been very attractive. Apparently, when Campisi's girlfriend let slip that she found him appealing, it was all downhill from there.

My grandparents, however, never liked to discuss the mob around me. I imagine they liked some and disliked others. Like most Italian immigrants, you lived in a community of Italians. You did not trust law enforcement from prior experience in Italy, word of mouth in the community, and shakedowns in the neighborhood.

As I got older, my father would occasionally tell stories involving crime and corruption in his own life—and from both sides of the law. My father also shared being a child and encountering a local gangster named Taccetta, a made member of the Luccheses. As Taccetta strolled down the street, my father watched him pull out the handle of his cane to reveal a blade, and stab someone.

"Did you see anything?" Taccetta then asked in Italian.

"No," my father replied.

And there the matter ended.

Like many young people growing up in the sixties, I had a somewhat fluid view of the extent to which the mob did or did not influence everyday life. Who was or was not a gangster or affiliated with a mafia family seemed nebulous. My dad was convinced that behind closed doors, undisclosed connections most certainly existed. According to him, Joe Kennedy, for example, was associated with the Genovese family. Likewise, he believed FBI Director J. Edgar Hoover was caught up in mob corruption. Both of my parents were loyal Democrats, and my mom, being Irish, couldn't stand to hear anything negative about the Kennedys.

My father also spoke highly of a local Genovese named Jerry Catena. He had resided in South Orange for decades, and my dad always insisted he was a "decent man." As I understood, Catena assisted financially in the construction of the all-girls Catholic High School—Marylawn of the Oranges—in South Orange. It was finished in 1956, one year before Catena was caught attending the historic Apalachin meeting (I discussed this meeting in chapter 5).

Catena was a historic mobster. He had a strong business sense and assisted in generating significant money for the Genovese. For a brief period, he was their official boss. With the rise of local manufacturing jobs in New Jersey, Catena took advantage to control trucking, shipping, vending machines, and many other opportunities. Whether or not it was true, the local wisdom was that "a quarter of everything manufactured" was either made in or transported through New Jersey, so the opportunities to profit were enormous. Barone described Catena as one of the brightest gangsters that existed in this criminal life. His business instinct was incredible. Catena stepped away from being the Genovese boss to a more inactive/retired role living in Florida.

Likely due to my adventurous streak, my parents tried to make sure I always had a job. One such job was working as a caddy at the Maplewood Country Club. I worked there six days a week. After about two years, I caddied for a local physician named Duffy who was notorious for trying to stiff people. At the end of his eighteen holes, Duffy thrust a very small wad of bills into my hands and headed for the locker room. As I unrolled the bills, I saw that the doctor had not only refused to tip me but was a dollar short of the minimal payment on top of that. Outraged, and not sensing that my actions were out of place, I immediately entered the "Members Only" locker room and asked him for the extra dollar. Duffy scolded me for entering a restricted area, and I replied that I would leave just as soon as I had my dollar. Some other members of the club interceded and gave me $5. I accepted the money but was still pissed off, so I grabbed the doctor's golf bag and threw it into the brook adjacent to the first tee.

Despite having been in the right—in my opinion, at least—I was out of my Maplewood job. But God closed a door and opened a big window, as I soon found another caddying gig at Cedar Hill Country Club, which was predominantly Jewish. Here, I made more money per bag, got bigger tips, and learned that the golfers traditionally bought their caddy a soda and hot dog at the ninth hole. Although I had to hitchhike two rides to get there, it was well worth the experience.

After working at Cedar Hill for a while, I raised the topic with my dad.

"I don't get it," I said to him one night. "Why do some people say Jews are cheap people? The Jews I caddy are some of the most generous people I ever met."

"You can't judge people by the things that a prejudiced person says," my father replied. "Anyhow, Jews have been generous to me, and they're some of my best customers."

I attended Seton Hall Prep, a Catholic high school located in town. In high school I did not make the freshman football or basketball teams. I was too small, only about ninety pounds. It was probably one of the *best* things that happened to *not* make those teams. That's because, during the winter, as I walked through the Seton Hall university campus, I could hear a roar from the gym. Seton Hall Prep was hosting the annual Christmas wrestling tournament that had the best local teams competing. After watching the finals, I decided the next year I would wrestle, and joined the wrestling team as a sophomore. The coach's philosophy was to train hard in preparing for every single match. Never quit on yourself or your team, and technique matters. If strength was everything, a bull could catch a rabbit. Wrestling had a huge impact on my life—the refusal to quit, and my aggressive approach in my later investigations.

I eventually attended Seton Hall University in South Orange for college. I wrestled there one season and played rugby all four years and a few years after college. After college I even traveled to England with a select group of rugby players representing the New York Metropolitan Rugby Union. This team had tryouts for two years and we played the best British teams on a three-week paid tour.

At Seton Hall, I began to have the sense that I wanted to do something that was worthwhile and interesting. Accounting, which I had thought would be my career, and was my major, was not what I wanted anymore. It was the 1970s, and the nation—and especially cities along the Eastern Seaboard—was in the middle of a crime wave. The mob was powerful. Street crime was everywhere. People who lived in cities were learning to live in fear. People were also still feeling the disruptions of the 1960s when Vietnam War protests had been rampant, and TV was full of college students burning the American flag.

I considered joining the Marines. Their recruiting advertisements promised adventure and travel, in addition to the chance to make a difference. However, my career trajectory solidified when I attended a backyard barbeque the summer before my senior year. My mother introduced me to a guest, the neighbor's brother, Jack McKenna. Jack was a special agent with the FBI. He explained that the FBI was currently very interested in hiring people with an accounting background. However, the agent promised, once you were aboard, you didn't have to stick with accounting work. If you wanted to, you were free to move into other types of investigation.

More than the descriptions of the opportunities to make a difference, I was also taken in by the agent's characterization of the culture at the FBI. These were regular guys and gals, but also people who gave a damn. They could be cynical and funny, but they were also genuinely patriotic. They were there to make a difference. This matched my deep need to spend my days doing something I found interesting and meaningful.

I liked what I heard and decided to pursue this opportunity. The agent further explained that there were entry-level support positions in a clerical capacity where you could experience the work firsthand. This interested me with an opportunity to view the work of FBI agents in a supportive role. I would apply for a position.

AFTERWORD

So that's what I know.

There are a couple of things I didn't discuss because they're just too sensitive, or because I'm not permitted to, such as some of the truly crazy stuff that took place before grand juries. But almost everything else is here. I hope I've contributed to a better understanding of what the mafia truly is—a hypocritical and cancerous group; they damage America, and they damage most of the young men who join in the delusional belief that the gang has values such as loyalty and honor. There is none. There is only treachery and an ever-present need to watch your back as another gang member looks to step on it and climb over you.

Because I've been completely honest and forthcoming, I've probably upset some people from the FBI and the "legitimate" world (as compared to the world of organized crime), who may claim that this book contains certain untruths. I understand some agents may wonder why I mention incompetent managers. A brief explanation would be my process to correct a deficiency. You cannot correct it until you identify the cause. Promoting agents to management positions without significant investigative experience results in huge risks. Some agents observe a supervisor who makes poor decisions leading a squad. They may believe they could make better decisions. They apply for a supervisory position before they obtain the experience of a competent "street agent." Competent street agents are why the FBI's reputation was so strong. The street is where all of the exciting action is.

My purpose in addressing the hypocrisy of the mafia criminal life is not to insult it. I want it to be a warning to discourage young men from getting involved in this life. The old-timers know this to be true. They have mentioned it many times in recorded conversations.

You probably appreciate by now that I am independent and don't care much for networking or politicking. I haven't led a life motivated by great riches or personal advancement. That frees me to provide the plain, unadorned facts. What you have read here is the full truth to the best of my memory (although many years have passed) and to the best of my understanding—what actually happened, warts and all. If I got any important facts wrong due to the passage of time, I apologize, but I don't believe I have. Despite incredible obstacles that many presented, I stand alongside the multitude of other good and patriotic law enforcement colleagues who contribute to a safer democracy and a safer and better country for us all. I want to stress the impact we all have on others, similar to the story I cited earlier in this book about my favorite movie, *It's A Wonderful Life*.

—Mike

APPENDIX A

Nelson A. Boxer letter accompanying insert photo with US Attorney Mary-Jo White.

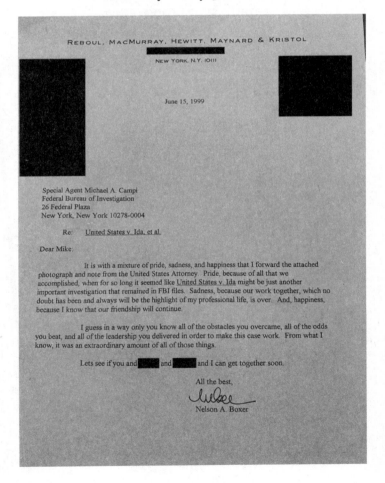

REBOUL, MACMURRAY, HEWITT, MAYNARD & KRISTOL

NEW YORK, N.Y. 10111

June 15, 1999

Special Agent Michael A. Campi
Federal Bureau of Investigation
26 Federal Plaza
New York, New York 10278-0004

Re: United States v. Ida, et al.

Dear Mike:

It is with a mixture of pride, sadness, and happiness that I forward the attached photograph and note from the United States Attorney. Pride, because of all that we accomplished, when for so long it seemed like United States v. Ida might be just another important investigation that remained in FBI files. Sadness, because our work together, which no doubt has been and always will be the highlight of my professional life, is over. And, happiness, because I know that our friendship will continue.

I guess in a way only you know all of the obstacles you overcame, all of the odds you beat, and all of the leadership you delivered in order to make this case work. From what I know, it was an extraordinary amount of all of those things.

Lets see if you and ███ and ███ and I can get together soon.

All the best,

Nelson A. Boxer

APPENDIX B

Kenneth N. Feldmen letter to Robert Mueller and Kevin Donovan

KENNETH N. FELDMAN
Attorney at Law
Suite 780
550 Biltmore Way
Coral Gables, FL 33134

Telephone (305) 445-0133
Fax (305) 443-0279
kenesq@bellsouth.net

January 27, 2003

Director Robert Mueller   Kevin Donovan, Asst. Director in Charge
Federal Bureau of Investigation   Manhattan Office of the F.B.I.
935 Pennsylvania Ave.   26 Federal Plaza
Washington, DC 20535   New York, New York 10278

Re: Letter to Acknowledge Manhattan Agent Mike Campi

Dear Mr. Mueller and Mr. Donovan,

This is to confirm my representation of George Barone who is a Defendant in the Indictment from the Eastern District of New York in Case No. 01-CR 416 in which my client was indicted about 18 months ago along with other members of the Genovese crime family. As I trust you are aware, my client's cooperation with the Government began immediately after his arrest and culminated in his providing testimony as a government witness last week in the trial of Peter Gotti et al.

What I wanted to specifically bring to your attention is that my client's continued cooperation with the Government would never had occurred had it not been for the total professionalism and dedication of Agent Mike Campi of the Manhattan office of the Federal Bureau of Investigation. Throughout this case, Agent Campi's actions have brought honor and respect to your Bureau. I know that not more than three days has passed in the last 18 months that Agent Campi has not contacted me to insure the safety and well being of Mr. Barone and his efforts should be acknowledged.

Respectfully submitted,

Kenneth N. Feldman
cc: Mike Campi

264

ACKNOWLEDGMENTS

My first thanks are to my parents, Mary and Anthony Campi, who provided me with a foundation in my Christian faith, family, stubborn genes, and work ethics that greatly assisted me as an FBI agent.

I would like to acknowledge the law enforcement community who I had the great pleasure of working with during my career at the FBI. This would include the FBI agents, NYPD detectives, prosecutors, and FBI support staff to include Jenny Ng, Ken Zoeller, Josephine Mauro and Steve Wagner, who played a significant role in our success.

I am especially thankful to "street agents" (SAs) like Jack Ryan, Cincinnati Division, who provided the best example to newly appointed agents. My initial time in this first office assignment was enhanced by my two partners Walt Wright and Bob "Haddie" Holmes. Dave Stone, my most supportive supervisor, SA Bob Doherty, FBI, Pat Maggiore and Joe Simone, NYPD detectives, for their significant role and partnership in the foundational evidence for the James Ida investigation. SAs Craig Donlon, Gary Uher, and Glenn Muenzer who worked with me on the Ida investigation and played critical roles in executing search warrants, arrests, and as witnesses who testified at the trial securing convictions of James Ida and the active hierarchy of the Genovese family. This complex Ida trial success was greatly complemented by the prosecutive team led by Nelson Boxer, and his partners, Maria Barton and Barbara Ward. Jim Bucknam, who was the Chief of the Organized Crime Unit who assigned Nelson Boxer as my

AUSA. SAs Jack Campanella, Kevin O'Grady, and Mike Sharkey who had overlapping investigations from bank robbery to frauds.

SAs Bruce Kamerman, Marybeth Pagliano, Pat Luzio, Mike Breslin, and Jim Walden, the FBI agents and prosecutor who secured convictions and cooperation of numerous witnesses in their investigation of Vito Guzzo and the Giannini crew. It was their investigation that charged D'Urso with murder. For the team who worked with me on this investigation providing security, surveillance, and consensual recordings that decimated all five New York organized crime families. This team consisted of SAs Craig Donlon, Tom Krall, and NYPD detective Bob Vosler. I also want to thank the prosecutors from the Eastern District of New York, Mark Feldman, Paul Weinstein, Paul Schoeman, and Dan Dorsky for their utilization of D'Urso's evidence in numerous indictments. An additional thanks to Katherine Hudak for all her work at the U.S. Attorney's office in assisting these prosecutors. I deeply appreciate the team members who worked with me during my career at the FBI and apologize for any omissions.

My greatest appreciation is for my wife and children. I am so thankful to them for their love and support during my career as an agent. I would not have agreed to participate in this book if not for their encouragement.

Last but not least, my thanks to Tony Lyons and Hector Carosso, Skyhorse Publishing, for their guidance, patience, and support in this project to tell this story. I feel it important that this story be told to help facilitate a change in those young men who don't realize the hypocrisy of this life.